DATE

MAP

The Heart of Dixie

[

The
Heart
of
Dixie

Frye Gaillard

Down Home Press, Asheboro, North Carolina

ISBN 1-878086-50-2

Library of Congress number 96-085573

Printed in the United States of America

Cover design: Tim Rickard
Book design: Beth Glover

Down Home Press
P.O. Box 4126
Asheboro, N.C. 27204

To the memory of Jim Batten,
who showed us the way;
and to Joseph B. Cumming,
with gratitude for his gentle critiques

ACKNOWLEDGMENTS

All chapters in this collection have appeared in other places, and some have appeared in more than one. In addition to those publications listed in the text, Chapter 2 appeared in slightly different form in the books *Race, Rock & Religion* and *Becoming Truly Free*. Chapter 4 appeared in *Race, Rock & Religion*. Chapter 5 appeared in *The Charlotte Observer*, *Southern Voices* and *Race, Rock & Religion*; Chapter 6 in *The Progressive* magazine; Chapter 7 in *The Chicago Tribune*, the *Miami Herald* and *The Philadelphia Inquirer*, and Chapter 10 in the books, *Southern Voices* and *Becoming Truly Free*. Chapter 14 appeared in *The Charlotte Observer* and *Carolina Lifestyles* magazine and Chapters 15, 21 and 24 appeared in *The Observer*. Chapter 22 appeared in *Southern Voices*.

PREFACE

Back around 1972, I was looking for a job. I had been working in Nashville for a magazine called the *Race Relations Reporter*—a publication funded by the Ford Foundation, seeking to provide a fair-minded account of the racial upheavals still sweeping through the country.

But the magazine folded when the foundation lost interest, and I wound up in a job interview in Charlotte. I was nervous about it. *The Charlotte Observer* was known in those days as one of the finest newspapers in the South, and it had become even better under the leadership of Jim Batten.

On the day I arrived to talk about a job, the conversation at first did not go well. Batten was not what I had expected. He was shy and soft-spoken, a handsome man with gentle eyes and hair beginning to turn grey at the temples. I suppose I was braced for an old-school editor— more aggressive and gruff—and I found myself disarmed, certain that my awkwardness was costing me a job.

But then the conversation turned serious. We began to talk about the South and the civil rights story that was still unfolding—particularly in Charlotte, which had become the test case for court-ordered busing. "This community," said Batten, "is trying to figure out what kind of community it really wants to be."

I said I thought that was true of the South, and I told him about a professor of mine who made me read a speech by William Faulkner, delivered when he won the Nobel Prize. In that address, the great Mississippi author spoke of "the problems of the human heart in conflict with itself which alone can make good writing because only that is worth writing about."

Batten nodded. "The heart of Dixie," he said with a smile, "is still in some turmoil."

In Batten's view, I would soon discover, that kind of turmoil—the search for a region's identity and soul—represented a sacred opportunity for the press. Not long after I was hired, he called me into his office one afternoon and told me I was being assigned to the school beat— as the busing controversy was rushing toward a climax.

"Your job," he said, "is to give the people of this community enough information to make good decisions in a time of crisis."

That admonition stayed with me through the years, as it did with most of Jim Batten's reporters. He planted the seeds with patience and care, wanting those men and women on his staff to understand the larger responsibilities of the calling. Ours was not an ordinary job. We lived on the cutting edge of the truth, digging for the kind of perspective and information that could enable our fragile democracy to function.

As basic as it sounds—and Batten's words, I admit, were less remarkable than the strength of his conviction—those early lessons at the *Charlotte Observer* have remained at the heart of everything I've written, and they reverberate, certainly, through the pages that follow.

But there's another influence in here as well. Joe Cumming, the Atlanta bureau chief of *Newsweek*, took me under his wing when I was first contemplating a career as a journalist. (He did the same thing for many other young writers whose talent was far more conspicuous than mine.) It's important to do your homework, he said—to try to report every story in depth. But it's also important to write it down well—to borrow a page from the novelists and poets and try to make certain that the story comes alive.

Again, it seems like basic advice, but I'm amazed looking back at how many reporters, myself included, were lovers of the chase, thrilled by the pursuit of a page-one story, only to regard the writing itself as nothing much more than a necessary chore. Joe Cumming cured me of that inclination, and I hope the stories that follow do credit to his influence.

Some of them are journalistic profiles; others are pieces of history or memoir, and there are one or two shorter essays and columns. The subjects vary—race relations, politics, religion, music, business, sports. But the stories are tied together in the end by the spiritual setting in which they were written.

They are snapshots really, each of them intended to stand by itself, but taken together, I suppose they are kind of a photo essay—a reflection on some of the people and moments that have helped shape the South, adding at least to its texture and style, and sometimes directly to its history and drama.

They are collected here as a gesture of thanks—to Jim Batten, Joe Cumming and other mentors along the way who believed that reporters, particularly in the South, were compelled to be good stewards of the craft.

—Frye Gaillard

TABLE OF CONTENTS

Coming of Age

Lessons From The Big House
1994

    I remember it simply as a warm, sunny day, though it must have been fall, for leaf piles were burning, the sweet scent drifting through the neighborhood. Robert Croshon was there with his wheelbarrow, and I was five years old and ready for a ride. It was something of a ritual for us by now. Every Saturday on his way to work, Robert would stop to pick up his "helper." That was me—the youngest and most favored of Palmer Gaillard's grandchildren.

    The old man was 90 by the time I was born, still full of vigor, though I remember his deafness, the deep wrinkles in his face, and the wispy white hair that tousled in the breeze. I called him Dad, the name permitted to anyone in the family, and I loved those hours that we spent together—just he and Robert and I in the garden. Robert was a black man, full of dignity and patience, hard-working and quiet, with a reassuring face, a broad, flat nose, gentle eyes, and a voice that was rich and resonant and kind.

    He and Dad worked hard and steady, while I practiced high-jumping across the rows of collard greens and chased away the Indians in the bamboo hedges. On one of those mornings in the 1950s, we broke for lunch around the middle of the day. The spread was impressive—fried chicken, greens, homegrown tomatoes, a platter of hot biscuits—covering every inch of the dining room table. But a funny thing happened as we sat down to the great cluttered feast: Robert found a chair at the table in the kitchen.

    To a five-year-old, it made no sense. "Robert!" I called, "come on in here."

    I knew immediately that I had made a mistake. The silence was sudden, and my Aunt Mary, who shared this house in Mobile with her father, shot me a withering look and hissed: "Shame on you. Shame on you for hurting Robert's feelings."

11

There were many different lessons contained in that moment—the most important of which was that however silly the world might appear, there were just certain subjects that we didn't talk about. Actually, it was easy enough to avoid them, for the diversions were plentiful for a boy growing up in Mobile. There were baseball cards to be traded in the summer and great limbs that beckoned from the live oak trees, some of them broad enough to walk. But the most passionate diversion was reserved for September, the date set aside for the beginning of football. We lived, of course, in the country of the Bear—Paul "Bear" Bryant, the football coach at the University of Alabama, who restored the fortunes of a losing program and became the biggest hero in the state.

There was something magical from the moment he arrived. He won five games in 1958, and three years later, a national championship—the first of five before he was through. He prowled the sidelines in his hounds-tooth cap, growling at everybody who came within range, and his mumbling mystique was Southern to the bone. He was humble in victory, gracious in defeat, praising his players whenever they won, and blaming nobody but himself when they lost. The boys on the team were a lot like he was. They played the game hard and mostly clean, never argued with officials or got into fights, and of course they almost always won. That was important in the state of Alabama, where winning was otherwise uncommon. We felt a little like the national stepchild—49th most years in what we spent for education, and sometimes lower in a few other categories. In addition to that, there was a revolution underway, and a great many of us, by the end of the '50s, were not at all sure we were on the winning side.

As far as we could tell, it began up the road in the city of Montgomery, this relentless intrusion of the outside world, compelling us to think about things that seemed better left alone. On December 5, 1955, a young black preacher named Martin Luther King, 26-years-old and fresh out of graduate school in Boston, made a speech to a rally at a Montgomery church. We had no way of knowing when we first heard about it that in the late afternoon before the speech, King was so overwhelmed by his doubts—his sense of inadequacy for the task that lay ahead—that he put his trembling pen aside and prayed that God would help him find the words. Such images were invisible to white Alabamians. What we saw instead was an insurrection, reaching far beyond the modest demands of the moment: courtesy on the part of white bus drivers, and a policy of first-come, first-serve seating—with blacks still filling the buses from the rear.

Imbedded in the majestic sweep of King's sermon were intimations of a shredded status quo—a radical recasting of the Southern way of life, with blacks leading the way on the road to redemption. And the most disconcerting thing was this: Despite his secret fears on that same afternoon, Martin Luther King seemed to be so sure. "We are not wrong tonight," he proclaimed, as the amens swelled and filled up the church. "If we are wrong, the Supreme Court of this nation is wrong. If we are wrong, the Constitution of the United States is wrong. If we are wrong, God Almighty is wrong....If we are wrong, justice is a lie."

I still remember the response of my family—the rage at the impudence of this middle-class Negro, who may have been raised in the state of Georgia, but picked up some funny ideas in Boston. As a child I didn't know what to think, though I did know better than to talk about it much. But then I saw him one day in Birmingham. It was seven years later, and I had come to the city on a high school trip. King was there as the civil rights movement was rushing toward a peak. He was afraid of Birmingham. He thought it was a place where he might be killed, for this was the city of Eugene "Bull" Connor, the infamous Commissioner of Public Safety who regarded brutality as a necessary tool. But for the civil rights movement, that was the point. King and the others intended to show that segregation in the South had never been benign—that it was not simply custom, or polite separation (as the Gaillard family, among others, liked to claim), but rather an ugly and violent stain, immoral at its core. They hoped that Bull Connor would not disappoint them.

The skirmishing began in April of 1963, just before Easter Sunday. I happened to be there as King was arrested, and at the moment it didn't seem particularly historic. The crowd of marchers was small, no more than 50, and by the time I wandered onto the scene, it was almost over. Somebody told me there had been some demonstrations at a lunch counter, and then the march, but the police now had it under control. They were hauling King away to a paddy wagon, and even to the whites who had learned to hate him, he didn't seem especially threatening anymore. He was a smallish man in blue overalls, with an expression that betrayed neither anger nor fear but a stoicism that seemed to shade into sadness.

The sympathy I felt for him came in a flash, almost involuntary at first. I don't remember thinking of segregation or civil rights but simply that I knew who the underdog was—the victim of a cruelty that grew more vivid in the next few days, as the snarling Bull Connor turned loose his dogs and aimed his fire hoses at the crowds of demonstrators. It was not always that simple and pat, for there were blacks who showered the policemen with rocks. But Connor and his troopers made no distinction between those who were violent and those who were not. The images flashing across the country were awful—German Shepherds tearing at a teenager's flesh, while another was knocked from his feet by a hose and blown along the ground like a piece of tissue paper.

It was exactly what Martin Luther King had hoped for—a demonstration of the violence at the heart of segregation—and yet he brooded about it in private. People were getting hurt out there in the streets, and some of them were barely more than children. The citizens of Birmingham blamed him for it, the white ones at least. Even the most moderate ministers in the city issued a statement condemning the protests, charging that King's non-violence was a mockery, for violence, after all, was precisely the point—the drama that kept the movement in the headlines.

King recognized the grain of truth, especially in September, when dynamite exploded at a Birmingham church. It was 10:29 on a Sunday morning, and the crowds were beginning to gather for worship. Four teenaged girls—Carol Robertson, Addie Mae Collins, Cynthia Wesley and Denise McNair—were especially excited on this particular morning, a balmy and peaceful later-summer's day, with the sound of church bells and the singing of birds. They and other junior high students were invited to participate in the service for adults. They had gone to the ground-floor rest room to primp, when the bomb went off and ripped through the wall—killing all four in a cascade of bricks. A civil defense team dug through the rubble, finding bits of clothing and a patent leather shoe before they came to the bodies. King was in Atlanta when the phone call came, bringing with it all the grisly details—four murdered girls, who were killed for one reason: Their church had been a base of operations for his movement.

The members of his family had never seen him so depressed. This was segregation laid bare, but he had never quite dreamed that this would be the price—the blood of four children barely older than his own. Was it really his fault? The irony of the question was nearly more than he could take, but whatever the answer, he also knew there was no turning back. He was the personification of the movement by now. A few weeks earlier, in the most triumphant moment of his life, he had spoken to a remarkable march on Washington, delivering the most powerful address that many of the people in the crowd had ever heard. It didn't start out that way. He was plodding at first through the printed text, almost reading, when he got caught up in the excitement of the day. The crowd was huge, maybe 200,000 people, a fourth of them white, spreading out from the base of the Lincoln Memorial. As he moved through the text, gazing out across the mass of jubilant faces, he remembered a passage he hadn't thought to include. He had used it before, and it had gone over well in Birmingham and Detroit, "and I just felt," he said much later, "that I wanted to use it here." So he pushed his printed text aside, and simply let the words pour out in a rush:

I say to you today, my friends, even though we face the difficulties of today and tomorrow, I still have a dream. It is a dream deeply rooted in the American dream. I have a dream that one day this nation will rise up and live out the true meaning of its creed—we hold these truths to be self-evident, that all men are created equal.

I have a dream that one day on the red hills of Georgia, the sons of former slaves and the sons of former slave-owners will be able to sit down together at the table of brotherhood... I have a dream today!

It was a vision that became his gift to the country, an antidote to the tragedies of Birmingham and other places. And for some of us growing up in those times, it became an image that we couldn't put aside.

For me, however, the final conversion on the issue of race—the moment at which there was no going back—did not come until the following year, when I left Mobile and went away to the campus of Vanderbilt University. For many who came from other parts of the country, Vanderbilt was a stodgy and conservative place, a tree-shaded retreat on the western border of Nashville, where the sons and daughters of the American rich set out to test their academic mettle. The student body was overwhelmingly white, and in fact until the day that my class arrived, there had never been a black undergraduate at the school.

The first group was impressive—earnest and bright—and I found it hard to explain to the student down the hall, making A's in calculus while I was fervently praying for a D, why his race was inherently inferior to mine. As basic as it sounds, it reinforced a sort of free-floating notion in my mind that I might have been raised on some faulty assumptions. But the moment of truth came later in the year, when George Wallace was invited to speak at Vanderbilt.

In the autumn of 1964, the Governor of Alabama had made a run for the presidency, and even though he lost, the people back home were proud of his spunk. He had the pugnacious aura of a boxer (which he had been in his youth), though he had built his curious career on losing. In perhaps his most publicized act as governor, he stood in the doorway of the University of Alabama to block the admission of two black students, knowing full-well that they would be admitted anyway.

Throughout those early years of his career, he became a lightning rod for the civil rights movement, almost assuring the kinds of changes he decried. But somehow it all played well in Alabama, a state still seething with lost-cause memories—the aftershock of the great Civil War. It was a feeling that Wallace understood how to tap, and his popularity back home was astounding, even among people who should have known better.

There was a theory circulating among the Gaillards and others that the Governor was really a moderate on race, making a principled stand on the issue of states rights. It was a theory that I badly wanted to accept—a gesture of loyalty, I suppose, to the family—but I was assigned during Wallace's visit to Vanderbilt to serve as one of his student hosts. We were standing backstage before the speech as the crowd began to gather at the gym: more than 3,000 people who were curious about him, with a few admirers and some others who had come to get a look at the devil.

"Do you think there'll be any niggers out there?"

The voice belonged unmistakably to Wallace, and the question was so bald and crude and startling that it took a moment to realize it was directed at me. I don't remember what I said, something about the speech being open to anyone, but Wallace merely shrugged and headed for the stage.

The ugly part came a few minutes later. There were, in fact, a few blacks in the crowd—a handful of students from Fisk University, well-mannered and brave, who had made the trip across town to ask him some questions. One girl rose with a trembling voice, and Wallace interrupted her question in the middle.

"What's that, honey? You'll have to speak up."

She tried again, and Wallace again cut her off with a sneer: "You're mighty pretty, honey. Go ahead with your question."

Many years later, George Wallace would change. Long after the murder of Martin Luther King, after he, too, had been crippled by a would-be assassin, Wallace paid a visit to King's church in Montgomery. It was a remarkable moment in the little brick chapel, barely a block from the Alabama state capitol, where Jefferson Davis had taken his oath and "Dixie" had been chosen as the battle anthem of the South. Wallace, still governor but confined to a wheelchair, spoke of the redemptive power of suffering and the ability of God to change a man's heart—and as he was wheeled down the aisle at the end of the sermon, the congregation wept, and a hundred black hands reached out to touch him.

But all of that was well-hidden in the future. At Vanderbilt in 1965, the only thing we could feel, my friends from Alabama and I, was a deep sense of shame that this man was one of us. The alienation was stark, and over the next several months, we found ourselves searching for a new set of heroes. Actually, we didn't have far to look. Martin Luther King was one possibility. He was the winner of the Nobel Prize by now, and the following year, when he also paid a visit to the campus, he seemed to be everything Wallace was not. He was gentle and gracious and patient with those who didn't agree. But there was a figure who stirred us even more than King, and the reason, I think, had to do with his race. Robert Kennedy was white, and in the 1960s that was critically important.

If black Americans such as King were posing the questions, the great moral issues that the country had to face, it was up to the rest of us to decide how to answer. That, at least, was how it seemed at the time, and Kennedy was clearly a man who was trying. But perhaps it was even more basic than that. Perhaps I simply needed a white man to admire, and for an Alabama boy in the 1960s, the number of choices at the moment seemed small.

Whatever it was, Kennedy soon captivated our attention. He came to Vanderbilt in 1968, five days after he declared for the presidency. It was a chilly March night with a misting rain that would soon turn to ice, but nearly 11,000 people turned out to hear him, and there were that many more waiting for him at the airport. His plane was late, but the crowd simply grew, surging forward as soon as he appeared—screaming, waving signs, reaching out to shake his hand or just touch him. The intensity of it was almost frightening, but Kennedy smiled and climbed unsteadily to an escalator railing, where he made a brief speech about the problems of the country. The electricity of it was hard to define, but somewhere imbedded in his Massachusetts twang, in the jab of his forefinger and the tousle of his hair, in the enigmatic intensity of his icy blue stare, there was an urgency that was reflected and magnified in the crowd. For this was 1968, when the country seemed to be flying apart. In our history, of course, we had seen it before—in the Civil War, certainly, and even at our founding, when the colonists had to choose between competing imperatives: liberty on the one hand or loyalty to the King. But the deepening divisions of the 1960s—over poverty and race and the escalating war in Vietnam—seemed so foreign to our recent experience. World War II had brought us together. We had responded as one when the country was attacked, taking our stand against the evils of Hitler, and in the course of those wrenching years of adventure, we had seen ourselves as both righteous and strong. Now it was different. Now our failures seemed to be laid bare, and some people wondered how the country would survive. Robert Kennedy, however, did not. He believed that the strengths of the nation ran deep, and because of that, he saw no need to gloss over its problems.

In Kennedy's mind, those problems were serious—not only the war, but the pain he saw among the country's have-nots. Kennedy identified with that pain, and according to some of the people who knew him, the empathy was rooted in the death of his brother. Before that terrible morning in Dallas, he seemed to be the consummate political operative, cynical and ruthless, a man who would do nearly anything for his family. And even in 1968, some people said he could still be ruthless, or at least so driven that you couldn't tell the difference. But he was not cynical. I remember the car ride from the airport to Vanderbilt. Three local politicians had squeezed into the front seat, while Kennedy shared the back with the former astronaut, John Glenn, and me. I had been assigned to introduce him that night, and I rode along in astonished silence, while the politicians tried to tell him what to say. This is a campus audience, they said, so talk about Vietnam if you want. But it's also the South, so go a little easy on the subject of race.

Kennedy merely shrugged and rejected their advice. At Vanderbilt and every other stop on his campaign tour, he spoke with passion about the wounds in the country—"the violence," he said, "that afflicts the poor...the slow destruction of a child by hunger, and schools without books, and homes without any heat in the winter...."

But despite his pleadings, the wounds grew worse. On April 4, 1968, Martin Luther King was murdered in Memphis. Kennedy heard the news on a plane to Indianapolis, where he was scheduled to appear that night at a campaign rally in a black neighborhood. All across the country the ghettos were burning, with looting and bombs and sniper fire from the high-rise apartments. But Kennedy insisted on keeping his appointment. Standing alone on a flatbed truck, hunched against the cold in his black overcoat, he told the crowd what had happened to King, and as the people cried out in disbelief, he told them he understood how they felt.

"In this difficult day," he said, "in this difficult time for the United States, it is perhaps well to ask what kind of nation we are and what direction we want to move in. For those of you who are black...you can be filled with bitterness, with hatred, and a desire for revenge. We can move in that direction as a country, in great polarization—black people amongst black, white people amongst white, filled with hatred toward one another.

"Or we can make an effort, as Martin Luther King did, to understand and to comprehend, and to replace that violence, that stain of bloodshed that has spread across our land, with an effort to under-stand....

"My favorite poet was Aeschylus. He wrote: 'In our sleep, pain which cannot forget falls drop by drop upon the heart until, in our own despair, against our will, comes wisdom through the awful grace of God.'"

There were no riots in Indianapolis that night. "I guess the thing that kept us going," said one of King's aides, "was that maybe Bobby Kennedy would come up with some answers."

For the next two months, a lot of people held grimly to that hope, especially as Kennedy did well in the primaries, and the thought began slowly to form in our minds that despite all the tragedy and despair of the decade—the war and the riots and the murder of good men—Kennedy might really be the country's next president.

And then he was gone, following unbelievably in the martyred path of Dr. King. In a way, it was a culmination of the '60s, the death of the promise that had been so strong. There was nobody now to give it a voice—unless, one day, we could find it in ourselves.

The Black Emergence: 1945-1965

Early in 1982, the Charlotte Observer *undertook a Black History series on the saga of race relations in North Carolina and South Carolina. I had covered civil rights for much of my career—a natural outgrowth, it seemed to me, of coming of age in the 1960s. But I was a journalist, trying to keep up with current events, and I was happy for the chance to go back in time in search of a bit of historical perspective.*

My assignment was to cover two decades, from 1945 to 1965, a time of ferment and an eventual sense of progress— a sort of We-Shall-Overcome momentum beginning near the end of World War II and continuing until the passage of the Voting Rights Act.

During that period—amid the sit-ins, marches and prece- dent-breaking lawsuits—blacks in the Carolinas and elsewhere were united in an assault on legal segregation. Jim Crow laws were abundant. North Carolina and South Carolina required segregated washrooms in factories and cotton mills, and both states were among 17 that segregated their schools.

In the next 15 years, a great deal would change. Dual public schools were ordered dismantled. Congress passed laws against segregated public accommodations, and after a blood- stained march from Selma to Montgomery, blacks secured sweeping protections under the Voting Rights Act. Those ti- tanic changes often began in the simplest of ways—with four frustrated freshmen in a dormitory bull session, or with a handful of farmers, country preachers and gas station attendants who wanted nothing more than a bus for their school children.

Here in those human terms, is a history of the period, be- ginning with the events in rural South Carolina that led, in the late 1940s, to the first successful challenge to segregated schools.

The Charlotte Observer
1982

The Schools

They began coming home from the South Pacific jungles, from Okinawa, Iwo Jima and the seas in between. Harry Briggs was one of them. He left the Navy after the surrender of Japan and returned to Summerton, South Carolina, where he had lived all his life.

Briggs, a solid, slightly round-faced man in his early thirties, was the father of five, a reliable provider who made his living pumping Sinclair gas at Carrigan's Service Station. He borrowed a little money from this preacher-friend, J. A. DeLaine, and built himself a house near Scott's Branch School.

Like other black people in Clarendon County, he was not especially impressed with the quality of the schools. He didn't know the statistics—how the whites who ran the public education system in that majority-black county spent $179 a year on each white student and only $43 a year on each black.

But he didn't have to know statistics to know that life was unfair in Clarendon County, a flat and tangled collection of hardwood forests and loamy cotton fields about halfway between Columbia and Charleston.

Political and economic power was in the hands of whites, and fewer than 300 of Clarendon's 4,600 black households earned as much as $2,000 a year. Harry Briggs understood the realities behind such figures, and like any rational man, he did not expect them to change.

Still, he had fought for his country during World War II. He had risked his life to defend American freedom, and it seemed that he and his people deserved something for that.

Like a school bus, perhaps.

In 1947, blacks in Clarendon County had petitioned for one—particularly to serve a small group of children near the community of Jordan, who had to walk nine miles around a lake, or else row a boat across it, to get to school.

But R. W. Elliott, a white sawmill owner and chairman of the school board, told the blacks simply: "We ain't got no money to buy a bus for your nigger children."

Harry Briggs didn't think that was fair. Nor did he approve when the chief petitioner for the bus, a fiftyish farmer named Levi Pearson, was denied credit by all of Clarendon's banks, nor when Elliott's sawmill refused to haul the timber that Pearson had cut to pay his bills, leaving it instead to rot on the ground.

21

So Briggs decided to fight back. He was not the leader in the fight; that task fell to J. A. DeLaine, the local spokesman for the NAACP. But Briggs did offer his house for strategy sessions, and alphabetically he became the first of 20 plaintiffs in the lawsuit of Briggs v. Elliott.

It was no ordinary lawsuit. Initially, it demanded equal schools for the black and white children of Clarendon County. But eventually, under the prodding of the NAACP's chief attorney, Thurgood Marshall, Harry Briggs and the other Clarendon blacks demanded a national dismantling of segregated schools—a move eventually affecting more than 11.5 million students in 17 states.

They paid a price for that demand. On Christmas Eve of 1949, Briggs was fired from his job at Carrigan's Service Station, and his wife, Liza, shortly lost her maid's job at a Summerton motel.

For J. A. DeLaine, the reprisals were worse. He was dismissed from his principal's position at a Clarendon County school and driven from his home by late-night gunfire. But Briggs and DeLaine would not relent, and their courage was supported by the thoroughness of the NAACP's legal staff and by the sympathetic ear of a federal district judge.

The judge was a patrician from Charleston, South Carolina. His name was J. Waties Waring, and he lived at 61 Meeting Street in a house that dated to the 17th century, nestled among the palms and wisteria and the stands of live oaks near the Charleston harbor.

Waring was a quiet man with sharply pointed features, his hair parted down the middle with aristocratic precision. He was 61 years old when he ascended to the federal bench, and from the beginning he had taken deep offense at civil rights violations.

Thurgood Marshall was aware of Waring's reputation. He was comforted by it, for the stakes were high and risky in Briggs vs. Elliott. Marshall knew that if he lost—if the courts affirmed the legality of segregation, as they had done at the turn of the century—the cause of black people would be set back irreparably.

Painstakingly, he constructed his case—first by documenting the inferiority of Clarendon County's black schools. Then, in a tactic that would later prove crucial, he set out to demonstrate the effects of segregation on the self-esteem of children.

Marshall asked for help from Dr. Kenneth Clark, a 37-year-old psychiatrist from City College of New York, who visited Clarendon County in 1951. Using a box full of black and white dolls, Clark conducted a series of experiments.

He asked 16 black children between the ages of six and nine which dolls they liked best. According to Richard Kluger, whose book Simple

Justice is the definitive history of the period, 10 children preferred the white dolls; 11 said the black dolls looked "bad."

In 1954, when Chief Justice Earl Warren wrote the Supreme Court's historic ruling, affirming Judge Waring's opinion that official segregation was unconstitutional, he was deeply moved by the tests Clark had conducted. They buttressed a feeling that he had, a simple gut certainty that segregated schools were damaging to children and inevitably unequal.

So, writing for the court, Warren declared them illegal.

The ruling applied to Clarendon County and to four other places where dual schools had been challenged—Prince Edward County, Virginia, Wilmington, Delaware, Washington, D.C., and Topeka, Kansas. In addition, the precedent affected 11,168 other school districts that practiced official segregation.

It was, morally and legally, the greatest victory that blacks had ever achieved. The problem was that nothing much came of it.

In Clarendon County, the schools quickly became all-black, as white parents—every single one of them before it was over—sent their children to private schools, rather than permit integration.

And throughout the South, most whites seemed embarked on a path of massive resistance. In 1957, for example, when Elizabeth Eckford and eight other black teenagers integrated Central High School in Little Rock, Arkansas, federal troops were required to protect them from the mobs.

The same year in Charlotte, a theology professor's daughter named Dorothy Counts—dressed in a prim checkered dress with a white bow at the collar—endured jeers and taunts as she enrolled in Harding High School. Two weeks later, she dropped out, after being spat upon regularly and pelted with rocks.

Most cities, meanwhile, simply ignored the Supreme Court's ruling, and segregation remained a reality in the South. So blacks grew impatient. They began to challenge Jim Crow laws and customs more directly than before: they simply refused to obey them.

In 1960, for example, four black college students demanded to be served at an all-white lunch counter. It was the first sit-in, and after it happened on that wintry day in Greensboro, North Carolina, the civil rights struggle gained a momentum it had never known.

This is how it came to be.

The Protests

It was cold that night. Too cold, they decided, to go anywhere. So they settled in about seven and began to talk and play chess. After a while, they could feel an all-nighter coming on.

They had had such sessions before—right there, in fact, in room 2123 with its drab green walls and off-white ceilings, the clutter of magazines scattered on the floor.

The room belonged to Joe McNeil and Ezell Blair. McNeil was studying physics, and the latest *Physics Today* had been tossed on the pile amid the old *Atlantic Monthlys*. There were philosophy texts and assorted paperbacks by Eric Hoffer and Nikos Kazantzakis.

But the talk that evening, January 31, 1960, seldom strayed to classwork. McNeil, Blair and their two friends from down the hall, Franklin McCain and David Richmond, were caught up once again in the central reality of their lives.

They were black students at NC A&T, a state university in Greensboro. All were freshmen—scholarship students from middle-class families—and from the beginning, they had sensed a philosophical affinity.

They would talk about the conditions afflicting their people, the insulting Jim Crow laws that had sprung up around the South at the turn of the century. They would rail at the patience of their parents' generation—people who had fought a world war to preserve American freedom, but who had failed to find a way to demand it for themselves.

The next day, these young men would make such a demand. They would make it in a way that commanded national attention, that generated a sense of movement and momentum for blacks across the South, and that tied in with earlier stirrings in Montgomery, Alabama—a bus boycott led by a then-obscure preacher named Martin Luther King.

Joe McNeil and the others were aware of that boycott. They approved of it, but gave it little thought for it seemed to them an isolated event. They were aware also of the legal strides in the field of education, the historic 1954 Supreme Court decision on segregated schools.

But what they felt most keenly was a sense of stagnation, at best of fits and starts, in the progress of their people. They had analyzed the subject from every conceivable angle—from the philosophical theories of Immanuel Kant and G. W. F. Hegel, to the social commentary of W. E. B. DuBois.

But as they noted that night, they themselves had done nothing. McNeil, more than any of them, kept pointing that out. He was the boat-rocker, the bright, impatient son of a cleaning company operator in Wilmington, North Carolina.

Blair and Richmond, both from Greensboro, were the steadiest of the group, and they insisted at least on a reasonable course of action, a carefully conceived plan, if they were to challenge the social order.

McCain, a chemistry major from Washington, D.C., tended to share McNeil's impatience, and he remembers the dynamics of the discussion that evening:

"The question kept re-emerging," he says. "'What are we going to do? Will we leave here as seniors still just debating? We can't sit back and wait. We've done nothing but engage in armchair rhetoric. We ought to feel badly about ourselves. It makes us less than men.'"

They began to talk about public accommodations—how nearby stores such as Walgreen's and Woolworth's would accept their money happily, but refused to serve them at their greasy spoon lunch counters.

"We said to ourselves," remembers McCain, "'if we tolerate it, to an extent, we probably deserve it.'"

Shortly after 5 a.m. on February 1, their bodies aching and eyes gazing blearily at the grayish streaks of dawn, they decided to "sit in"—a term that would soon become popular among blacks across the South—at a nearby lunch counter.

They thought of Walgreen's but chose Woolworth's instead because it was a much larger chain with stores across the country. They agreed to meet at the campus library at four that afternoon.

McCain remembers being distracted that day. He made it through chemistry and geometry and a discussion of James Thurber in English Composition. But he picked up several demerits in ROTC, his last class of the day, for speaking without permission.

Finally at 3:30, he headed for the library where he met the other three. At four, having given up on a handful of friends who promised reinforcements, they started off on the 10 minute walk to Woolworth's.

They arrived at the store and began meandering among the aisles, buying school supplies and keeping the receipts. As it happened, McCain and McNeil were closest to the lunch counter, and McCain recalls the strange mix of feelings:

"Apprehension. Anxiety. A fear of the unknown. I can't define explicitly what I had anxiety about, except that it's hard to plan an adequate defense if you don't know what will happen.

"So we just looked at that counter. We stood there maybe a minute, maybe five. Then McNeil and I looked at each other, looked at the counter again and then stepped toward it.

"The moment we sat down at that counter...well, I just can't tell you what it felt like. Never have I experienced such an incredible emotion, such an uplift in my life. My good friend from Atlanta, (journalist) Howell Raines, probably said it best: 'My soul was rested.'

"Everything else that ever happens is probably downhill from that. I don't think it's possible for me to crystallize that feeling, and in most

25

conversations I don't even try—because the words are not adequate, because they can sound very foolish and pretentious."

In any case, says McCain, they took their seats on the padded swivel stools, beneath the signs for 10-cent coffee and 15-cent lemon pie—McCain still in his ROTC uniform, with his black-rimmed glasses and small, thin mustache; McNeil more boyish and slightly sad-faced—waiting for the waitress to come and tell them to leave.

She did come and tell them, a slightly flustered white woman, brown-haired and average-sized, maybe 40 years old with the look of middle age. She said, "We don't serve Negroes here."

That had happened before at Woolworth's. What was new was the resistance—McCain speaking softly with a manicured politeness: "I beg to disagree. You do serve us and you have." And McNeil added stubbornly: "We have the receipts to prove it."

A policeman arrived about that time and began to pace near the scene, tapping his nightstick firmly in his palm. The waitress, meanwhile, went to fetch the manager, James Harris, as Blair and Richmond, who had been across the store, arrived to take their seats at the counter near McCain.

The tension grew.

"I just can't serve you," said Harris, obviously the man in charge, with his blue suit, white shirt and tie.

Why? he was asked.

"Because it's custom," said Harris, his frustration mounting, but also a pained confusion, a collision between his decency and the logic of the argument that now confronted him. Still, he would not relent:

"There's a counter downstairs. It's custom. You can get anything you want."

The crowd began to grow as word spread of the stand-off. Maybe 200 whites were watching near the counter, their mood a mixture of curiosity and resentment. More were gathering on the sidewalk outside, staring in through the windows that faced Elm Street.

Harris left and the crowd still glared. But one of their number, an aging white woman with a feisty air about her, approached the four young men still sitting at the counter. She patted their backs, and told them loudly enough for anyone to overhear:

"Boys, I'm so proud of you. The only thing is, it should have been done twenty years ago."

That was the high point. The low point came when a black kitchen worker berated the four for their impatience and presumption. "Why don't you just get up and leave," she pleaded with them finally.

"At that moment," says McCain, now an executive with Celanese in Charlotte, "we literally hated her. Later, I felt differently. I came to understand how we threatened her world and the order she was used to. She could see no good coming out of what we were doing."

The good came, however.

The four left that day when James Harris closed the store. But they returned the next morning with maybe 20 of their friends, and by that afternoon, every stool at the counter was occupied by blacks.

The national press arrived. Woolworth's eventually gave in, and the sit-in tactic spread across the South, as blacks—middle-class and poor—took common offense at official segregation.

Their primary spokesman, in the eyes of the national press, and increasingly in the eyes of Southern blacks as well, became Martin Luther King, an eloquent preacher of some reluctance, who, at the least, had been trained for his role.

Some of the training came from his father, Martin Luther King, Sr., an Atlanta preacher who dreamed of revitalizing the Southern black church, making it a force for social change.

The younger King's other mentor was a South Carolinian named Benjamin Mays, a sharecropper's son, born in Greenwood County near the end of Reconstruction, when the presumed inferiority of his people became a matter of law—of official policy in his home state and elsewhere.

"I never did accept what my eyes saw and what my ears heard," says Mays, now in his late eighties and living in Atlanta. "Everything around me said to me that I and my people were inferior. Negroes were constantly cringing and kowtowing in the presence of white people.

"I remember when I was four years old, a mob of whites came by my father's house. They were on their way to the town of Phoenix, where a black man had tried to register to vote.

"But they stopped and made my father take off his hat, bow down and salute. They were armed, and they made him scrape and humble himself. I didn't think that was right."

The episode, which offended a four-year-old's sense of fairness, stayed with Mays as he made his way through school, then to South Carolina State College in Orangeburg, Virginia Union, predominantly white Bates College in Maine, and finally to his doctorate in theology from the University of Chicago.

As the honors piled atop each other, Mays began to absorb not only the learning itself, but a lesson so fundamental that it became an obsession: "I was trying to demonstrate," he says, "that I was not inferior."

Eventually, he believed it and set out to teach other blacks as well.

He became president of Atlanta's Morehouse College, and one of his most willing students, in the years following World War II, was Martin Luther King, Jr.

Mays thought the religion he experienced as a child in South Carolina was a barrier as well as a solace to blacks. He wrote:

"I heard the pastor of the church of my youth plead with members of his congregation not to try to avenge the wrongs they suffered, but to take their burdens to the Lord in prayer. Especially did he do this when the racial situation was tense or when Negroes went to him for advice concerning some wrong inflicted upon them by their oppressors." The pastor assured them "that God would fix things up" and "would reward them in heaven for their patience and long suffering on the earth.

"Members of the congregation screamed, shouted and thanked God. They felt relieve and uplifted...they sang, prayed and shouted their troubles away. This had telling effect on the Negroes in my home community. It kept them submissive, humble and obedient. It enabled them to keep on keeping on."

Like the elder King, Mays believed in the potential of the Southern black church; it was, after all, the only institution that blacks had been allowed. And he brought black scholars to Morehouse College, who instructed the students in the tactical non-violence of Mahatma Ghandi.

In 1956, the younger King was able to put his training to use. The opportunity, however, took him by surprise, for unlike the four students in Greensboro, his friend Rosa Parks had given it little advance thought when she refused, on a Montgomery bus, to relinquish her seat to a white man who demanded it. She was simply tired.

And after she was arrested and taken off to jail, Montgomery's black community was almost universally insulted—shocked that a woman like Mrs. Parks, a respected seamstress with an air of great dignity, could be treated so shabbily.

They rallied to her defense by boycotting the buses, and they chose King as their spokesman. He was a good choice. He was only 26 and completely untested by the trials of leadership. But already he had a gift that would continue to develop over the next 12 years—an oratorical flair that was probably unsurpassed by any man of his century.

Partly it was a simple question of pulpit showmanship, the sense of cadence and momentum, the dramatic rise and fall of his voice. But more than that, he had a certain perspective, an ability to reassure his people through all the victories and tragedies that made up the movement—the church bombings in Birmingham, the murdered civil rights workers in Alabama and Mississippi—that "the arc of the moral universe is long, but it bends toward justice."

He told them such things in Washington in 1963, on a late summer's day when 200,000 black people and their white allies marched peacefully on the capital. There were only three arrests that day—two thugs and a Nazi—as King proclaimed improbable thoughts and dreams about the future of the South:

"I have a dream today...that one day on the red hills of Georgia, the sons of former slaves and the sons of former slaveowners will be able to sit down together at the table of brotherhood."

For a while, it almost seemed possible. Congress passed a strong civil rights bill in 1964, outlawing segregation in public accommodations.

Then, in 1965, King led his most important march—a trek from Selma to Montgomery, an occasion in which one of his followers, James Reeb, was beaten to death outside a Selma cafe, and another, Viola Liuzzo, was killed by gunfire on an Alabama back road.

Congress responded by passing the Voting Rights Act, assuring blacks in the South of access to the ballot. The result over the next 15 years was a stunning increase in the number of black elected officials —from fewer than two dozen in the Carolinas to 485 in 1980.

Things, however, began to sour after that. The summers exploded as blacks rioted regularly in major cities around the country, burning the neighborhoods in which they felt themselves trapped. For even though they could vote or eat where they chose, millions of them experienced little improvement in their lives.

They were as poor, and felt as victimized, as they ever had before. And that feeling was at the heart of an uncertainty, a dilemma and a division, that began to afflict the black movement.

Until the Voting Rights Act and other gains of the '60s, blacks were united by a common reality: the shared insult of official segregation.

But that bond was broken—ironically enough, by the progress of the movement—and blacks found themselves in a subtle new period. The challenge was now economic, and some of them met it nicely: During the 1960s, black family income increased by 141 percent in North Carolina and nearly 162 percent in South Carolina.

But millions of blacks remained desperately poor—and no longer, it seemed, were their interests indistinguishable from these of the middle class. Ralph Abernathy, who took over Martin Luther King's organization after King was murdered in 1968, offered this summary of the new dilemmas of leadership:

"It's a difficult period," he said as the '60s drew to a close. "Very hard to get a handle on exactly what to do."

September 1957

The civil rights movement was always a mixture. From Benjamin Mays to Martin Luther King, there were people of erudition and brilliance, extraordinarily prepared for the leadership roles that came their way. But there were others who were even more heroic—the ordinary people who simply took a stand. One of those was Dorothy Counts, who became a pioneer for integration at the age of 15. I learned her story in the 1970s, when I was covering the continuing struggle in Charlotte to completely desegregate the public schools. The controversy began in the 1950s, and this account of those earlier times was pieced together from newspaper archives, and from long interviews with Dorothy Counts.

The Dream Long Deferred
1988

It was always a city of two minds about itself. As Dorothy Counts discovered, on September 4, 1957, while the mob of white people closed in around her, with their threats and petty violence and cries of "nigger," Charlotte was a deeply Southern city. It was caught up in all the prejudice and racial fear that defined life in the region, and those emotions, being powerful and basic, were easily stirred. But even at the time, there were glimmers of something different. Brock Barkley, a florid, barrel-chested, chain-smoking lawyer—a man of great intensity and conviction who had once chaired the school board and was now its attorney—had persuaded local school officials that integration was inevitable. The best course of action, he said, was to begin it voluntarily. He had relied on an argument of enlightened self-interest—"begin the process before somebody sues you"—but he found more than mere self-interest in Superintendent Elmer Garinger, who would tell his principals in the late spring and early summer of 1957: "Desegregation is not only the law, it is also right."

The history of race relations in Charlotte is the history of Garinger's point of view in a life-and-death collision with its volatile opposite. When that struggle began in 1957, black leaders had no illusions about which view was in ascendancy. Certainly, Herman Counts had none when Kelly Alexander, the head of the local NAACP, approached him the summer of 1957 and asked him to volunteer his children as desegregation pioneers. Counts, the father of four, was a family man first of all. But if he believed, as he often told his children, that they could be what they wanted to be, and go where they wanted to go and the chains of prejudice did not have to bind them, Counts recognized that his was a view with political implications. Somebody had to be first. And, if one of the pioneers had to come from his family, he probably felt the most confidence in Dorothy. The third of four children and the only daughter, she was uncommonly levelheaded for a girl of 15. There was a certain serenity about her that was hard to define, a feeling of confidence and optimism that may have been in part a reflection of her father's. But wherever it came from it was so deeply rooted as to be unobtrusive: she did not have to flaunt it, it was simply there.

Earlier in the summer of 1957, Dorothy had spent a week at a Presbyterian youth conference in Grinnell, Iowa, rooming with a white girl who had never encountered a black person before, not at least as an equal. The two of them had talked for many hours exploding racial myths and developing a bond that gave Dorothy confidence about the challenge that now confronted her. "I told my father," she remembers, "that while I was in Grinnell, I met kids from all over the country, and I never felt anything in the way of hostility. I said, I'm sure there were some negative feelings, but I didn't experience them while I was there, and I didn't think there would be a problem at Harding."

Herman Counts was proud of his daughter's courage, and quietly pleased with her view of human nature. He was, however, also a man who understood the risks, and he called the family together on the night of September 3, beginning the discussion with a prayer about what lay ahead. Such meetings were common in the Counts household, and they occurred most often at the dinner hour usually between five and six, after Counts had returned home from his office on the nearby campus of Johnson C. Smith University.

Counts was a tall and imposing man, 6-feet-4 and 220 pounds, and with his dark suits, white shirts and carefully knotted ties, he carried himself with an air of great dignity. He came from a family of achievers, people who understood the realities of slavery and the system of white supremacy that became its natural heir, but who were determined,

31

nevertheless, to carve out the foundations for the family's self-respect.

As Counts began to speak, gently and informally on that night in September, his words, his opening prayer, even the setting itself, all evoked a sense of the legacy he was seeking to impart. They had gathered, as it happened, around a family heirloom, a mahogany dining table handed down for generations, and though they would not have put it this way at the time, the table was a sturdy and cherished symbol of continuity and achievement. It had belonged most recently to Dorothy's great-uncle, the late headmaster of a black academy in Cheraw, South Carolina, a Presbyterian institution, dedicated to the notion that blacks could make it in America. So as his wife and children quietly took their places, heads bowed and eyes closed, Herman Counts prayed briefly for unity and strength. He told the others that while Dorothy was the one who would be on the line, they must all be available to offer their support. And then he said to Dorothy: No matter what happens tomorrow, remember who you are. Remember the things that you have been taught. Hold your head up. You're the same as they are. You can do whatever you want to do.

Then the morning came, and Dorothy and her father, accompanied by a family friend, Edwin Thompkins, drove to Harding High School. They were astonished at the size of the crowd—maybe 400 people, many of them students, clogging the street leading up to the school. Thompkins and Dorothy got out of the car, and while Herman Counts went to find a parking place, they began the short walk to the Harding auditorium. The crowd immediately closed in around them, hatred twisting the young faces, as they spat at her and pelted her with ice, demanding that she return to the continent of her ancestors. She walked through them calmly, feeling, she remembered later, a strange mix of emotions, though oddly enough, fear was not among them. She felt enveloped, somehow, in the strength of her family and in the Sunday school certainty that God would protect her. And there was something else as well—an emotion that would have infuriated the mob, driving its members toward an even greater frenzy if they had only detected it. She felt pity for them, a conviction, tinged with the traces of youthful self-righteousness, but also with a genuine compassion, that they would not do these things if they had been raised better, if they had grown up in a family as loving as her own.

Even that evening, as the threatening calls began (mixed with a few that were sympathetic) and carloads of white people cruised past her house, she persisted in feeling that it would be all right.

Meanwhile, the photographs of her reception that day were transmitted by the wire services throughout the world. Eventually, the events at Harding would be overshadowed by the rioting in Little Rock, Arkansas, where federal troops were required to assure the safety of eight black students at the city's Central High School. But for those who saw them, the pictures of Dorothy Counts and her youthful white tormentors were etched deeply in the mind, a testament to the ugly futility of the hour.

The next morning, she was sick. Plagued with chronic tonsillitis, Dorothy developed a sore throat and fever that would keep her home for two days, and even though her father went to school and picked up her homework assignments, word quickly spread that she was not coming back. Apparently as a result, there were no mobs to greet her when she returned to Harding on Monday. Encouraged, she went to her locker, picked up her books and moved on to class. There were a few shocked stares and murmurs of surprise, but the thing she remembers most was the silence of her teachers. They basically ignored her, even when she knew the answers to their questions and eagerly raised her hand. "That's OK," she told herself, "because they don't know what you know. You've just got to work a little harder."

She made it through the morning, and then came lunch. There were racial slurs as she waited in line, and when she got her food and sat down at a table by herself, several boys came up and threw trash on her plate. She got up quietly and went outside, walking by herself up a grassy hillside. In a little while, two white girls came up and introduced themselves. Their names were Jean King and Betty Broom, and they told her they were glad that she had come to Harding. Jean King, especially, seemed deeply affected by the meeting. Years later, she would remember the size and softness of Dorothy's eyes, the light-skinned delicacy of her youthful complexion. And she remembered also what they talked about—how they had sought to assure her that the hostility would pass. Then they settled on the grass, crinolines rustling beneath their calf-length skirts, and began pulling family pictures from their overstuffed wallets. Jean was particularly impressed with Dorothy's older brother, handsome and serious in his military uniform, and Dorothy remembers thinking that she had found a friend. When her father came to pick her up that day, and asked her how it had gone, she told him she was encouraged. "I had a good experience," she said, and she told him about the noon hour spent on the hillside.

Then came the third day—and things were suddenly worse. There was more pushing and shoving in the halls, more name calling, teachers still treating her as if she wasn't there. At lunchtime, she looked for

33

Jean and Betty, who seemed to ignore her. Puzzled, she walked outside, where the two girls stopped her and told her that they would have to back away. The pressure and the ostracism were simply too great. Jean King thought for a moment that Dorothy might cry. But she didn't. She told them instead that she understood what they were saying, and that she would always remember their generosity and kindness.

The next day, the fourth, was the worst and the last. Devoid of allies, Dorothy discovered that morning that her locker had been ransacked. There were more racial slurs as she walked through the halls, more pointed silences from her teachers in class. Later at her locker, a small metal object struck her in the head, and a blackboard eraser, thrown by a student, hit her in the back. Her brother, waiting in the car to pick her up for lunch, was startled by the shattering of the rear windshield—crushed by a mock orange, a hard piece of fruit, thrown from nearby.

Herman Counts hurried home as soon as he heard the news. He called several friends, including his minister Dr. J. W. Smith, Kelly Alexander of the NAACP, and Dr. Reginald Hawkins, a fiery young dentist who was beginning to emerge as Charlotte's leading black militant. They talked to Dorothy and discussed it among themselves, and with the concurrence of the others, Herman Counts decided that enough was enough. He turned to Dorothy, a full participant in the discussions and told her simply: "Dot, I really don't think it's worth it."

The next day, Thursday, September 12, Counts called a press conference and issued a written statement, explaining his decision in the simplest terms: "It is with compassion for our native land and love for our daughter Dorothy that we withdraw her as a student at Harding High School."

For the Counts, however, there were, in the end, a few consolations—heartening expressions of support and good will that left them believing there was hope for the future. One of those came from evangelist Billy Graham, a Charlotte native who had already made public his opposition to segregation. In 1952, he had personally pulled down the ropes separating the white and black audiences at a Graham crusade in Chattanooga, Tennessee. Five years later, after reading the newspaper accounts of Dorothy's first day at Harding, Graham sat down and wrote her a postcard. Dated September 6, 1957, and written in pencil, the message was stiff and awkwardly sympathetic, a curious mixture of Christian compassion and Cold War patriotism: "Dear Miss Counts," Graham wrote. "Democracy demands that you hold fast and carry on. The world of tomorrow is looking for leaders and you have been chosen. Those cowardly whites against you will never prosper because they are un-American and unfit to lead. Be of good faith. God is not dead. He will see you through. This is your one great chance to prove to Russia that democracy still prevails. Billy Graham, D. D."

Far more touching, and more gently Christian, was a much longer letter from Mary Bowers MacKorell, a Presbyterian Sunday school teacher who also taught Bible classes at Harding. Apologizing for an illness that had kept her away from school during much of Dorothy's ordeal, Miss MacKorell wrote on September 13:

Dear Dorothy, I thought things were going to be all right for you at Harding. I am writing this note just to tell you how deeply I regret to hear of the events there this week which have caused you and your family to think it wise that you withdraw from our school. I can understand your decision in this matter and do not blame you for it. You have made a very courageous and dignified effort to serve your people in this just and righteous cause. Your efforts will not be in vain for as your father so well expressed it in his excellent statement for your family, the cause is just and it will win. Perhaps the victory will be slow in coming, for that is the way God's kingdom moves forward on this earth. When I return to my Bible classes at Harding it will be with an ache in my heart that we have failed you.

However heartening such letters may have been—whatever their foreshadowings of the eventual triumph of good will in Charlotte—the most striking, the most healing, gesture toward Dorothy Counts may have been one that occurred much later. Nearly 28 years after her departure from Harding, in February of 1985, she was interviewed by a television station in Charlotte. Returning home that evening in the nearby town of Gastonia, Jean King saw the interview and the old footage from Harding, and she decided immediately to write Dorothy a letter. For years, she said, she had wanted to explain why she had withdrawn her friendship after sharing the pictures on the Harding hillside. In that letter and the conversation that followed it, she told Dorothy the details of her own ordeal. Jean, like Dorothy, had been a new student at the school. She had come to Charlotte that summer from her hometown of Easley, South Carolina, newly married at the age of 16, a little nervous perhaps over the changes in her life. Her childhood had been unusually free of the prejudice that afflicted most of her peers, the Southern worldview that even her young husband would begin to struggle with, and she was grateful to her parents for the example they had set. Her father, the hard-working proprietor of a tile and flooring company, simply did not believe that white people were superior to blacks, and indeed the experiences of Jean's childhood suggested otherwise. Several of the neighborhood children were Negroes, and they were, as Jean remembered them, "high-caliber people," one of them growing up to be a doctor, another a psychologist. So when Jean spoke warmly to Dorothy Counts on her first day at Harding, or when she admired Dorothy's family pictures several days later, she did not intend either act as a political gesture. She simply felt compassion for a girl who was the brunt of such rudeness, and in a way that was hard to define at the time, she identified with Dorothy: Dorothy was black, Jean was married, and that made both of them different.

But such simple motives were incomprehensible to many of the white students at Harding, and bizarre rumors quickly spread: Jean King was a plant from the NAACP, a spy to monitor white resistance to integration. Because of such perceptions, Jean's ordeal in September of 1957 was nearly identical to that of Dorothy Counts. She was shoved in the hallways, eggs were thrown at her car, and rocks at her upstairs apartment. And after her picture appeared with Dorothy's, first in the *Charlotte Observer* and later in *Life* magazine, her parents were harassed in South Carolina and her husband taunted on his job at Capitol Airlines. Then one day in the bathroom at Harding, other girls held the door shut and refused to let her out; and after she returned home from school, she found a menacing note attached to her door: "We know where you life."

So in a frightened gesture that she has regretted ever since, Jean King told Dorothy they could not be friends. ("I was sixteen," she says. "I wasn't mature enough to cope with it.") But they are friends today—a happy and symbolic ending to a story that began in a very different way. As the years would reveal, it was both the blessing and the curse of Southern life that the noblest instincts—the well-springs of decency that coexisted with the meanness—were buried most deeply. There were places where, in time, the better instincts would rise to the surface—but never easily, and seldom without a head-on collision with all of the ugliness that stood in the way.

In Charlotte, eventually, simple decency prevailed. Three decades after her own ordeal, when Dorothy's daughter and nephew and other members of the family made their way through the schools, the Charlotte-Mecklenburg system was one of the most integrated in the country.

The Other Side of Southern Justice

The South's racial progress of the past 30 years, fragile but dramatic, might never have happened if the civil rights movement had not found an important ally in the courts. Back in 1979, I wrote about that for the Charlotte Observer, *tracing the origins of a judicial era in which precedents established in Deep South courtrooms began to affect not only this region, but the nation as a whole. In seeking to understand that era, I relied on numerous interviews of my own, as well as the writings of judicial scholars—particularly Richard Kluger, whose book, Simple Justice, is a brilliant account of the Brown vs. Board of Education lawsuit.*

In the course of that research, I was impressed by the ironies surrounding federal judges in the South. They struck me as real-life Atticus Finches—men who never sought controversy, but who simply planted their feet, behaving with a certain grace, stubbornness and aristocratic certainty.

A part of the story of federal judges in the South has been told earlier in this book, primarily in chapter two. But that was the black man's side of the story. What follows is an often overlooked segment of the white man's response—the legacy of a handful of highly principled Southerners who, for more than 20 years, exercised enormous sway in the affairs of the country. The legacy, however, is beginning to fade.

The Charlotte Observer
1979

There is a tiny brass plaque at 61 Meeting Street in Charleston, South Carolina, a tarnished reminder that the house is old—a certified piece of tradition in a neighborhood dating to the 17th century. But the plaque says nothing about the man who lived in the house, which seems an odd and deliberate oversight.

Charleston is famous for the homage it pays to aristocratic heroes —to secessionists, Civil War generals, and warriors of the American Revolution. But there is a crucial difference between the rebellions of Francis Marion or John C. Calhoun, and the more recent heresies of Judge J. Waties Waring.

There is a comfortable quality about revolutions that have faded into history. The violence and the sense of upheaval are absorbed and gentled by the passage of time.

And so it is that chiseled stone monuments—shrouded by wisteria vines and twisting live oak branches—still honor the rhetoric of secession. Antebellum cannons still aim their malevolence across the Charleston harbor, pointing to the spot where the Civil War began. But the legal and social revolution that gained momentum (some would even say it started) in the somber, pine-paneled courtroom of Judge Waring is the object of official neglect. Its effects are too unsettling, too much a part of today, to permit much homage.

Waring became, in his 61st year, a U. S. District Judge—the first in America to hear an overt challenge to the segregation of schools or to hand down a pair of sweeping, bluntly worded rulings giving black people the right to vote.

It was not a role that he sought or expected to play. For the first six decades of his life, he was a pillar of Charleston's tranquility—an aristocratic lawyer and mildly ambitious politician, who belonged to all the right clubs, believed all the right things and was honored and admired by his fellow Charlestonians.

Like so many of his colleagues in the federal judiciary, he had achieved his lofty position precisely because he never rocked any boats. But he came to the bench in the 1940s—the beginning of a period of judicial history that was one of the most wrenching the country had ever known.

Federal judges, particularly in the South, were compelled to deal over the next 30 years with a bewildering array of constitutional issues —from voting rights to school segregation, from police brutality to the future of nuclear energy. Because of rulings by Southern judges—precedents set in deep South courtrooms—cities from Boston to Los Angeles have wrestled with busing and school integration for the better part of a decade.

A whole race has been given access to the ballot, mental patients have been guaranteed the right to treatment, and legislatures across the country have been reapportioned—shifting the balance of political power from rural America to the nation's cities.

For all of that, the judges themselves have paid a price. If their rulings often tore at the domestic tranquility of their region and nation, there have been similar effects on the comfortable, uneventful lives that most of them had known.

"Federal judges," concludes Robert Merhige, a district judge in Richmond, "don't start lawsuits. But the cases began, and they started coming to all of us. That's what the federal courts are for. They are places where minorities can come, where they ought to come. In the South, of course, that often meant blacks, and the racial issue was probably the most unsettling we had to deal with. Because of the laws we had in our region, the attack on legal segregation—especially segregated schools—began in the South."

More precisely, you could argue, the attack began on a dusty backroad in Clarendon County, South Carolina, in a creaky, paint-chipped cabin belonging to Harry Briggs. They met one night in 1948— a half dozen black men, frightened at the potential consequences of their rebellion, but knowing in the end there was no turning back.

Their concern was schools—the gaping disparity between the facilities and opportunities afforded to Clarendon County's white children, and those afforded their own. The county, in those days, was one of the state's most primitive—a swatch of picked over cotton fields and murky, black-water swamplands that yielded a meager and reluctant living to the people who clung to the land. And overlaid against all of that was the specter of segregation.

"It seems unbelievable when you look back at it," affirms Billie S. Fleming, a longtime leader in the Clarendon NAACP, a large and genial black man who exudes the dignity and assurance that his people were striving for in the 1940s.

"I remember when I was a boy, coming through schools in the twenties and thirties, almost all the money went for white schools. Blacks got only what was left over—and that was nothing but some money to pay a few teachers. The state and county did not provide us with bricks and mortar, and when we built facilities for ourselves, the county didn't even furnish fuel and utilities. Public-spirited citizens would chop wood and haul it on wagons so the children could have some heat.

"In the majority of cases, there was only one teacher per school, usually teaching six or eight grades. Public transportation was provided only for white students, even when blacks lived ten or twelve miles from high school. It seems unbelievable," he concludes with a tug at his graying mustache. "But that's how it was."

Conditions had changed very little by the 1940s, and in response, Clarendon's black people decided to take their concerns to federal court

39

—to Judge Waring, who was rapidly emerging as a man with a sympathetic ear.

When they first arrived in Waring's court, the Clarendon plaintiffs weren't asking for anything radical. They simply wanted decent and equalized facilities—such basic amenities as indoor plumbing and heated buildings on cold winter mornings. But when the dust finally settled, they had, at Waring's urging, redrawn their suit—demanding nothing less than the total dismantling of a segregated school system.

The decision to pursue such a drastic course did not come easily. It became intertwined with the national policies of the NAACP, which had entered the Clarendon case at the request of the Rev. J. A. DeLaine and the county's other black leaders.

The NAACP's chief strategist in those days was a tough and aggressive attorney named Thurgood Marshall, later a justice on the U. S. Supreme Court. He had long understood the pitfalls of an outright attack on segregation itself—the potential for disaster if such an all-or-nothing course were to fall flat on its face.

He knew that in 1896, the Supreme Court had handed down the Plessy v. Ferguson ruling—affirming the constitutionality of separate but equal facilities for blacks and whites. Throughout the 1940s, the NAACP's primary strategy was to seek an implementation of the Plessy precedent—to file a series of lawsuits charging that while schools for black and white were officially separate they were also decidedly unequal.

The strategy was proving effective in cases throughout the South, most of them higher education suits in Texas, Louisiana and North Carolina. Gradually, Marshall and his fellow attorneys were chipping away at the problem, dramatizing the hypocrisy of separate but equal and securing a steady stream of rulings requiring better black schools.

The attorneys knew that the cost of providing segregated—but truly equal—public schools systems would prove to be exorbitant. Eventually, they hoped, the South would find the price too high.

Marshall, however, was consistently uncomfortable with such a gradual and circuitous approach to breaking down the walls of segregation. He began to declare in his public speeches that the NAACP was committed to a reversal of the Plessy precedent, to a ringing affirmation by the U. S. Supreme Court that separate was inherently unequal.

As it happened, his public declarations coincided with the NAACP's entry into the Clarendon County case—a fact that Marshall found disturbing. He couldn't imagine a worse test case for total integration, since Clarendon was a poor, rural and majority black county with a history of racial hostility.

He knew that if he abandoned his strategy of the past, he would be asking not only for the radical, unheard-of step of integrating public schools, but also for the busing of whites into a minority situation. He decided to hedge his bets, arguing in passing that separate could never be equal, but emphasizing that in any case, Clarendon's black schools should be drastically improved.

Fleming remembers the response of Judge Waring, how he peered from the bench with a somber expression on his round, friendly face. He summoned Marshall forward, and then, according to Fleming, "He told us, 'You're going down the wrong road. If you really want the courts to declare segregation to be unconstitutional, you need to draw your arguments exactly that way.'"

Marshall and the blacks of Clarendon County would have been dumbfounded by such advice from a Deep South judge if they had not watched the gradual transformation of Waring from the time he was appointed to the bench.

Born in 1880, the judge was raised in a time when Reconstruction had left its scars on South Carolina. His was a genteel lineage, running back through eight generations of Charlestonians, and while he was never an out-and-out race-baiter, neither did he question the social order of the day.

"Most of the Negroes I knew were ex-slaves," he would later recall. "You loved them and were good to them. We didn't give them any rights, but they never asked for any rights, and I didn't question it. I was raised in the atmosphere that we ought to take care of these people."

Waring's noblesse oblige sensibilities were deeply offended early in his tenure on the bench. It began with a peonage dispute, a case in which a white man was accused of detaining a black and forcing him to work for almost nothing. Waring ordered the white man to jail. Later, he would order South Carolina's Democratic Party to allow blacks to vote in statewide primaries and would require equal salaries for the state's black and white teachers.

His life, at that point, began to change. Hate mail poured into his office. Late-night telephone calls brought threats and promises of bodily harm. And one October evening in 1950, three pistol shots rang through the Charleston night—the ricochet narrowly missing Waring and his wife, Elizabeth, as they played canasta in the living room.

But at least as unsettling as the threats were the more sophisticated retributions of Waring's fellow bluebloods. During more tranquil times, when he was Charleston's city attorney, he would step out his front door and stroll briskly past the swaying palms of Meeting Street,

41

smiling, waving and chatting with friends during his one-block walk to city hall.

Such strolls soon became lonely. Party invitations, once numerous, dried up entirely, and even Waring's own family reacted as if a leper had appeared in its midst. The change was sealed by his role in the school case, and at age 70, Waring found his life transformed—found himself wholly alienated from the people and values of his first 60 years.

It did not help—in fact the situation became more nasty—when the Supreme Court affirmed Waring's view that segregation was unconstitutional, declaring in 1954, and in a follow-up ruling in 1955, that America's schools must be desegregated with all deliberate speed.

Following the high court's sweeping proclamation (which was based on the Clarendon case and four others, including Brown v. Topeka, Kansas), Waring resigned his judgeship and moved to New York to spend his remaining years. He had been sustained in Charleston only by his wife and a few black friends, and the loneliness eventually took its toll.

It was a peculiar, and in some ways tragic, scene in 1968 when Waring returned to Charleston for the final time—to be buried in one of the city's oldest cemeteries, lowered to earth in a plain pine casket. A handful of whites—his wife, a minister and an efficient-looking undertaker—watched in silence, while behind them nearly 300 blacks lowered their heads in a final gesture of respect.

Many of them were from Clarendon County, and like the judge, they too had felt the sting of retribution—at times had felt it even more acutely, as the white man's counterattack cost them homes, farms and the ability to make a living. But it was a price they paid in behalf of themselves, and never had they they seen a white man willing to match their sacrifice.

"I remember one time the judge and I were talking," recalls Fleming. "He was always a gentleman, never bitter about the things he went through, and one day he asked in his quiet way. He said, 'Mr. Fleming do you really believe that I have helped your people?' I said, 'Yes sir, Judge, I do. More than any man since Abraham Lincoln.'"

The same year Waring was buried, an equally unimposing, unthreatening man was taking the oath of office 200 miles away in Charlotte. James McMillan, a respected lawyer who grew up in the flat, tobacco country farmlands of Robeson County, North Carolina, knew from the beginning that a federal judgeship had its pitfalls. He was

42

aware of the examples, not only of Waring, but dozens of others around the South—particularly Frank Johnson, a stubborn, independent Republican from the hills of northern Alabama.

Johnson was appointed to the bench in 1956, and since that time had been called upon to decide the legality of nearly every conceivable aspect of Alabama society. He had desegregated buses, bus terminals, jails and prisons, museums, mental institutions and more than 100 school systems in his district.

But controversy came in other forms as well. He declared that Alabama's mental institutions had a responsibility to treat, as well as confine, their inmates and ordered them emptied if they didn't attempt to do it. He abolished the Alabama poll tax and ordered the reapportionment of the state legislature—following the one-man, one-vote precedent established by his fellow Southern Republican, Judge William Millor of Nashville.

For those things, of course, Johnson paid a price. His former classmate at the University of Alabama, Governor George Wallace, declared him political enemy number one. Death threats were common, and Johnson was shunned by proper Montgomery society, just as Waring had been in Charleston.

McMillan was aware that similar consequences could come his way, but he didn't dwell on the prospect. He was not a man with a martyr complex, and he certainly didn't expect hard times and bitterness to descend in the form that they eventually took.

But in 1968, a group of Charlotte blacks, represented by civil rights lawyer Julius Chambers, re-opened the local school desegregation suit, contending progress to that point had been minimal at best. McMillan was unsympathetic at first. But Chambers' carefully prepared case turned him around, and he issued, in 1969, perhaps the most stunning school desegregation ruling in the history of the country.

He ordered the Charlotte-Mecklenburg school system to use "any and all known ways of desegregation, including busing" to completely desegregate the schools by the fall of 1970. And when the U. S. Supreme Court unanimously sustained him in 1971, it raised the possibility of meaningful—that is, total—school integration nearly anywhere in America.

Not long ago, McMillan parked himself behind a table in a Charlotte restaurant and offered a wistful and typically low-keyed assessment of his role in Swann v. Charlotte-Mecklenburg Schools.

"Legally speaking," he explained in his muted Carolina accents, "I've had a number of cases that were considerably more challenging. The Swann case was simply a matter of absorbing the education and then working up the courage to act on what I absorbed. It took me a little while to do it."

It was, as usual, a brief and understated monologue. And McMillan —never very expansive when the conversation centers on himself— found his train of thought continually disrupted by people passing his table and paying their respects. Though he didn't say so, the disruptions had to contain a certain measure of ironic satisfaction, for there was a time only a few years ago when such pleasantries would have been a rare occurrence indeed.

When the community began to grasp that his ruling was for real, McMillan was hanged in effigy. There were demonstrations at his modest brick home near the Charlotte Country Club, and death threats became an accepted part of his life.

McMillan doesn't like to talk about such things today, and even at the time, he retained a remarkable level of dignity and calmness. He has a Presbyterian's fatalism—a sense, as he puts it, that "God has a plan for our lives, and we're a lot better off if we can try not to fight it."

He also discerned, in a short time, some heartening signs that Charlotte was adjusting to the change. In 1975, an ad hoc citizens group, working with the school system's staff, devised what McMillan considered a fair and stable desegregation plan, and the judge closed the case as an active piece of litigation.

He praised his fellow Charlotteans for their maturity and restraint and announced he was "retiring from the education business." But if McMillan held doggedly to his perspective and good humor during his own personal ordeal, he was deeply disturbed by other judicial developments during the same period.

By the mid '70s, he believes, there had been a major alteration in the rules of the game—of the Supreme Court precedents that govern his job. It bothers him, for deep down, McMillan believes in the march of judicial and social history that began in the courtroom of J. Waties Waring. And so it was with a deep sense of gloom that he watched it all end—in the illustrious, one-time Civil War capital of Richmond.

Above the mantel in the homey, judicial chambers of Judge Robert Merhige, there hangs a large and gilded portrait of a famous Virginian. His light brown hair is long and flowing; his steady eyes are gazing toward a window and beyond it the stately form of the Virginia state capitol.

It has been 170 years since the man in the portrait, Chief Justice John Marshall of the fledgling U. S. Supreme Court, walked up the steps of that very building to convene one of the most historic trials his young republic had ever known. The defendant was a former vice president by the name of Aaron Burr—a man accused of plotting and leading a violent attempt to overthrow his government. As part of his defense, Burr asked the court to subpoena his chief accuser, President Thomas Jefferson.

After much soul searching, Marshall decided to grant Burr's request—an act of judicial impudence that helped transform the federal courts, making them, for the first time, a coequal branch of government with Congress and the President. Rarely has that transformation—the legacy and prestige flowing from the muscle flexing of Justice Marshall —been as important as it has in the past 25 years.

Throughout the '50s, '60s and early '70s, the U. S. Supreme Court was a critical, sustaining force for the district judges on the Deep South firing line. In some cases, it was out in front of them, pulling them reluctantly down a path of judicial and social change. At the very least it was behind them, providing support.

But Chief Justice Earl Warren, a Dwight Eisenhower Republican who had gradually emerged as a hated figure to America's conservatives, resigned in 1969 and was replaced by a man named Warren Earl Burger. Almost everyone, from President Richard Nixon on down, expected a different philosophy from the Burger court. It took a while for the philosophy to jell (it was Burger, after all, who wrote the opinion sustaining the busing decree of James McMillan). But eventually, Nixon and the others proved correct in their expectations, and one of the earliest, most definitive indicators came at the expense of the man who presides in John Marshall's old courtroom, Judge Robert Merhige of Richmond.

At about the same time that the Supreme Court affirmed McMillan's ruling on busing, Merhige was carrying the logic a step further. He ruled in a case affecting Richmond city schools, and those of surrounding suburban school systems, that busing across school district lines was a permissible tool to achieve integration.

News of the decision was received with alarm in the big cities of the North—in places like Boston, Detroit and Indianapolis, where inner city schools were carefully set apart from predominantly white suburban systems that wanted no part of total integration. Court-watchers and proponents of desegregation knew that in many cases, Northern integration would hinge on the Supreme Court's response to the Merhige ruling.

Merhige thought he was on firm legal ground for a number of reasons. For one thing, he had handled more than 40 school desegregation suits, and it seemed a short and easy step from his earlier ruling to the conclusion he reached in the Richmond case—that if the existence of suburban school systems, with their heavy white ratios, made it impossible to integrate the whole Richmond area, then busing between the suburbs and the city was a necessary step.

The judge was surprised, perhaps even stung, when the Supreme Court rejected his logic in 1972. Among his peers, Merhige is widely regarded as a fair-minded jurist, who rarely suffers reversal by a higher court. It's logical that it would be that way, for despite a layman's reputation for judicial activism—for aggressive and sometimes unsettling rulings on everything from integration to prison reform—Merhige brings a conservative, almost civics-teacher definition to the nature of his work.

"My job," he says simply, "is to interpret the Constitution the way the Supreme Court says it should be interpreted. Whether I personally agree or disagree is of absolutely no consequence."

The more you talk to him, the more genuine the humility seems to be, and the more it appears to spring from a deep fascination with history. Merhige has spent more than his share of hours pacing and pondering beneath John Marshall's gold-framed portrait. He is sometimes overwhelmed by the power of the legacy. And yet, in his times of trial, it has also sustained him—has left him with a sense of the past that provides perspective on his own ordeals.

Sitting behind his cluttered wooden desk, glasses perched precariously on the end of his nose, Merhige reflected recently about his years on the bench. He had been, before his appointment in 1967, a hard-working trial lawyer—a transplanted Yankee with a thriving practice and a passion for his work.

It was a safe and lucrative occupation compared to his current calling, but Merhige seems to have had few regrets—even during the raging controversies that left him a household name in Richmond, sometimes hated, sometimes grudgingly admired, but a man who is known to almost everyone.

The notoriety came quickly. He had been on the bench for less than two weeks when black revolutionary H. Rap Brown was arrested in Virginia on a firearms charge and came before Merhige seeking release until his trial. Merhige let him go.

"There was a big hullabaloo about it," the judge recalled. "It was the first time I had given any thought to public reaction. There were pickets around the courthouse, some kooky calls, but that's all part of it."

As the controversies continued to pile on top of each other, so did the vehemence of the public reaction. But Merhige hung in with a feisty, low-keyed tenacity. He refused to acquire an unlisted phone number, despite the hate spewing calls that came late at night. And one day in a restaurant, when a matronly Virginian called him a son-of-a-bitch and spat in his face, he simply wiped away the damage with a hand-kerchief and walked away.

Later he would bring the same kind of stubborn resignation to his Supreme Court reversal. "It so happens I agree with the rulings we were handing down," he explains quietly. "But that, I don't think, is of any consequence. The law is what the Supreme Court says it is, and whatever labels you put on the court—conservative, liberal—it changes. But that's what brings balance."

Merhige paused for a moment, absently flicking a ballpoint pen, as his deeply rooted Catholicism and his almost mystical view of the American system intertwined themselves in his mind. "I thank God we had the courts," he continued. "They are not places where pleasant things happen, but they are the final peaceful forum in this country.

"I think," he concluded finally, "that God has a very special view of America. Lord knows if He didn't, we would have made a pretty big mess of it ourselves. And all of these changes, I'm satisfied, are for the good."

Good or bad, the changes have been dramatic and have come in a clump. In the five years following its reversal of Merhige, the Supreme Court handed down rulings approving capital punishment, allowing teachers to spank their students, making it harder for minorities to bring class action lawsuits, and permitting the use of property taxes to finance education—even when the results are unequal, underfunded schools for low-income children.

If Merhige brings a long-run, blind-faith optimism to those kinds of trends, his Charlotte colleague and admirer, James McMillan, does not. "A lower court judge," McMillan says bluntly, "is bound by higher court decisions. But he is not bound to keep his mouth shut on the wisdom of those decisions."

And McMillan does not, in fact, keep his mouth shut. In his soft-spoken way, he has publicly chastised his fellow jurists—usually in speeches at various legal conventions. The thing that troubles him most, he says, is the growing tendency of some judges (including those on the Supreme Court) to dodge the basic issues of a case through the use of legal technicalities.

McMillan felt the result of that tendency in 1976 in the most recent landmark case to come his way—a complicated suit that temporarily clouded the future of the nuclear power industry.

Legally, the primary issue was the constitutionality of the Price-

47

Anderson Act, a 20-year-old law that limited the liability of power companies in the case of a nuclear disaster. Duke Power Company, the defendant in the suit, argued that the act was an essential piece of protection—that without it, power companies would lose necessary investors and might find themselves unable to operate nuclear plants.

The company also argued that the chances of a nuclear disaster were extremely remote—an argument McMillan rejected in a ruling that declared the Price-Anderson law unconstitutional. "The court is not a bookie," he wrote. "The significant conclusion is that, under the odds quoted by either side, a nuclear catastrophe is a real, not fanciful, possibility."

Despite the sweeping implications of the case, most of the legal maneuvering centered on an issue that was far more trivial. "The most seriously litigated point," McMillan later recalled with a shrug of frustration, "was not the constitutional issue that was being raised, but Duke Power's contention that under recent Supreme Court precedents, the plaintiffs had no right to be in court."

Eventually, the Supreme Court ruled with Duke, adding to McMillan's frustration. He believes that federal courts must be accessible to almost anyone—that legal fees alone make it hard for most people to get there, and that the Burger court's attempts to add to the difficulty are a stab at the heart of democracy.

McMillan holds that view even though his own district has dispensed with more than 1,700 cases—an average of at least three a day—in the past two years, leaving him wobbly under the load. But the answer, he thinks, is more judges, rather an fewer cases or the dodging of complicated issues.

"It seems clear to me," he concluded recently at the end of a hearty lunch, "that a judge's first duty is to decide the primary issues of a case for the people who have brought it to court."

He paused and fell silent after that, pondering what to him is an unhappy fact: that America's courts—and therefore the U. S. Constitution—are no longer the instruments he believes they should be, and that the judicial legacy of J. Waties Waring has slowly begun to fade.

Judge McMillan died in 1995, still deeply saddened in the final days of his life by the changing philosophy of the federal court system.

The Scandalous Gospel
of Will Campbell

In addition to the law, the other twin pillar of the civil rights movement was the tradition of Christianity that prevailed in the South, a fact that came home powerfully to me when I was asked about 15 years ago to do a profile of Will Campbell. Campbell, as it happens, is a white Southern Baptist preacher and civil rights advocate, who has been one of the most important religious figures in the region. He is a gadfly at heart (some say a prophet), offering genial offense at one time or another to nearly every creed, denomination and political ideology in the country. That is simply the nature of his calling, and we are all, I think, the richer for it.

The Progressive
1982

I stopped off in Nashville a short while back for a few days of R & R with my friend, Will Campbell—a Baptist-bred drinking buddy and spiritual advisor who has emerged over the years as a Socratic Southern gadfly, a thorn in the flesh of the conventional wisdom. I arrived a little late for the christening—the spiritual dedication of the newborn son of Waylon Jennings (an event attended by, among others, Muhammad Ali). But I did catch a glimpse of the burial of Bill Jenkins, which was in itself a remarkable occasion. Jenkins was a neighbor of Campbell's— an 85 year-old black man who lived alone and who would peer from his farmhouse porch across the rolling Tennessee countryside, recalling the days when it all belonged to him, before the depression came and the banks foreclosed and his children grew up and moved away. "The younger generation," he would say, "they so crazy. Always causin' trouble 'bout this or that. Me," he would say, "I ain't ever been in no trouble..." then adding for the sake of clinical accuracy after gazing discreetly at the curling, light-skinned scar that ran across his wrist and left thumb, "'cept when I killed my wife."

But all that was a long time ago, and Jenkins had long since done his time and paid his debts and lived hard and clean for more than 50 years. Then he died, and as the mourners poured into the sandstone church, making their way across a rubble-strewn field of briars and Johnson grass and Queen Anne's lace, Campbell stood before them, grimly buoyed by the swelling amens and the grief-stricken moans, and he declared in sonorous tones: "He was my neighbor. We used to lean against the fence and swap stories in the evenin' time, but that wasn't enough. No it wasn't enough because he was also my friend. It didn't matter that he was old, and I was not so old, or that his skin was black and mine was white, or that he owned a lot of land and I owned a little. He was my friend. But that wasn't enough either 'cause he was also my brother..."

And later, when a friend with no connection to the event beyond curiosity offered lame compliments on the quality of the sermon, Campbell simply grunted and cleared his throat. "Hell," he affirmed, his boot kicking idly at the Tennessee sod, "if you can't preach to a bunch of broken-hearted people, there ain't much use in trying to preach...."

Campbell can preach, of course, He's been at it now for more than 40 years, ever since the steamy June Sunday in south Mississippi, when he preached his first sermon at East Fork Baptist, a tiny wooden church near the town of Liberty—hidden away in the murky Amite County bottomlands, amid the stands of pine and the shadowdy streams of gray Spanish moss. He gazed out nervously across the upturned faces —a skinny, soft-eyed kid of 17, with oversized ears and a runaway shock of dark brown hair. He peered through a pair of black-rimmed glasses, and after checking the hand-me-down pocket watch on the lectern beside him, he launched a short, fiery sermon on the first verse of Genesis.

Later, after thinking it over and praying about it some, the elders of the church—preacher J. Price Brock and a half-dozen others—took him aside and declared him ordained to go and preach the gospel. He made a few detours along the way, through Yale Divinity School, among other places, but he has emerged in the end as one of the South's leading preachers—an earthy, erudite theologian and author who takes satisfaction in giving offense, in proclaiming a kind of scandalous, radicalized vision of the faith, producing shock and astonishment nearly everywhere he goes.

He is not a William Sloane Coffin. Nor is he Billy Graham. He is instead an odd and unsettling combination of the two—a radical, slow-moving Bible-belt preacher with a hand-carved cane and a floppy Amish hat, meandering his way through the crises of life. He's developed a kind of cult-figure fame in American theology, partly through his books, but mostly through his unpretentious, one-man ministry to the nation's dispossessed. He's an ardent proponent of black civil rights, a friend to the bigots in the Ku Klux Klan, and most recently, an unlikely champion for the men and women of death row.

He began in the '50s with the issue of race. First as chaplain at the University of Mississippi, and later as a Deep South staffer for the National Council of Churches, he allied himself with the civil rights movement—traveling the bumpy Southern backroads from one upheaval to the next, from Montgomery to Nashville to St. Augustine, Florida.

It's hard to say exactly what he did. He was simply there, moving among the people and offering what he could. In 1957, for example, he was one of three white ministers with Elizabeth Eckford, walking by her side as she and eight other black teenagers made their way through the Little Rock mobs, braving taunts and rocks and bayonetted rifles, seeking to enroll in an all-white school.

Gradually, he became a friend to the leaders of the movement—Andy Young, John Lewis and Martin Luther King—but also to the bright young radicals of lesser charisma, some of them filled with foolhardy courage, others simply quiet and determined, as they drifted into Selma or Marks, Mississippi, defying the wrath of the most brutal South. Campbell was awed by the bravery of it all, and yet he couldn't shake a feeling in the back of his mind—a troublesome sense that however right and righteous it was, however important that the South be confronted with the sins of its history, there was something simplistic and shortsighted about the whole crusade, some failure to understand, as he would put it later, "that Mr. Jesus died for the bigots as well."

So he began to work the other side of the street, mingling with the racists and Klansmen, as well as the blacks, setting out from home in the early morning hours, rumbling through the Delta in his cherry-red pick-up. Armed with a guitar and a Bible and an occasional bottle of Tennessee whiskey, he would point himself toward the flat and muddy fields of Sunflower County, toward the straight and endless rows of picked-over cotton and the barbed-wire fences of Parchman Penitentiary.

At Parchman, he would visit a young friend of his—a terrorist, as it happened, whose name was Tommy Tarrants. He was a Klansman, a tough and lanky young man in his middle twenties, with scruffy brown hair and a head full of hate. He had moved to Mississippi from Mobile,

Alabama, becoming, while he was still in his teens, a leading strategist in a campaign of violence. But he was shot and nearly killed in 1968, ambushed by the FBI, as he sought to bomb the home of a liberal Jewish merchant. For his trouble, he was sentenced to 30 years in prison, and at the time Campbell came along, he was still in a struggle with the passions of his youth.

They spent a lot of time behind the barbed wire of Parchman, settling occasionally under the shade of an oak and letting the conversation ramble where it would. Eventually, after visits from Campbell and a handful of others who took an interest in his case, Tarrants began to change. He renounced his racism, proclaimed a newfound belief in the Christian faith, and got himself paroled. He enrolled in Ole Miss, got a degree, and became a kind of free-lance missionary to the prisoners of the South.

Campbell is pleased by that, but takes no credit for it. Conversions, he says, are not his calling. He is embarked instead on an unconditional ministry, a simple reaching out to angry young blacks, Kluxers, draft-dodgers and alienated rich—leaving it to them what they do with the message. That's a little unsettling to many fundamentalists, and also to his liberal friends, to the people who are involved in a push for social change. But for Campbell, it's all very clear, and he will rummage through the clutter on his rolltop desk, producing a well-worn copy of the *King James* Bible, fumbling through the parchment to the writings of Paul.

"Here," he will say, "it's all right here in Second Corinthians, right down here at the end of chapter five: 'God was in Christ, reconciling the world unto himself, not imputing their trespasses against them....'

"There," he continues, with a fierce, sudden swipe at this gray fringe of hair, "that's what it's all about. You can read it there, or in Mark or Matthew, or over in Luke. But what it all means is so damn simple: we are bastards, but God loves us anyway. We're forgiven, and if we can somehow manage to get hold of that fact, we can find the power to go and do likewise. Go and hate no more, go and kill no more. Old Tommy Tarrants got his mind around that one, and if the rest of us could do the same...but of course we don't want to do the same 'cause it would change the way we all do our business. So we keep foolin' around with all the false messiahs..." and he shrugs philosophically, folds up the Bible and returns it roughly to the clutter on his desk.

But despite his fatalism and occasional despair, Campbell has set out to proclaim the message—giving little thought to measurable results, for if he did much of that, he would give up the ghost. He is a peculiar sort of gospel existentialist, like some strange character from the mind of Camus, behaving as if the odds were not insurmountable—as if the world were not full of murder, mendacity, executions, and prejudice.

It is, he admits, a mission so pure and pitiful that it's almost a joke. But it isn't a joke, for not everyone is amused when he pays a visit to a rich liberal church, surveying the stained glass window, and the prosperous people in the hand-carved pews—and suggesting, when they ask how their faith should be applied, that they leave the door to the sanctuary open, so the downtown winos will have a place to sleep.

"I agree," he says, "that they'll use bad language, and maybe piss on your rug. But it's scriptural."

And if that sounds outrageous to the point of buffoonery, there are other moments when he can't be dismissed, when the scandal of his message is so inescapable that the people in the audience will wince, or even cry, as the words tumble out. He is strangely unimposing as he stands before them, looking thoroughly uncomfortable, tugging at his earlobe or the end of his sideburn, ignoring, or trying to, the knot of fear and insecurity that is there in his gut. There is the trace of a tremor around the edges of his voice, and yet through it all a kind of resonant, stentorian certainty as he begins to tell the story.

It is a brutal story and the telling is as wrenching as Campbell can make it

"Thirty-four years ago," he says, speaking this time to more than 12,000 teenagers, Lutherans as it happens, who are gathered in Kansas City for their annual convention, "I stood with my buddies on the island of Saipan, overlooking the crystal blue waters of the Pacific Ocean. Not far from where we stood was a little island, looking to us almost like an aircraft carrier—a little island called Tinian. We used to stand in the early morning and watch the big airplanes take off and gather in the afternoon to watch them return. That day, August sixth, nineteen forty-five was no ordinary day. It was the day two hundred thousand human beings would die. It was the day the first atom bomb was dropped...

"We knew as we gathered that afternoon that the bomb had fallen, two hundred thousand people left dead in its wake...and I cheered! My young brothers and sisters, I yelled and cheered and slapped my buddies on the back and threw my Army helmet into the sea at the news that two hundred thousand people, those for whom Christ died, no longer lived. Because I wanted to go home. Fry the bastards. Kill the slant-eyed, slope-head sons-of-bitches. I want to go home...."

He pauses now to let the words sink in, his expression a mixture of outrage and grief, eyes glistening, his hand trembling slightly at the side of the lectern. But his words are soft and sure as he resumes the narrative, shifting the scene to another cheering crowd of more recent vintage—to the people who gathered May 25, 1979, to applaud the excruciating end to the life of John Spenkelink. Shortly after 10:00 on that sunny May morning, amid the taunting of guards and the jubilant chanting of the people outside, Spenkelink was strapped to a white wooden chair at the Florida state prison. And on the final orders of Governor Bob Graham, 7,500 volts of electricity were sent through his body, causing his flesh to burn, and six minutes later, his heart to stop beating.

In the aftermath of that execution, Campbell has emerged as one of the nation's leading opponents of capital punishment—denouncing it, testifying against it wherever he can. For he knew John Spenkelink's history, knew that he was guilty of killing another man, but also that in his nearly six years of facing death himself, he had become caught up in a quiet Christian search, not showy or pious, but a final private grappling with what it all means. He was the acknowledged leader among the men of death row—aggressive in defense of other prisoners' rights, but with an emerging sensitivity that was sometimes startling. Two hours before his death, for example, he turned to his minister and friend, Tom Feamster, and said, "Let's pray for the governor..." adding when the prayer was over, "Don't tell the press. That's not why I did it...."

Campbell told all that to his young Lutheran audience, then compared it starkly to the things that happened next.

"When all was in readiness," he said, his voice low and husky, but strangely calm, "when Brother John, bound and gagged, was strapped in the electric chair, the curtain was opened for the witnesses. The first surge of twenty-five hundred volts of electricity, singed the skin off his right calf, sending smoke into the death chamber. He clenched his left fist, then his hands began to curl and blacken. Listen to me now. The doctor stepped forth, unbuttoned his white shirt and placed a stethoscope on his chest. He was not yet dead. The doctor stepped back. Another surge of twenty-five hundred volts of electricity, then another and the deed was done. And outside the walls, a group of teenage hecklers about your age, fifteen, sixteen, nineteen years, were chanting in unison, again and again: 'Spark Spenk, Spark Spenk, Bring On The Barbecue Sauce.' I wanted to cry, to run, to vomit. And I did cry, for I was hearing myself, thirty-four years ago, cheering on the cliffs of a faraway island...'Fry the bastards, kill the sons-of-bitches. I want to go home....'"

And there in the auditorium filled with silence and shock, just before the outburst of a standing ovation, Campbell added six words—

sounding at first like an afterthought, but making, he says, the only real point that he knows how to make: "May Christ have mercy upon us."

That is his hope, his pitch, his final affirmation when it all gets crazy. Though his thinking is systematic in its own peculiar way, it is more than an abstraction from St. Augustine or Paul, more than an echo of his professors back at Yale. There's a kind of brutal intuition about reality and religion, a sure wrathful instinct that keeps him on course. But where does it come from? What is it, finally that saves him from despair, yet removes him as well from the pristine and pious?

To get a sense of that, it helps to tag along on a swing through the South—when he strikes out from Nashville in a small rented car, heading southwest toward the state of Mississippi, humming through the Delta on the long flat road, toward the town of Yazoo where the hills begin, past the cotton and the rice and the dingy green pastures where the cattle are grazing. There'll be a few stops along the way—a dinnertime visit with a liberal lawyer-friend, a strategy session with a young black activist—but his real destination lies deeper in the state. He is headed toward the homeplace down in Amite, singing country songs or telling bawdy tales, backseat driving while a friend takes the wheel....

"Dammit," he says with peevish good humor, "will you please slow down? How you gonna see when the countryside's a blur? There're some historic sites along in here. Right over there, on up around the curve, is where old man Tweet McKelvin used to live. He was the only Republican I'd ever seen 'til I was grown. I remember the first time an automobile ever came by his place, he said, 'My God, son, the automobiles are gonna be the ruination of this country.' God, that ole guy had it all figured out, right down to what we are talking about today. He didn't call it an energy shortage, but he knew...and then he'd want a ride into town....'"

He laughs and spits tobacco toward the chilly night air, and then begins to talk about his family. "Right down there," he says, "down at the turn at the bottom of the hill, that's where my daddy let me drive the old thirty-four Ford right into the ditch. I was going too fast, but he didn't say a word, just sat there, and when we landed, he said, 'Well, I guess there's nothin' to do but go on up to the house, eat a little supper and come back tomorrow with the chain....' He never even raised his voice. How you gonna rebel against that? I tell you, he's one of the gentlest, most generous human beings I've ever known. He got it from his daddy, and he did what he could to pass it down the line."

He is rolling now, and as the stories tumble out, we pause for awhile at an ancient-looking farmhouse, tidy and green, set back from the road on Highway 24. It has a TV antenna and a fresh coat of paint, but other than that it's changed very little since Campbell's grandfather, known in the family as Grandpa Bunt, raised 10 children in its four small rooms. He was a stoic Baptist deacon of determined good cheer —a small-time cotton farmer, gaunt and slightly stooped, with a sun-crinkled face and wispy gray hair that grew thinner with age.

In his later years, when the children grew up and the grandchildren came, he would lean against a stump in his barren front yard, smiling to himself at the games that they played. They were a hearty consolation against the tragedies of the past—against the unrelenting memories from his early years of marriage, when his first three children, Murtis, Claudie and little Sophia, all died within weeks from the same disease. But he came through it all with no trace of bitterness—with a kind of dogged, undismayed understanding that the world is full of suffering and caprice, and that the mission of a man is not to add to the total.

"I remember one time," says his grandson, Will, "we were playing in the yard over there by the fence. It looked a little different back in those days, which was right during the heart of the Great Depression. The road was made out of gravel and clay, and it was farther from the house than it is today—kinda curling past us toward a thick stand of pines. We were playing tag or some such game, me and about a dozen cousins and friends, when we noticed a black man coming up the road. His name was John Walker, and we thought he was a character. He had recently been beaten for stealing a sack of corn, and some of us laughed at the way he told the story: 'Lawd, they got me nekked as a jaybird. Took a gin belt to me. Whipped me til I almost shat." So when he came shuffling by us on this particular day, we began to taunt him: 'Hey nigger, hey nigger.' But he didn't even look up, kept his eyes pointed straight at the road, as if he hadn't noticed. But Grandpa noticed, and he called us over and said very quietly: 'Now hon'—that's what he called everybody in that way that he had—'now hon, there's no more niggers. Those days are dead. All that's left is the colored people.'"

And suddenly as you listen, it begins to make sense. You begin to understand what Campbell is about—to see why his diploma from Yale is no longer on display, and why, pasted over it on the wall above his mantel, is a certificate of ordination from East Fork Baptist—lying slightly crooked in its simple black frame, but affirming that in the eyes of his fellow believers, of people like his grandfather, he is now ordained to go and preach the gospel.

He has tried to do simply that, armed with gritty understandings of the Sermon on the Mount, of the last being first and the meek and humble emerging triumphant. And the radical causes into which it all thrust him—his strategy sessions with Martin Luther King, his prison visitations to death row killers—never seriously estranged him from most members of his family. He could always return from his travels through the South, his free-lance pastorate to the centers of turmoil, and he would know that on some level—often more instinctive than openly expressed—his father and his brothers would approve of his calling.

He usually spared them the harrowing specifics, the nerve-racking scenes in the midst of demonstrations, when he was threatened occasionally by mobs of whites or trailed by deputies in the middle of the night. But there was one particular story that he related in detail, for it was, he said, a kind of conversion—a sudden, agonizing moment of truth when his faith took on a heightened sense of clarity. He learned that a friend named Jonathan Daniel—a gentle-spirited Episcopal priest who had spoken out for civil rights in the dusty reaches of rural Alabama—had been murdered, torn apart by a shotgun blast in the little town of Hayneville. Campbell was devastated. But in the midst of his grief, he found himself forced by his own theology to affirm that the sins of the murderer were already forgiven—that the shower of grace rains down upon us all, and the astonishing opportunity is simply to accept it.

"It was a revelation," he says. But it was also something more personal than that; it was a rediscovery of the things that his grandfather knew—that in a world full of tragedy, you don't choose sides; that you can stand for what's right and yet reject condemnation for those who are wrong. So when an all-white jury freed Daniel's killer, Campbell made a point of endorsing the verdict. It was shocking news back in 1966 when he wrote in a liberal Christian quarterly, "Jonathan can never have died in vain, because he loved his killer—by his own last written words. And since he loved his murderer, his death is its own meaning. And what it means is that Tom Coleman, this man who pulled the trigger, is forgiven. If Jonathan forgives him, then it is not for me to cry for his blood, his execution. Any act on my part which is even akin to 'avenging' Jonathan's death is sacrilege.... For when Thomas killed Jonathan, he committed a crime against the State. When Thomas killed Jonathan, he committed a crime against God. The strange, the near maddening thing about this case is that both the offended parties have rendered the same verdict—not for the same reasons, not in the same way, but the verdict is the same—acquittal."

Later, he admits with a sort of rueful self-bemusement, "A whole bunch of my civil rights friends came to me and said, with considerable embellishment, 'Good God, Campbell, you stupid idiot, you can't go saying things like that to a bunch of rednecks. Man, that just gives 'em license.' But of course, I told 'em, that's not true. What the jury told Tom Coleman was, 'You are forgiven. Go thou and kill again, if you want.' But what the gospel says, and what we are obliged to say is, 'Your sins are already forgiven you, brother. Go thou and kill no more.' That's the difference, and it's all the difference in the world."

And for those who regard such words as the ravings of a madman or the babblings of a fool (and there are many who fall into each of those categories), Campbell has a different answer. Instead of arguing the efficacy of conversions through divine compassion, he shifts his ground and attacks the alternative. "The law," he says. "We are forever arguing that people must be restrained, so we pass a law and set about enforcing it. But if the law is for the purpose of preventing crime, of securing a just and civilized society, then every wail of a siren calls out its failure. Every civil rights demonstration attests to the inability of the courts to provide racial justice. Every police chief who asks for a larger appropriation because of rising crime rates is admitting his own failure. Every time a law has to be enforced, then it has failed to do what we hoped it would. So what I am saying is, for God's sake, let's try something else."

He has built an organization on precisely that premise—a haphazard collection of like-minded people, ranging over the years from John Spenkelink to novelist Walker Percy. It's an otherwise ill-defined group called the Committee of Southern Churchmen, subsisting year-to-year on patched-together budgets of $30,000—most of it coming from small foundations. The committee publishes a quarterly Christian journal, with contributors ranging from Percy to Robert Coles. But its primary function is to provide a base for Campbell—a subsistence salary, a generous travel budget and a log cabin office in the hills near Nashville.

People often ask him exactly what he does, and the answer isn't easy. He listens to the problems of bewildered individuals, writes magazine articles and occasional books. The first major seller, *Brother to a Dragonfly*, was nominated for the National Book Award in 1978, and the one after that, a novel called *The Glad River*, drew widespread acclaim.

But one of the clearest indications of the nature of Campbell's calling occurred in 1980 when Billy Graham came to Nashville, arriving on a warm summer Saturday and sending word to Campbell that he'd like to get together. Graham was preparing for a crusade at Vanderbilt, and through an intermediary, he invited Campbell to meet him backstage— "just to get acquainted," the intermediary said.

Campbell considered it a strange invitation. He had never met Graham, though he'd tried on occasion, and he knew that their differences had been well-publicized. Some eight years earlier, at the height of the killing in Vietnam, he had written an open letter in a Christian magazine, chastising Graham for his support of Richard Nixon. And more recently than that, speaking to a convention of ministers in Graham's hometown, he had scoffed at the blandness of mass market evangelism. But despite such differences, and despite his theology, Campbell is inclined to like Billy Graham—to respect him grudgingly for his personal decency and for his stubborn refusal, nearly 30 years ago, to allow his crusades to be segregated racially. So he looked forward to their meeting for many of the same reasons that Graham proposed it— he wanted an opportunity to discuss their disagreements, but also to affirm that they were brothers in the faith.

It looked for awhile, however, as if it would all fall through. For as Graham preached to the multitudes at Vanderbilt, inveighing against divorce and pre-marital sex, Campbell was absorbed in his own Christian witness. He had a wedding, a baptism and a visit to death row; then a counseling session with a troubled seminarian. And then came the funeral of Bill Jenkins, where he preached a sermon and cried with the family—cursing his lapse of pastoral detachment, while one of Jenkins' daughters, a big, friendly woman with a robust grin, patted him on the arm and consoled him gently: "Now preacher, we all know how you loved Papa. You just go ahead and cry."

But the most wrenching moments came later in the week, just a few hours before he was supposed to meet Graham. He traveled to the town of Lebanon, Tennesse, a medium-sized hamlet some 30 miles from Nashville, with flat-roofed stores along its downtown streets and a Confederate monument in the center of its square. And there in the shadows of early afternoon, amid the tension and humidity of a crowded courtroom, he pleaded for the life of Tyrone Bowers.

Bowers was a black man, 22 and stocky, with close-cropped hair and hard, steady eyes that stared straight ahead. Though he insisted he was innocent, five separate witnesses linked him to a murder—to the death of an amiable white man whose name was Glenn Taylor, a 41-year-old father of two and a popular figure among the people of Lebanon. According to the witnesses, Bowers admitted robbing Taylor on a cold winter midnight, leading him through a field of waist-high sedge and putting six bullets in the back of his head. They said he pulled the trigger until the gun failed to fire, while his victim moaned and begged for his life.

Campbell knew Taylor and was shocked at his death. But as an opponent of capital punishment, he makes no exceptions; and when an all-white jury found Bowers guilty, Campbell agreed to testify at the sentencing hearing. He was asked to appear as an expert witness—a Christian ethicist who had studied at Yale and written extensively on the subject of justice. And the testimony began that way, with Campbell offering theological arguments and recounting his history of opposing executions—his occasional appearances at legislative hearings, his televised debates and his private pleadings with assorted public officials.

But when he acknowledged participation in public demonstrations, the character of the testimony began to change—to become less cerebral and considerably more emotional, as attorney general Tommy Thompson, tall and sandy-haired, with a penetrating mind and an overbearing style, sought to paint Campbell as an out-of-step radical. But in the jousting that followed, Campbell simply sidestepped and presented himself as something very different—a God-fearing, Jesus-loving preacher who takes it all seriously.

Thompson: So you were one of the masses in the streets that we see on television? Would that be fair to say?

Campbell: It would not be fair to say.

T: Well would it surprise you to know that eighty-five percent of the general population is in favor of capital punishment?

C: Of the general population? No sir, it would not surprise me. It may well be, sir, that we say one thing in church and another thing outside of church.

T: All right, well let me ask you this. Would the fact that eighty-five percent of these people are for capital punishment make them any less of a Christian than you, sir?

C: It would not make them any less the people for whom our Lord died.

T: Yes sir. Well you are so concerned about capital punishment, I want you to look at that picture right there (*showing him a photo of the dead man, his right arm folded beneath his head, mud on his clothes and six bullet holes in the base of his skull.*)

C: I have already looked at it, sir.

T: And if I told you that the evidence in this case indicated that this was a hard-working man, fifteen hours a day....

C: I know, I know. I was in his business many times.

T: Well, what do you think would be an answer to a person who would not only rob him, but have him walk through a sedgefield, make him lay down, put his head in his hands, and sit there and shoot him once with a pistol, and when he started moaning shoot him five more times? What is the answer to that, Reverend?

Campbell paused before he offered a response, and for a moment it seemed as if he had nothing to say. But he did, of course, and the reaction was stunning in the small country courtroom, with the people jammed into the rough wooden pews, fanning themselves against the Tennessee heat and gazing steadily in the direction of the bench.

"Mr. Thompson," said Campbell, with his thoughts now collected, "apparently we do not know the answer to your question. I believe the answer is to evangelize the country in the name of Jesus Christ, so that it will simply not occur to anyone to commit the kind of violence that is shown in that picture, or the kind we are contemplating in this courtroom today. Until we do come to that kind of commitment and understanding of the Christian faith, I believe the spiral of violence will continue in this country. We have tried everything else we know to try. So I'm citing the only answer I know. I'm a Christian minister."

And in the astonishment that followed, Campbell knew that the point was made. The jury seemed absorbed in his simple proclamation, and several hours later he received word of the verdict—life imprisonment, instead of death in the chair. "The Spirit," he said. "Maybe it got loose in the Court of Mr. Caesar."

He considered telling the story to his brother, Billy Graham, for he thought it was possible that they could find a common ground, some mutual, substantial affirmation about the gospel—that it is effective and powerful amid the tawdriness of life, and that it's a sacrilegious shame to bury it in sweetness. But when he arrived at the stadium at seven that evening, with the choir and the crowds and the floodlight falling on the artificial turf, he immediately understood that it would not work. He found himself amused at his own presumption—at the notion that he, Will Campbell, could evangelize the best-known evangelist in the world. So he simply smiled at his own private foolishness. And after basking backstage in Graham's friendliness and charm, he moved to the stands for the public performance—staring in dismay at the slickness of it all. Then he shook his head sadly at what religion has become, and laughed a little wanly when a friend turned and said: "Let's get out of here and go get drunk."

"Well, how was it?" Brenda Campbell demanded.

She is a formidable woman of 56 years, 33 of which she has spent with Will Campbell. She has become accustomed, she says, to the odd array of people who stream through her kitchen—an unsuccessful songwriter who needs a place to stay, a frightened young marine who has run away from boot camp. But on this particular night, it was just a

61

pair of journalists, and she seemed more relaxed as she gave her husband a drink and informed him again in her booming Southern voice: "I want to hear all about it."

"Well," he said, burping discreetly and settling in beside her on a lumpy brown couch, "there ain't much to tell. He's a nice guy, but it's easy to be nice when you're in that position. And the problem with it is that people see how nice you are, and how pure you are, and they get to focusing their attention on you. I even have that problem from time to time; somebody'll read what I write or hear some sermon, and before long they'll be callin' me up, or some seminarian will be comin' along to write a Ph.D. on Will Campbellism. And I try to tell 'em, 'Don't do that. There's nothin' here. You don't look to me, and you don't look to Billy, because that ain't where the Christian faith is. It ain't in niceness or eloquence or even social commitment, and we seem to have some trouble gettin' hold of that point....'"

Then a writer-friend who was, as Campbell put it, "well into the hops," cut into the soliloquy to demand a clarification: "You keep saying what the Christian faith isn't. Well, what the hell is it, if it isn't those things?"

So Campbell smiled and picked up his guitar, and he began to answer with his own graphic parable. He told a story from eleven years ago, about a journey he made over to North Carolina—to the town of Granite Quarry in the lush, wooded flatlands just east of Charlotte. His purpose in going was to be with Bob Jones, then the Grand Dragon of the Ku Klux Klan, on the night before Jones was shipped off to prison. It was a strangely festive occasion, with all the kinfolk and Klanfolk gathered in the Dragon's cinder block home, telling funny stories and trying to be jolly and unconcerned. The whiskey flowed and the laughter continued until about two in the morning, when Campbell proposed communion. "Hell yes," said Jones, "let's have communion." So the people gathered in a circle, and Campbell unpacked his guitar and said: "I'm gonna sing a song that to me is the essence of the Christian faith. It's called 'Anna, I'm Takin' You Home,' and it's about a whore and a lover who forgives her and takes her home. That's what Christianity is all about—being forgiven and taken home to where you're loved." Then, strumming softly on his guitar, he began to pray.

"Lord, ole brother Bob is going off to jail for a while. We gonna ask you to kind of keep an eye on him. Lord, you know he's not a saint. And you also know that we sho ain't. But the Book tells us that's why you died. So that God and sinners could be reconciled. And we gon' drink to that and if it's all the same, we gon' sing our song in Jesus' name:

"Anna, I'm takin' you home...."

In the nearly 15 years since I wrote this piece, Campbell has emerged as one of the South's leading writers, with books like Providence, Covenant and Forty Acres and a Goat. But he is still a gadfly most of all, thundering his own prophetic warnings about the direction in which the country is headed.

"Just watch every serious contender for high office," he declared in a speech in 1995, "rush to the TV studios seeking the blessing of the right-wing electronic soul molesters who hurl to hearth and household, not the radical and revolutionary message of Jesus regarding the downcast, but rather a milquetoast gospel of, 'Take up the cross and relax.' 'Take up the cross and get rich.' 'Take up the cross and find self-esteem in an edifice made of glass.' Great Godamighty! I don't know where this country is headed. But there comes a time to fret."

The Death Row Preacher

When I was working on the story about Will Campbell (preceding chapter), I paid a visit to death row in Tennessee. Campbell is a staunch opponent of capital punishment, seeing it as simply another piece in the escalating violence in America.

While the morality of the death penalty may be complicated, this much is clear: Strapping people to electric chairs and pumping enough electricity through their bodies to set their flesh on fire is a violent thing to do—as coolly calculated and utterly premeditated as killing ever is.

After talking to a half dozen death row inmates in Tennessee and several more in other states, I developed a kind of macabre fascination for the doomed men and women of our society. Many of them are terrifying people. That's why they are facing death. But others seem remarkably ordinary, and one of the people in the latter category is Bill Groseclose in Tennessee.

I met Groseclose in 1980 and have visited with him four times since then. I found him articulate, funny, sensitive and mostly cheerful—all of which surprised me. I don't mean to idealize him. He may be guilty of one of the most hideous murders in the history of Tennessee. On the other hand, he may be innocent.

His trial was sloppy and he was poorly represented. But that is not my point in the story that follows. I am simply convinced that Groseclose is worth knowing—particularly to those of us who, by proxy, are planning to kill him.

Whatever else you can say about him—and in this piece I let him speak for himself—Groseclose puts a human face on an unsavory abstraction, one that most of us try not to think about.

Race, Rock & Religion
1982

Unless something changes, they're going to kill Bill Groseclose before very much longer. It'll go something like this: Some people he barely knows will lead him from his cell at the Tennessee State Prison. They'll strap him to a tall, wooden chair and attach some electrodes to his thighs and so forth. Already, they'll have shaved his head to keep his hair from catching fire. Then they'll pull a switch, which will send maybe 2500 volts of electricity through his body.

Nobody knows how bad it will hurt, since nobody has ever reported back after the experience. But if recent precedents hold true, several things are likely. Groseclose's flesh, particularly around his legs, will begin to burn. His fists will clench involuntarily, and his hands will blacken. In addition, he might not die right away. If he doesn't they'll repeat the dosage as many times as it takes.

The people who do this will have very good reasons. They will know some of the details of Groseclose's history. They will know that he was arrested in 1977 after his wife was discovered in the trunk of a car. They will know that she was stabbed and raped and beaten, and they may also know that she did not die from those things. She cooked —probably over a period of several days—beneath the July sun in the river town of Memphis.

They will know these things, and they will feel that they are doing what they should—for theirs will be an awesome duty. But there are also things that they will not consider. Harmon Wray will consider them, and Abel Adams, but they will not be able to convince the people in authority. They will believe Bill Groseclose is innocent—that he is not vicious and cruel, and that he could never have done the things that the State says he did. But they will not dwell on that point, for they are Christian ministers, and their interest is in redemption. So they will talk instead about Groseclose's life: his correspondence studies at a small Bible college, his ordination as a Church of God minister only a short time after his conviction for murder.

They will try to tell the governor, who will not want to listen, about their conversations with Groseclose over a period of e years. They will use words like kindness, faith and humor, and they will speak of his desperate consolations in the writing of St. Paul. But they will certainly fail, for their words will have the soft and simple ring of sentimentality— and others in their grief will cry out for revenge, and time will pass slowly until his waiting will end.

Groseclose enters the room with a bounce to his step, clad in jeans, a T-shirt and a faded denim jacket; the numbers 83408 are stitched on the back. He is 34 years old, though he looks much younger. He wears wire-rimmed glasses and his hair and beard are scraggly. But the thing you notice most, and the thing that stays with you, is the lopsided grin.

Ask him a question or two, and his thoughts flow freely, the feelings tumbling out with punctuations of laughter, moving inexorably from the light to the heavy. This is what he says:

Man, it's cold in here—just about back up to the shivering point. We got a leak back here, and water comes pouring into the cell behind the commode. Then it freezes on the wall in this little thin layer of ice that you can't really see.

So you're standing there in front of the john, and you've already started, and you lean against the wall, and zap, you're sliding all over the place, and the stream's goin' crazy, and you're laughing like a madman, and then you say to yourself, "Man, how weird can things get?"

It's hard sometimes, but everybody tries to keep each other up. It's just something everybody seems to do. If someone is down and he likes something on TV, someone will say something about that show. If that don't work, you're quiet for a half hour, then you try another subject. If that fails, you straight out ask, "Hey, man, what's happenin'?"

Always, always, you look for the humor. The hatred is there, it's a constant; you don't have to look for the hatred. But you do look for the way to laugh, and often enough we find it. We have a good sense of community.

Down the road there's Richard Austin, he plays cards—plays cards and gambles. He'll take bets on anything—football, baseball, basketball, how many bullets they'll shoot on *Bonanza*. He took fifth in the world billiard championships one time, but he hardly ever discusses playing pool. He keeps pretty much to himself. Got a bad heart.

Ole Richard, he's short and fat; he's balding and got this mustache. But he don't like to think of himself as fat. He'll say, "I am muscular...." He's O.K.

I don't have one best friend. Everybody is pretty close. It's who are you hanging out with this week? I sat back there all day a while back and played chess with Houston—that's Richard Houston in the cell next to mine. It was one good, full, hard day of chess. It'll be a while before I do that again.

Houston is black. He's well-educated, very smart, a pretty handsome dude. We been next-door neighbors for three years. One time—I forget what we was mad about—I cut out this cross out of an envelope, you know, then I licked it and stuck it to his door and set it on fire.

So he cut himself out a cross, and for the next little while, he worked at it with a burned match, rubbing the carbon on the cross until the whole thing was black. Then he stuck it on my door.

Well, I couldn't let it drop at that point. So the next day, I painted a watermelon and stuck it on his door and burned it. Some of what we find to laugh about is pretty weird. But any time you can give somebody an excuse to laugh, you do it.

We don't start stirring till about 10 or 11—usually about the noon meal. Everybody just says no to breakfast. The dinner today was...well, how can I say it? Only one guy took anything. I've fed a lot of dogs a lot of things. But none of them were that bad.

The problem is time. Sometimes you don't know if you want it to pass, or you don't want it to pass. But it hangs pretty heavy sometimes. You'll do anything to fill it up. Jeff Dix down there, he placed third in the cockroach race. Jeff's a soap opera freak. We call him Swamp Monster. He's about 6-feet-2 and weighs 260 pounds. And a nose—man, Jimmy Durante would have to hide. This guy has a beak.

Jeff is a non-violent, violent person. He has weird ways of expressing himself. 'Course he says the same thing about me, but one time he put a TV set through the bars of his cell with one blow—plastic and tubes and crap all over the place. I just kept on with what I was doin', trying to be nonchalant.

I paint a good bit, particularly with James Earl Ray. Ray's all right. He's a good guy. He's not on the row, but he's one of our best buddies. Me and him and Joe Buck paint together. Joe's the best portrait painter I ever seen. I can paint mountains in my sleep, 'cause that's where I was raised.

So we started painting this collective picture. Ray painted the sky and some clouds—he was experimenting with how to accent the clouds, whether to use reds or greens or whatever. Then he gave it to me to do the mountains, and I'll give it to Joe to do the foreground.

We got a good laugh out of trying to figure out a name to sign to the painting. We were trying to decide between Billy Joe Ray and Billy Buck Ray. We tried to imagine the painting hanging in some art gallery, and everybody sees it and can't wait to meet this Billy Buck Ray.

We don't want any trouble back here on the row. We've got all we can use. So we do what we can to help each other out, to keep each other's spirits boosted. We've got one back there who can't read and write. We're teachin' him. Whenever he gets a letter, we go over it with him. He reads the letter, then somebody else will read it, and they'll say, "O.K., what did it say?" He spits it back out. If he can't, we go over it with him.

Mostly, though, we just sit and watch the world go by. I've been behind bars five years. I was arrested July 1, 1977.

I made it here in April, 1978—April Fool's day. At first, it ate at me—especially with the situation as crazy as it is. But then you say, "What am I going to do about it? Am I going to scream or cry the rest of my life? What is going to come of it?"

So, you have to learn to live with it. You have to get rid of the superfluous, and you have to keep control of your mind. I have lost control a time or two. Of my mind, yes, and of my emotions. But I've been fortunate not to lose control of both at the same time.

Still, you think about things. Like sometimes I think about Vietnam. I was there in the Navy, and the things that happened, man...I mean the thing you ask yourself about Vietnam is, Why? You answer that a million times, and then you turn around and disregard the answer and say, Why?

One time when I was over there, I came upon this torture scene. I was driving a supply truck, and I came to a hut where this Vietnamese peasant has been castrated and tied to a tree. They stuck his penis in his mouth and sutured it shut. They had cut his wife's abdomen open and pulled out a fetus and used it to beat her children to death.

I stopped and said, "My God, human beings could not have done this to other human beings." Then I saw five Vietnamese regulars running up a hill behind the hut; they were giggling. I pulled my sidearm and emptied it in their direction. I saw three go down. I said "Did I, or didn't I?" Over the years, I had time to think. I asked myself, "Do I have so little control over my emotions I would shoot somebody in a moment like that?"

I got more serious about religion in Vietnam. Death is so imminent, you can't really help it.

We also talk about it a lot on the row. About everybody back there is anti-religious. I don't mean by that that there aren't any believers. In fact, I don't think there are any non-believers. There's some that say, "No, I don't." But when the believers are having their conversations, there's always close attentiveness among the non-believers. They are the ones that keep the conversation alive. Opinions back there are straight from the heart and cold as ice.

The guys would see these ministers on TV with all their fallacies. Jerry Falwell is our pet. Oh, we love him. They're building some crap, and he's wanting me to send him $50 for one memorial brick, and for $500 he'll put gold on it or something. Or look at Oral Roberts with his multi-million dollar prayer tower. How many hungry kids could you feed for that?

But to err is human.

I've tried to put across the idea of Christianity vs. religion, and I think the general feeling back there is that religion is of man; it stinks. Christianity is of God; it's all right.

A lot of the guys have said, "If I was on the streets, more likely than not, I'd be just like 'em." But in here, it's a peculiar situation. In my case, it has strengthened my faith. I have not been confronted and bothered with the pressure of the outside world—with prices going up, or how am I going to make more money? I can devote more time to being still and listening.

I read the Bible a lot—underline verses and think about their meaning. Romans 8:18 is my favorite, but you can keep going from there. Ol' Paul could write: "I consider that what we suffer at this present time cannot be compared at all with the glory that is going to be revealed to us. For we know that up to the present time all of creation groans with pain, like the pain of childbirth.

"But it is not just creation alone which groans; we who have the Spirit as the first of God's gifts also groan within us for God to make us his sons and set our whole being free.

"If God is for us, who can be against us?...Who will accuse God's chosen people? God himself declares them not guilty. Who, then, will condemn them? Who, then, can separate us from the love of Christ? Can trouble do it, or hardship or persecution or hunger or poverty or danger or death?...

"No in these things we have complete victory through him who loved us. For I am certain that nothing can ever separate us from his love; neither death nor life, neither angels nor other heavenly rulers or powers, neither the present nor the future, neither the world above nor the world below—there is nothing in all creation that will ever be able to separate us from the love of God which is ours through Christ Jesus our Lord."

That's some pretty heavy stuff, and I think about it sometimes, and then I just listen. There's a difference, I've discovered, between wants and needs. I think I know that now. If I get out someday, there's a lot I'm looking forward to. But in or out, it's God's will that matters.

He was born in 1948 near Salt Lick, Virginia, growing up in a two-story house with twin chimneys and a covered porch on two sides. There was a good-climbing sugar maple near the picket fence out front, and he would climb to the point where the branches became frail and stare off at the colors on the mountain behind his house.

69

Boyhood had its idyllic moments, but there were also hard times. After his parents divorced, his mother, a round-faced woman with a receding chin like her son's, took a job as a payroll clerk at a gypsum mine. She lost it when the mine caved in, and after that, she moved around in search of other work. When Groseclose was 12, she remarried, and the family wound up in Kingsport, Tennessee.

Her new husband, Walter Taylor, was short and heavyset—a storeroom worker at an Eastman Kodak plant, who learned from his stepson how to write his name. Groseclose says he and Taylor got along well—"I learned from him, he learned from me"—and adolescence passed with only normal scrapes and mischief.

At 17, Groseclose joined the Navy and spent four years in Vietnam. He survived and came home, and after a failed marriage that produced two children—freckle-faced boys now 10 and 8—he moved on to Memphis. He worked as a Navy recruiter, and on April 4, 1975, two years after his separation and divorce, he remarried.

His new wife, Deborah, was 5-feet-2, blond and rather pretty. "Like any marriage," says Groseclose, "this one had its problems. We had no joys or difficulties that other married couples don't experience."

They did fight, however, and on the night of June 28, 1977, they had quite a row. The next morning, Groseclose took his infant son for a routine trip to the doctor and then to the Navy office so they could pick up a paycheck. When he returned, his wife was gone. So was their green Plymouth Fury, a 1973 model. Groseclose says he wasn't worried, since Deborah, a medical receptionist, was due at work that morning.

"I put the kid to bed and cleaned up the breakfast dishes," he says. "I was off that day. I was sitting in the family room, and the phone rang. It was her office asking if she was coming in. I said, 'What do you mean, is she coming in?' They said she wasn't there, and my natural assumption was that the car broke down. It just didn't hit me what was going on. Then several hours passed, and she didn't call, didn't show up. I called the police. I called the hospitals, her parents, even the jail. Nobody had seen or heard from her."

Six days later, on July 4, they found Deborah's body in the trunk of the Plymouth—mutilated and decomposing where the car had been abandoned. "It was like a straight right to the face," says Groseclose. "There for about two or three minutes, it just wasn't real. Even after the funeral, it was just a void, empty, like now what?"

Prosecutors for the State of Tennessee tell the story differently. They say that Groseclose, working through a young intermediary named Barton Wayne Mount, hired two men to kill his wife—paying Phillip Britt and Ronald Rickman $100 apiece so that he could collect on a $32,000 insurance policy.

The prosecution case is based largely on the testimony of Mount, who in return for his account of the crime, plea-bargained a sentence of 10 years in prison. Britt also confessed and was sentenced to life. Rickman, a South Carolinian whose failed ambition was to join a motorcycle gang, admitted that he and Britt kidnapped Deborah Groseclose, but said she was still alive when they left her.

He was sentenced to death.

For a time, Rickman and Groseclose were compelled to share a cell. But they fought, and the arrangement was altered. Today, Groseclose is three cells away, living with one of two realities: Either he is guilty of a monstrous act of violence, a brutal aberration from his life before and after, or he is innocent—facing death because of the murder of a woman he once loved, living in proximity to a man who may have killed her.

"It's a crazy situation," says Harmon Wray, a Nashville minister who has visited Groseclose regularly over the past five years. "It's remarkable, really, that he has managed to stay sane. He's serious about his faith. He studied the Bible and was ordained as a minister after his conviction. I think that and his sense of humor have kept him together."

Wray says he is uncertain about Groseclose's future. He hopes for the best from the appeals process, now half completed. But he believes that if it fails, Groseclose will die. Because of the horror of the crime, and because members of Deborah Groseclose's family are calling in their grief for rapid executions, Wray says no governor of Tennessee would be inclined to commute the sentence.

In January of 1982, Groseclose came within four days of his execution date. He became increasingly morose as the time drew near, more cynical and self-pitying, and it had an effect on the morale of the row. Even the guards became gloomy, and when the word finally arrived that Groseclose had gotten a stay, one of them—a burly black veteran of the prison force—hurried in with the news. "Hey Groseclose," he said, "we're glad you're gonna stick around."

"Bill's style really does have an effect on people," says Jeff Blum, a staff member with the anti-capital punishment Southern Prison Ministry. "He plays the role of mediator. He's a leader, pretty up most of the time, someone who is in control of his situation. He is not an extraordinary person. He has his ego and his foibles; he's very ordinary. But in his circumstances, that's not an easy thing to be."

For his own part, Groseclose is fatalistic. "This whole thing has endowed me with a lot of patience," he says. "If you are truly going to let the Lord lead you, if it's his wish that I burn in that chair, I will. Death is just a doorway.

"But when I think about all the things I've learned and thought about, all I've grown, all the listening I've done, I just can't imagine wasting all that for five cents of electricity."

As this book goes to press in the summer of 1996, Bill Groseclose is still alive, still a prisoner on death row, where he has lived for more than 18 years. Because of problems in his original trial, he has been granted a new one, but the State of Tennessee has appealed. The end of the process has not yet arrived.

In Search of Billy Graham

The Rev. Billy Graham has long been an object of fascination for American journalists—a mass market evangelist in an age of excess, determined to be a good steward of his calling. And yet there has been a certain blandness about him—a tendency to avoid even those controversies where it would seem that his faith might lead him. One of the most controversial attempts to understand Graham was a book by Marshall Frady, a tough-minded journalist, whose biography, Billy Graham: A Parable of American Righteousness, *was published in 1979. In the spring of that year, I was asked to write about the painful dispute surrounding Frady's efforts.*

The Charlotte Observer
1979

Marshall Frady took a swipe at his bushy black hair and grinned a little wanly. "Never," he said, as he fumbled through a sprawl of cardboard boxes, "never in fourteen years of this kind of work have I run into anything like this."

He scooped his hand into one of the boxes and withdrew a few dozen spiral-bound notebooks, dusty and battered, but jammed with scrawling, ball-point notations—transcriptions from his urgent, four-year delving into the life and ministry of the Rev. Billy Graham.

It was, for Frady, an arduous undertaking—a professional challenge far more subtle than his blistering biography of George Corley Wallace in the 1960s; far more demanding than the stream of articles he has produced over the years for *Esquire*, *Harper's*, *Life* and *Newsweek*.

"It has been," he said with the resonant, honey-toned accents of southeastern Georgia, "absolutely the most consuming enterprise in which I've ever been engaged."

The result of it all is a book—546 pages, published by the Little, Brown company in Boston. The critics, so far, have been ecstatic—calling it a "massive, brooding, open-minded" work, unlike anything ever written on Graham.

The problem is that Graham himself doesn't much like it. After perusing an advance, typewritten copy—provided after elaborate negotiations among a battery of New York lawyers—he wrote to Frady in tones of deep and genuine hurt:

"Dear Marshall: You have certainly done a considerable amount of work over a long period of time. Some of the things I checked were accurate, but many were absolutely inaccurate. Several incidents that I read really had no basis of foundation in fact at all.... One of the interesting things all of us noticed was how few notes you took when talking to us, and often no notes at all...."

From the day that letter was mailed, Aug. 28, 1978, Frady and Graham have felt themselves mutually wounded—their relationship, once so giddy and brimming with boundless good will, turning suddenly sour, lapsing into excruciating months of legalistic carping.

Perhaps they both should have known, both should have seen from the beginning, that it was almost certain to end that way. For they came from far different places—Graham the proper, Bible-thumping, good-hearted son of a Mecklenburg farmer; Frady, the rebellious, urbane, prodigal offspring of an old-fashioned preacher.

But still there had been a time when they sensed a kindred spirit—some mutual, compatible preoccupation with the witness of Jesus; but more than that, an immense and simple liking for each other that still leads Frady to say:

"From the very first moment I met him, I thought this was as good a man, basically, as I had ever sat in the presence of."

Graham knew Frady felt that way, and it left him with an acute and heightened sense of betrayal when he saw in the end what Frady had written.

Working through a savvy Madison Avenue lawyer, he accused Frady of frequent misquoting and an almost willful misreading of motives. During the course of the furor, which stretched out through the autumn of 1978, the *Atlantic Monthly*, after expressing an interest in excerpting the book, suddenly backed off. In his darkest moments, it crossed Frady's mind that his editors at Little, Brown might follow suit. But they didn't, and *Billy Graham: A Parable of American Righteousness* hit the book stores in May of 1979, six weeks after some 10,000 words appeared in *Esquire*.

During the weeks leading up to that publication, both men took a few steps to repair the damage—a cautiously cordial exchange of letters that left Frady muttering with uncertain conviction: "It's absolutely an improper concern—appallingly unprofessional to hope that your subject is pleased with what you have written."

But Frady did hope that, and in a note in February, he confided to Graham: "I'm really sorry there has been all this preliminary static, Billy. ...I think you're going to find the alarms have been hugely inflationary to the actual effect the book is going to have. Just watch."

There was a time in the beginning when such familiarity seemed anything but likely.

In his initial approaches to the Graham organization, Frady encountered polite rebuffs. He managed a brief telephone conversation with Graham's confidant, T.W. Wilson, a boyhood friend from the old days in Charlotte, who helps sift through the roughly 8,000 interview requests that deluge the Graham organization in any given year.

Wilson, acting in Graham's behalf, was consistently cordial but thoroughly non-committal—emphasizing on Frady's first approach in 1974, and again two years later, that Graham was a very busy man and Frady would simply have to hope for the best.

Frady was disappointed, but not really chagrined. He had assumed from the beginning that the book would be written from the outside—a literate critique of Graham's ministerial style and meaning.

His thoughts were already pretty much in order. He was put off by Graham's celebrated coziness with Richard Nixon, the awesome gullibility he seemed to exude as he made his way through the halls of power. And there was also, Frady believed, a sort of "clunking banality" in Graham's message—a flatness and absence of dimension that robbed it, somehow, of a final kind of relevance.

Still, even from a distance, Frady had caught that driven, ingratiating sense of conviction about the ministry of Graham—an earnest, absolutely sincere spirituality that deserved, he thought, to be accosted and understood on its own peculiar terms.

So Frady was delighted when Graham stumbled upon an article in the *Charlotte Observer*—a column on Frady by book editor Dannye Romine. Graham decided after reading it that he and Frady should meet, and on April 17, 1976, they shared a fruit salad lunch—settling into rocking chairs at Graham's Montreat, North Carolina, home, staring out across the dizzy, rolling, hazy-blue expanse of the Appalachian mountains, and talking together for more than two hours.

The following August, Frady spent 10 days with Graham at a San

Diego crusade—"sitting there," he now remembers, "amongst all the admirals and football coaches"—and then, in the breezy chill of late October, returning to Montreat for a pair of all-day marathon interviews.

The discussions were intense, and the flow of information went both ways. Frady found himself explaining to Graham how, as a teenager in Anderson, South Carolina, he had rebelled against the Sunday school preaching of his minister father—stalking, raging, lashing out at his parents as he tore himself loose from the regimen of Wednesday night prayer meetings.

But in the end, his rebellion failed. He couldn't get the Jesus story out his system. "That story," he explained years later, "is the most fascinating thing in the world, and matters more than any other thing in the world."

Billy Graham was reassured by statements like that. As he and Frady passed their hours together, the feelings of trust became tangibly stronger—their conversations ranging from matters of faith, to people of power, to the heartbreak flowing from Graham's early loves.

One story in particular caught Frady's fancy. It was the saga of Emily Cavanaugh.

A student with Graham at Florida Bible Institute, Miss Cavanaugh was a serious and substantial young woman with whom Graham fell deeply in love. Eventually, she left him for somebody else, and it was during the tearful, absolute devastation that followed that Graham made his celebrated midnight submission to Jesus, kneeling on a golf green and turning over his life to the will of higher powers.

Later, upon returning to Atlanta, Frady would gather around him a cadre of writer-friends—people such as author Pat Conroy, or *Newsweek's* Joseph Cumming—and he would tell them, passionately, again and again of "Graham's Gethsemane of the flesh."

The stories were invariably devoid of condescension, and his friends were often somewhat startled—surprised by the intensity of Frady's narratives, the utter absorption and identification he was obviously feeling with his subject.

Graham, apparently, got a sense of it, too. For as Frady began making the rounds among Graham's friends and family, the evangelist would often call ahead of him, urging cooperation and painting Frady as a man they could trust.

And they did.

"Oh yes," said Graham's 87-year-old mother, Morrow Graham. "Yes, I remember him very well. He seemed a very nice man."

She was sitting when she said it in her Park Road home in Charlotte, on a plush, pale couch of Carolina blue, peering at a visitor through thick bifocals. She is a handsome woman, with lively, twinkling eyes and curling ringlets of soft white hair.

"No, she said, "this may surprise you, but I don't exactly feel proud of Billy. I don't think pride has any place in a Christian family. I would say I'm grateful—thankful that the Lord has blessed him as He has."

She offers such sentiments with an un-pious sincerity that Frady, after talking to her, found deeply impressive. "I've just returned from over two weeks in Charlotte," he wrote Graham on November 17, 1976, "and I began to feel almost a part of the family before I left. Your mother is an uncomparably civilized lady...."

To which Graham responded seven days later: "My dear Marshall, My family was delighted with you, and your ears would have burned at my mother's statements about you."

There is a touching momentum in the correspondence between Frady and the Grahams, a gathering warmth that culminated, it seems, in a January 1977 letter from Graham's wife, Ruth. Included were several poems she had written—well-crafted pieces of simple blank verse—appended to the shy and tentative request that Frady critique them.

And then she said:

"I am just astounded at the amount of ground you are able to cover, the number of people you have interviewed, and the fact that you probably know more about us now than we know about ourselves."

However sincere such gushings may have been, the relationship began to change as Frady completed his research and retreated to the cloister of his helter-skelter office—the jumbled corner of an attic, really, where he and his typewriter become locked in a struggle to tell it as he sees it.

Despite his genial effervescence, there is about Frady some final sense of distance—personally and professionally a feeling of detachment, a loyalty not to his subject, but to his own understanding of the calling of truth.

"For the sort of biography I wanted to do—the only kind I know how to do," he would later write to his editor at Little, Brown, "you just naturally, without premeditation, enter into an eager personal rapport...with your principal. So far as possible you become for a while who and what you are writing about.

"The problem is, when you eventually disengage again to sit down and tell, from a point now of detachment, what it all was...the result to your principal is usually a bit of a bump, one might even suppose an icy shock, at having been apparently betrayed after what seemed such warmth and affinity.

"That's what's happening—God, once again—with Graham."

Frady, in short, may say the Jesus story is the most important thing in the world. And in his head—in the far-flung scope of his cerebral fascinations—that may be the truth. But at some deeper level it is not the truth. For in his heart, he worships at the shrine of his craft, and there is nothing—absolutely nothing—more important to him than the anguished products of his old battered typewriter.

But Billy Graham, of course, had no way to know.

The final result of Frady's obsession is a book in tension, a rich and demythologizing narrative that stops far short of writing Graham off.

The most knee-jerk criticisms—that Graham is insincere or a profiteer—seem never to have crossed Frady's mind. On the contrary, his 546 pages are filled with expressions of regard—flat and unambiguous assertions that Graham must be respected and accepted on his own spiritual turf.

Frady describes a time in Sydney, Australia, where Graham was gearing for another crusade, when the evangelist knelt with an associate and prayed before confronting still another crowd: "Oh God, you know I'm not prepared for this service tonight, and there'll be people out there who need thee.... Please don't let my unreadiness and my inadequacy cause you to blot out your blessing from these people."

Frady accepts absolutely the sincerity of that, and he writes, "In his own way, Graham himself indisputably partakes, in some measure, of that limitless and unaccountable compassion that compelled Jesus, sitting one night overlooking Jerusalem, to begin weeping for those who were soon to murder him."

Ever since his boyhood, when telephones would ring in the middle of the night and his father without question or complaint would spend hours just listening, mumbling reassurances and sharing the anguish or loneliness of an elderly widow, Marshall Frady has marvelled at the dimensions of Christian compassion.

It is a feeling he holds in awe—and it is, ironically, precisely that awe that leads him to his most serious critique of Graham's ministry.

In Frady's understanding a certain mass market blandness has crept into Graham's witness, a simplistic pulpit rigidity that has made him acceptable to the rich and powerful, but has left him far too removed from the poor, the hungry, the whores and the prisoners—all the unlovely people Jesus would have called "the least of these."

In one 25-page segment of the book, Frady compares the 60-year-old Graham to a Southern Baptist preacher of about the same age—a man named Will Campbell whom Frady had profiled a few years ear-lier and had come to regard as a 13th apostle.

Campbell, an earthy, tobacco-chewing son of Mississippi, preaches a gospel of reconciliation—a radical vision rooted in the writings of Paul and leading him into one-to-one ministry to draft resisters, militant blacks, Ku Klux Klansmen, death row prisoners and anybody else he thinks might need him.

For Campbell, the Christian faith took on a sudden, agonizing clar-ity on a bleak summer day in 1966. He learned that a close friend named Jonathan Daniels—a gentle-spirited Episcopal priest who had spoken out for civil rights in the dusty reaches of the rural South—had been murdered, torn apart by a shotgun blast in the slumbering, sun-baked village of Hayneville, Alabama.

Campbell was devastated. But in the midst of his grief, he found himself forced to affirm that the sins of the murderer were already for-given—that the undeserved shower of divine forgiveness rains upon us all, and that the astonishing, common-thread human opportunity is simply to accept it.

Frady contends there is a power in that—a profundity that far over-shadows Billy Graham's pronouncements against the evils of drink, or his "shabby" public appearances with Richard Nixon during the height of the killing in Vietnam.

"Campbell's ministry," asserts Frady, "seems a good deal closer to the original"—meaning, of course, the wandering, first-century preachings of Jesus.

There have been times in the past when undertones of delight have crept into Frady's unminced words—when, for example, his writing about Wallace betrayed a kind of bottom-line contempt.

This is not one of those times. If Graham winces at Frady's under-standing of him, Frady himself takes no delight in being critical. That becomes abundantly clear in the waning moments of an evening with friends, when the wine is flowing, the hour is late and tongues are not quite as guarded.

Frady, a bit more reflective now in the looming shadow of his 40th birthday, will lean forward across a candle-lit table, his elbows propped near the remnants of veal, and he will say: "I really think this kind of journalism, where you try to tell the story in its fullest human dimension and registers, could become a new American literary form.

"I think it could. But then you have to ask yourself if it's worth it. Is it really worth it to inflict that kind of hurt, to take that kind of liberty with someone's feelings?"

He pauses to let the question sink in, pondering the ethics of it all, but you know what his answer is. He is doing the thing he knows how to do, and there is simply no chance that he is going to stop.

Billy Graham, too, is certain to continue. Whatever the limitations of his witness, he will stand at the podiums in Washington, Paris, Amsterdam or Moscow, as the arena fills with the sound of his voice— rich and honey-toned and gently pleading, the words familiar after so many years:

"You come forward now, men and women, black or white; you come, hundreds of you. It'll only take a moment to come. Mothers, fathers, young people too. The ushers will show you. You may be an elder or a deacon in the church, but you come."

And they will come then, moving forward in numbers that are startling—some weeping softly, others holding hands or gazing curiously at the people around them, but coming, streaming down the aisles, drawn by the certainty—the absolute conviction—they can hear in his voice:

"You come now. It's important that you come."

And whatever the whole thing means or doesn't mean, whatever the limitations of his witness, there is never any doubt in Billy Graham's heart. He is, he says, simply trying to obey—doing what he thinks that God has in mind.

As this book goes to press, Billy Graham, his health inevitably beginning to fail, is still calling people forward, preparing for a crusade in his hometown of Charlotte. Marshall Frady is working as a writer in California, having recently completed a biography of Jesse Jackson. An updated version of his book on Graham is being released in 1996.

The Lonely Crusade of Karen Graham

In 1990, I left the Charlotte Observer *to write books, but I was persuaded by an old friend, John Grooms, to write a regular column for his weekly newspaper,* Creative Loafing*. I found the experience a breath of fresh air. Grooms was an editor, unlike many at the daily newspaper, who seemed unconcerned about political correctness or the possibility of causing discomfort among readers, advertisers or company executives with their own points of view. Several pieces in this book were written for Grooms, and the one that follows, about an anti-abortion activist in Charlotte, could not have been written for the daily paper.*

Creative Loafing
1994

Karen Graham stood before the grave, running her hands through her wind-blown hair. It was her first time back since the day of the funeral. She folded her arms across her faded t-shirt, then squatted and stared at the grave some more. It was a warm spring day at Belmont Abbey, with the smell of honeysuckle on the breeze, and a cloud bank moving in from the west. Graham was nearly alone in the Catholic cemetery, and she said it was hard to know how to feel—hard even to remember the day of the funeral. Was it sunny? Cold? How big was the crowd?

The details were receding now in her mind, but even in her current state of derpession, it was easy to remember what had happened just before. Starting in the summer of 1992, Graham was a member of a grisly expedition. She had clearly emerged in the previous four years as Charlotte's most talked about pro-life radical, and was regarded by some as an important national leader in Operation Rescue.

Privately at least, she had always acknowledged the complications of abortion—how it was a reflection of the conflicting values of the culture and the private desperation of individual women. But she also thought it was simple at its core: These were babies being killed in the clinics, tiny human beings with fingers, toes and a heart—and perhaps more terrible in a great many cases, the ability to feel pain as they were being ripped apart.

She knew that many people didn't see it that way, but she was also convinced that if they did—if they could somehow see the evidence for themselves—then the pressure would build for abortion to stop. That was essentially her article of faith, and if it was wrong, what hope was there anyway?

So in the summer of 1992, she set out to prove it. She and several other people from the movement began sifting through the contents of plastic bags they had found in a dumpster behind a Charlotte abortion clinic. She says they made seven expeditions in all, and in every case their discoveries were appalling. They found discarded medical waste —bloody sheets and suction bags from abortions, and inside the bags there were pieces of tissue, many of them recognizable as human.

One night in August, she took two reporters on the expedition with her. They found a human hand in one bag—a right hand, 2 1/2 inches from elbow to fingertip. The thumb was distinct from the other four fingers. The fingernails were tiny. They also found a left foot and a hand with a broken forearm and a right foot torn and severed at the ankle.

The reporters wrote the story in two different papers—the *Charlotte Observer* and *Creative Loafing*—and Graham was expectant, hoping that at last her message was clear. But the operators of the clinic fought back, suggesting that Graham and other pro-life zealots had planted the material in the dumpster themselves.

She tried to argue that the charge was absurd. As the reporters who wrote the original stories could attest, these weren't body parts taken from a jar. The blood from the abortions was not yet dry.

"We couldn't have planted this material," she said, "unless we performed the abortions ourselves."

But it semed that almost nobody believed her, and the story quickly died with no apparent change in the public attitude. For Graham it was a startling moment of truth—evidence of the power of the backlash against her, created in part by her movement's own failures: its insensitivity and shrillness and the scattered acts of violence by people on the fringe.

In the months after that, the backlash grew, with a new administration in Washington signing tougher laws against abortion protests. By the spring of 1994, Graham was suddenly disillusioned and tired, frustrated with the struggle and her own place in it.

"We have been stonewalled," she said. "We are at this turning point in the movement, whether we want to face it or not.... I have to ask myself now, why am I in this? What is my role?"

In her search for answers she came in May to the windblown cemetery at Belmont Abbey—the place where they buried the remains of the babies from the dumpster. Squatting there bside the granite headstone, which had no names like the others around it, she sifted through the years of her lonely crusade, and hoped that maybe the answers might come.

She knows it was an unlikely role in the first place. Private and shy, Karen Graham was never born to be a public figure. She is a frail-looking woman of 29—5-feet-6 and about 100 pounds. She was born in Florida, but raised in Charlotte by her mother, graduating from South Mecklenburg High School.

At the University of Florida, where she took her bachelor's degree in journalism, she often thought of herself as a liberal—and still does on many social issues. She opposes capital punishment as well as abortion, calls herself a pacifist and chafes at the sexism found in her movement.

But it was at the University of Florida that she first began to brood about the subject of abortion. She says it took on a reality one night when she saw a fetus that someone had thrown in a dumpster.

"I got there about the same time as the police," she remembers, "and there it was, lying on a blanket on the ground. We couldn't tell for sure if it was a miscarriage or an abortion. But the baby was a girl."

When she graduated in 1988, with the issue of abortion now on her mind, she went to Atlanta to offer her support to Operation Rescue. The organization was making its first wave of headlines—blockading the doors to abortion clincis while the media was in town for the Democratic Convention.

During the week that Graham arrived, the frustration of Atlanta's police boiled over. They had already spent more than 38,000 man-hours and a half-million dollars hauling protesters away from clinic doors.

The police decided to take off the gloves. As screams rang out through the streets of downtown, the officers did the work that they had been assigned, twisting arms, gouging pressure points on the demonstrators' necks.

"We know," explained one officer in charge, "how to get people from point A to point B."

Whether it was the drama of the moment, or the theology that was

83

preached in the Rescue rallies—a theology of sacrifice and a resistance to the lures of self-righteousness and pride—Graham was hooked. Later, she would see a widening gap between the preaching and the practice of many people in the movement, including its leaders. But in the autumn of 1988, she said she saw it as "a move of God."

She came home to Charlotte, and on October 29, 1988, she organized the first in a series of rescues. They were often tense and chaotic affairs, with protesters swarming toward the doors of the clinics, then lying inert as policemen hauled them away on stretchers.

With the passage of time, and the rise of frustration and anger in the streets, Graham found herself becoming more shrill.

"They like to kill babies!" she began to scream, and many of her opponents came to see her as extreme. More than that, they regarded her tactics as a final indignity against women whose lives were already full of pain.

Graham understands that there is truth in the charge. She remembers one scene from a clinic in Atlanta, when a group of three young women arrived for abortions, looking pale and terrified, as they were led through a crowd of Rescue demonstrators. One of the women held her jacket to cover her face, the way criminals often do in the presence of a camera, while the protesters screamed, "Don't kill your baby!"

Privately at least, Graham has admitted that insensitivity to women is one of the great failings of the anti-abortion movement. Too many times, she says, she has seen disdain instead of compassion for women who are pregnant and don't want to be. But she also turns the issue around.

"A lot of feminists," she argues, "seem to be saying that women are strong and can handle anything—except a pregnancy that they didn't intend."

Graham sees her movement as having deep roots, reaching back at least to the Underground Railroad—the attempt to free black slaves just before the Civil War. In Graham's mind, the analogy is this: The people who supported the Underground Railroad went beyond a simple advocacy of abolition. They also broke the law, risking their lives or time in prison to help the runaways make it to freedom.

That, she says, is essentially the stance of Operation Rescue—an attempt to save the lives of unborn children, even if it means defying civil law.

But there is another analogy from the days of abolition. The ultimate casualty of that crusade was the plantation economy of the antebellum South—a fact that produced powerful arguments of necessity. So it is, too, with the pro-choice side of the debate on abortion—which argues not that abortion is good, but that terrible, real-life circumstances arise that make it simply the least tragic option.

"That's the point they don't understand," said one young woman, standing on the fringes of one of Graham's demonstrations. She explained to a reporter that she had once been raped—impregnated by a man who had been her husband. But despite the horror of that ordeal, she said she decided in the end to keep the baby.

"I coudn't do it," she explained. "I couldn't bring myself to get an abortion. But I'm also a clinical psychologist. I hear the stories all the time of women who are raped, or abandoned, or young girls overwhelmed by an older boyfriend. I have my own views. But I can't impose them on other people in a crisis. So I guess I believe in the morality of choice."

So do most Americans, and it is against that reality that the anti-abortion movement has stalled, splintering into factions in the dispute over tactics. The most extreme of those factions has favored an escalation into violoence. According to abortion rights activists, there have been at least 36 bombings at clinics since 1977—an average of at least two bombings a year.

But the most notorious act of violence came in 1993, when Dr. David Gunn, who performed abortions in Florida, was shot and killed by an anti-abortion activist. Graham regarded the murder as an outrage, and said so frequently in the counsels of the movement.

"This needs to be denounced and stopped," she said. "It makes no sense to shoot someone and claim to be pro-life. But the level of frustration is much higher today. You have people now talking themselves into believing that what we need to do is become violent.

"They say to people who refuse to make the distinction between murder and bombing on the one hand, and blockading the doors of a clinic on the other, 'if you want to see violence, we'll show you violence.'"

But the distinction now seems permanently blurred, even by the President of the United States. When Bill Clinton signed legislation in 1994 imposing tougher penalties for clinic blockades, he denounced in one lump "obstruction or intimidation or even murder from vigilantes who take the law into their own hands because they think they know what the law ought to be."

There are those who say that law won't work, that Operation Rescue will go on undeterred, even if it means longer terms in prison. But Karen Graham isn't so sure. She has participated now in more than three dozen rescues, going to jail on many of those occasions, but she doesn't know if she's ready for federal prison, and she's certain that many in the movement won't be.

"It's like we are starting over," she concludes. "After all this time, we are back at square one."

Graham isn't sure where to go from here, but there was a clarity, she said, at the edge of the cemetery at Belmont Abbey—standing there beside the gray granite marker with no names on it.

"There are 128 babies buried here," she said, "together now in one grave. I still believe if we can make them human, the people out there will not want to kill them."

But Graham admits that it won't be easy, for even she, in her unintended way, denied the humanity she is seeking to proclaim. After gathering the remains from the dumpster at the clinic, she kept them floating for months in a jar, seeing them as possible evidence in a trial, not as human beings in need of a funeral.

But now that error has been corrected, and she says there are others she can work on as well.

She reflects a lot these days on a recent trip to Norway for pro-life protests during the winter Olympics. The Norwegian pastors that she met on that occasion had a different philosophy from those in this country—a longer view of history perhaps, as well as a different understanding of God.

They were gentler people, less given to extremes. As Graham puts it, "they didn't seem to worship our American God, who's only into winning."

She says she also heard the story of a minister in Tennessee who was once asked by a group of civil rights activists—people frustrated by the slow pace of change—what he thought they ought to do next.

"Do?" he replied. "Nothing. Just be."

Graham smiles as she tells the story. At the moment, she says, it has the ring of good advice.

As the anti-abortion movement became more violent—and even less effective—in the months that followed the publication of this story, Karen Graham pulled away from it. She is seeking, she says, to build a normal life and to look for ways to witness more quietly for the rights of children who are not yet born.

A Farewell to
Ralph David Abernathy

Among the people whose activism was inspired by their faith, there were none more conspicuous than the early leaders of the civil rights movement. I've always thought that one of the heroes among those leaders was the Reverend Ralph David Abernathy—the pastor of the movement and the number one assistant to Martin Luther King Jr. He was never a favorite with the American media; he lacked the polish and erudition of Dr. King, which may have caused some reporters to underestimate his strength and contribution. But I was proud of the fact that when Abernathy died on Tuesday, April 17, 1990, the Charlotte Observer, *where I was working, recognized the importance of that passing, and stripped the story across the top of Page one. Here, expanded slightly for the book* Southern Voices, *is what I wrote on that occasion:*

Southern Voices
1991

Ralph David Abernathy leaned against the lectern, a smallish man with sleepy eyes, his hair now gray, his speech a little slurred after two strokes and an operation on his brain.

In the posh banquet room of a Charlotte hotel, more than 250 people were caught in the ebb and flow of his rhetoric. He joked and teased, then pounded the lectern three times with his fist.

"I need to be in church now," he said. "I need some amens." And then he roared: "America has never been America to me, but I am staying on the case."

Such were the images that came tumbling back on April 17 with the news that Ralph David Abernathy—preacher, activist, and loyal partner to Dr. Martin Luther King—had died in Atlanta at the age of 64.

By virtually all accounts, he left a legacy of courage, controversy and sadness.

Abernathy published an autobiography in 1989—a poignant re-counting of his Alabama childhood and his turbulent years as friend and alter ego to King.

Some reviewers, including the *Washington Post's* Juan Williams and civil rights historian David Garrow, praised the warmth and honesty of Abernathy's story.

But others focused on roughly a half dozen pages, in which Abernathy acknowledged King's sexual infidelities—the slain leader's "temptations of physical pleasure."

In October, 1989, 27 prominent black Americans signed a statement denouncing the author and his revelations and predicting he would lose his "place in history."

By most accounts Abernathy fretted about that place. During the final 22 years of his life, the years that followed the assassination of King, he seemed to be haunted by a painful irony—that his own contributions to civil rights were overshadowed by the legacy of the man he most loved.

"The people around King thought of themselves as a group," said Garrow, author of the King biography *Bearing the Cross.* "They shared the same vision and endured the same dangers." And none of them, least of all Abernathy, wanted to be left out of the story.

He was born in Marengo County, Alabama, and came of age on a family farm. "A plantation," he liked to call it—some 500 acres that were a source of his family's independence and pride.

In the early 1950s he moved to Montgomery and at the age of 26 took over as pastor of the First Baptist Church. Soon, he met Martin Luther King, Jr.—a young intellectual who believed that the fervor of black Christianity could be transformed into a movement for social change.

"We used to talk about building such a movement," Abernathy remembered during an interview in Charlotte. "We knew the church was the only institution that black folks had. We weren't the only ones with those ideas. It just happened that history chose Montgomery."

The story today is widely known—how a respected black woman named Rosa Parks refused to relinquish her seat on a Montgomery bus. Black community leaders called a bus boycott, and in the movement that followed, King and Abernathy emerged as the leaders.

"Most times," said Abernathy, "we would both speak. Dr. King's job was to interpret the ideology and the theology of nonviolence. My job was more simple and down-to-earth. I would tell them, 'Don't ride those buses.'"

King with his flair and rhetorical polish, became the visible figure in the movement's dealings with the press, and before long, he was firmly entrenched as the symbol, the preeminent leader. But if Abernathy chafed at being Number Two, it never showed.

"Over the years," says Andrew Young, a former mayor of Atlanta and also a top aide to King, "Ralph was really the pastor to Dr. King. He was a source of strength to us all. Dr. King never went anywhere without him, and Ralph often did the dirty work that Dr. King found distasteful. But more than anything else, Reverend Abernathy was, and is, a great preacher. He knew how to relate to the masses of black people."

So the role was established, and as Martin Luther King moved from confrontation to confrontation—Montgomery, St. Augustine, Birmingham, Selma—Abernathy was always at his side. Those were heady, dangerous times, and for a decade the victories piled on top of each other. But after the Voting Rights Act of 1965, the movement began to flounder. The forces of separatism and violence gained momentum, and by 1968, Abernathy remembered, "Dr. King told me, 'Ralph, maybe we should step aside—temporarily—and let the forces of violence have their day.'"

Soon after that conversation, King was murdered, and Abernathy found himself the new president of the Southern Christian Leadership Conference (SCLS), King's organization. It was perhaps the most difficult period of Abernathy's life.

"I probably could have done a more effective job," he said in 1978, "if I had realized this was not my staff. It was Dr. King's staff, and people simply cannot transfer loyalties. Dr. King always felt, always told me, that we were partners. But the staff did not see us as such.

"He also had that ability with words. I can preach. I do fine in the pulpit. But there was music in his voice." Abernathy smiled and fell silent after that. Despite the depth of his love and admiration, the memory of King had long been a weight. He knew that he suffered in most comparisons, and he did not always handle it with grace.

After a 1969 campaign on behalf of hospital workers in Charleston, Abernathy called it "the greatest victory in the history of SCLC." The implication seemed to be that his achievements ranked with any of King's—a claim that was offensive to most of King's admirers.

But even without such lapses of tact, the '70s were a difficult time for any civil rights leader. The dramatic issues had begun to disappear, and as Abernathy conceded not long before his death, "It was very difficult to know what to do."

In 1977, he finally stepped aside, resigning as president of SCLC to run for Congress. He lost.

It was no doubt, a bitter moment, but it thrust him then, at age 52, back into the role he had played the best. He became, once again, a full-time pastor—preaching regularly in Atlanta's West Hunter Street Baptist Church, visiting the sick and serving communion in the homes of the elderly.

During those same years, he also preached often around the country—sometimes at civil right rallies, other times at old-fashioned revivals.

In 1978, at one of his most rousing appearances in Charlotte—a deafening reminder of an earlier day—he stalked back and forth in the pulpit, the sweat dripping from his face as he gripped the microphone and proclaimed, "My God is here and we gon' have a good time."

Finally, after more than an hour, he called the faithful forward to the altar, and sank back wearily to a chorus of amens. Softly he whispered what could be his epitaph:

"I have done the best I could."

Jesse Jackson:
The Long Road From Home

People disagree about Jesse Jackson, another of Martin Luther King's lieutenants. When he ran for president in 1984, and again in 1988, proclaiming visionary notions of justice and peace and a conservative message of self-help among blacks, the critics came at him from all directions. Some people said he was opportunistic, while others saw him as too wary and untrusting to evoke much trust among the voters. Still others said he should have groomed himself for the presidency by seeking lesser office—and more than a few merely noted that Jackson is black, a fact that, for many Americans, is still sufficient grounds for disqualification.

But it was also true that during the presidential election of 1984, Jackson hurt his own cause with a lapse into ethnic street talk. It was a blow to his brash and legendary confidence, but he picked himself up, and in that election—and again in 1988— put together campaigns far more successful than his critics would have dreamed. I was assigned to try to find the source of Jackson's resilience—and also of his soaring ambition. It seemed to me that the source of each of those traits was the same.

The Charlotte Observer
1984

It was cold in New Hampshire. The wind was whipping up outside the Manchester Sheraton, and the snow would soon fall and mingle with the soot, blocking out the foothills rising toward the north.

Somewhere around midnight, with his spirits sagging lower, Jesse Jackson decided to call home. The truth was, he was extremely depressed. He knew he would not do well in the next days' voting (when it was over he had finished an unimpressive fourth in the Democratic presidential primary), but the worst part was, it was all his fault.

Less than two months had passed since his Damascus triumph, when he had negotiated the freedom of an American pilot in Syria, and when reporters from the *National Review* to the *New York Times* marvelled at his rhetoric—and perhaps also at the vision it contained:

"This is not about one man running for the White House. It is about ten thousand people running for everything—school board, mayor, tax assessor, sheriff. It's about a whole people being lifted from the bottom.

"Everybody must assume their role. We as a people must get free. We have a power we must not forget. It's the power of being morally right. We overcame slavery. We were morally right. We came forward from the back of the bus. We were morally right. We won the right to vote. We were morally right.

"America is not a blanket, all of one piece. It is more of a quilt, and every piece and every color fits somewhere. I want this campaign to be the conscience of a nation, to set a new direction. We must measure character by how we treat our children in the dawn of life, how we treat poor people in the pit of life, how we treat old folks in the sunset of life. And we must have character to be a great nation.

"We tell the Democratic party: The delegates you choose expire in July, but the rainbow lives on. Never again will the Democrats take us for granted, or the Republicans write us off. We have changed our minds, and there is nothing so powerful as a mind that's made up."

Jesse Jackson means it absolutely when he says such things, means it more deeply than most people could imagine—and his need to speak is at least as urgent as the things he has to say.

But now in New Hampshire, it was all coming apart, and the cruelty of the truth was that the blame was all his. During a casual conversation in early February, he had referred to Jews as "Hymie" and New York as "Hymietown." It might not have been much of a problem if it had occurred in a vacuum, but it didn't. The quotes were not the first from Jackson that had disturbed Jewish leaders, and his views on the Middle East—he favors a Palestinian state as a step toward peace—were already controversial.

For a time, he compounded the insensitivity with non-denial denials. And when his confession finally came and the controversy faded, he was left with an attack of depression and self-doubt—emotions that have seldom risen to the surface in his life. "He was going through a thing with himself," says Rex Harris, a longtime friend and campaign coordinator in North Carolina. "Sort of like, 'How stupid can I be?' Jesse kicks himself awful hard sometimes."

So on the night of February 27, in the midst of the candidate's internal ordeal, the telephone rang in Greenville, South Carolina.

Because of the hour, Leroy Griggs knew who it would be. "Jesse," he said, "usually calls when he's down."

Griggs is a soft-spoken man with an air of authority, a youth counselor by trade, and a friend of Jesse Jackson's since their Greenville childhoods, when they roamed the housing projects and segregated schoolyards, or scrambled into the "Colored Only" section of the old Center Theater.

During Jackson's latest call, they didn't talk about a lot. "Just old times and nonsense," as Griggs remembers it. But that telephone connection from the winter chill of New Hampshire put Jackson in touch with something at his core—with a time and a place and a set of circumstances that haunt him and sustain him and occasionally trip him up. But they also force him to say:

"We can't stop running. If we run, we may lose. If we don't run, we're guaranteed to lose. We got to run on."

And Jesse Jackson wasn't talking about merely an election.

He was born in Greenville on October 8, 1941, spending his first few years on Haynie Street, a neighborhood of pitted dirt roads and small wooden houses where most of the people were as poor as the soil.

Jackson's father was married, but not to his mother, Helen Burns, a 16-year-old high school girl with almond eyes, a pretty face and a voice that served her well in the choir of her church. Two years after the birth of her son, she married Charles Jackson, a janitor at the post office, who later adopted Jesse and gave him his name.

Though the family was stable, they had to scrape to get by. And for every black in Greenville, there was the added offense of official white supremacy: the back-of-the-bus rides, and "White Only" signs, and bathrooms off limits to the aching of the bladder.

"Segregation was total," says Leroy Griggs. "Maybe not as mean on the surface as it was in some places. But it could get mean when you threatened the system. I remember one time Jesse and Arthur Adams and I had a game of basketball going at Greenville High. That was the white school. These three white youths asked to participate, and the coach yelled out, 'You niggers get off the court before I call the police.'"

Jesse Jackson has never strayed very far from those memories— from the poverty, illegitimacy and all the instruments of segregation that together pointed at him and told him he was nothing—and they are never far from his mind when he stands before a crowd of young black people, many of them as poor as he was, and leads them in a chant of "I am somebody."

"Like Jesus," he proclaims, "we were born in a slum. But the slum was not born in us. You can explode through riots, or implode through drugs, or be delayed by teen-age pregnancy or simple indifference. You can watch five hours of TV every night, or you can use your minds to become educated. You can vote or you can complain. The choice is yours."

Jackson understands about choices, but he didn't teach himself the lesson. He learned it from a community held together by need—and by the improbable strength of the extended black family. A former teacher, Xanthene Norris, puts it this way:

"Quite often, the matter of not having can make you hope for better. It can crush you, but it can also turn you on. If you had one parent, or one grandparent, or a coach, a minister or a teacher—somebody with a pride for education and a vision of something better, somebody to take an interest—it made you feel that you could be somebody. Jesse had all of those things."

Among other people, said Norris, there were Jackson's English teachers, Anna Richardson and Julius Kilgo, who planted the seeds of metaphor and language. There was his Baptist minister, D.S. Sample, with his salt-and-pepper hair and Flip Wilson features and a permanent half-smile that made a child feel important, and his grandmother Mathilda, with her faintly freckled skin and poetic understanding of the nature of religion, who could take a grandson aside and assure him with conviction, "Put your hand in God's hand and you can be somebody."

But one of the most important people in Jackson's young life—the prototype, in many ways, for his message of self-help—was a gruff and gentle man by the name of Joe Mathis, now a Greenville minister, but then the football coach at Sterling High School.

Mathis, like Jackson, had grown up poor and illegitimate, and football had been his ticket out. When he finished playing at Allen College in Columbia, and came back to Sterling as a coach, he would disappear on occasion to coaching clinics around the South, poring over the X's and O's until the bleary hours of semi-dawn. He once roomed next to Ara Parseghian, the great coach at Notre Dame, swapping strategy with him until it was almost time for breakfast.

Mathis insisted that his players be as driven as he was, though he expected their ambitions to extend beyond football.

"I would tell the kids when they were getting dressed for practice, 'You need something in your heads, not just on your heads.' We took pride in our program, won all our games in 1957, Jesse's sophomore year. But we took a defeat with our heads up. Never complained. We'd say, 'Next week.'

"As a coach, I tried to expose players to college centers. We would schedule games in Charleston, Orangeburg, Atlanta, Columbia. We tried to combine football with an exposure to a better life. We pushed very hard for the football team to be winners—to act like winners, dress like winners.

"Jesse often wore ties, and none of them walked around with their shirttails out. They could get off from practice for having a classroom assignment. It was all part of the strength of Sterling High School. Black teachers would take a personal interest in every child in their class. No hour was too late or too long, and the constant thome the constant theme—was, 'You can make it.'"

By the time he left Greenville, Jesse Jackson believed it. He was a good-looking kid, athletic and self-assured, polite toward his elders and cocky among his peers. But there was something else about him—a certain urgency to his drive that has been a blessing and a curse, leading him headlong into the dizzy realms of the ego, where self-absorption and opportunism can emerge from ambition, and where critics find a reason to sharpen up their knives.

On January 31, a bitter cold night in 1960, four students in Greensboro, North Carolina, prepared to make a little history. They had no idea that it would turn out as it did, but Franklin McCain, Ezell Blair, Joe McNeill and David Richmond were tired of doing nothing.

They were black students at North Carolina A&T, bright middle-class freshmen who were offended by the durability of Southern segregation. They decided to go the next day to the lunch counter at Woolworth's, politely taking their seats on the padded swivel stools, beneath the laminated signs promoting lemon pie.

Their "sit-in," as it was called, gained national attention, and the tactic soon spread across the South—chief weapon in the assault on lunchtime apartheid. In Greensboro itself, the movement continued for several more years, and before it was over, Jesse Jackson was its leader—polishing his oratory at the A&T commons, marching with young protestors in the direction of their targets.

But at the time it all began, when the risks were the greatest and the rewards uncertain, Jackson was far from the scene. He was a frustrated student at Champaign-Urbana, trying to play quarterback for the University of Illinois.

According to some accounts, he was told that even in the enlightened Midwest, the world was not ready for a black at his position. Whatever his reasons, Jackson was unhappy at Illinois and transferred to Greensboro for his sophomore year.

Several things happened after he arrived at A&T: He made some lifelong friends that he continues to see, their relationship unchanged by his own soaring fame. ("He's always been Jesse, straight up," says Wylie Harris, an A&T classmate, and later a coach at Johnson C. Smith University in Charlotte.) But as time went by and Jackson's visibility propelled him to the student body presidency, there were others more skeptical of his flair for self-promotion. One of those people was Franklin McCain, the sit-in pioneer, who was once asked by Jackson to critique a paper Jesse had written on the civil rights movement—seven or eight pages exploring one essential theme: the role of Jesse Jackson in the future of civil rights.

"It was sort of amusing to us," says McCain, "that you sensed from Jesse: Hey, this thing started when I came."

Still, McCain liked Jackson, and admires him today. But it is critical admiration, tempered by major differences in personality and in the way they were raised. McCain, now a supervisor at the Celanese Corporation in Charlotte, was middle class from the beginning, the fourth generation of his family to go to college. He is an unassuming man with the frame of a bear, and he has an air about him of soft-spoken candor.

"In his early years at A&T," says McCain, "Jesse was sort of a nondescript fellow—a tiny bit loud, I suppose, which may be the only reason I remembered him. For most of his first year, we didn't see much of him in the movement that was going on. You'd find him holding hands with the girls while we were downtown picketing.

"But I think it's fair to say that once he became involved, Jesse served to kindle and rekindle some enthusiasm on the part of latecomers and reluctant participants. He served as a catalyst in year Number Two of the movement.

"There was a different group of people in phase two. People saw there weren't any more unknowns. You knew damned well that you were not going to jail, or if you did, you'd be out in twenty-four hours. You knew policemen were not going to knock you over the head or hoodlums string you up. You actually heard people say, 'I'm not going to get left out.'

"Jesse was already a fairly decent speaker, and that is pretty much the role he began to play. Still, I always felt something about Jesse: not a sense of mission, but a need for accomplishment. The mission was there, perhaps, but it was overshadowed by other things—the sense that I need to be there. What I wanted to feel more of was a sense of the we.

"But you have to consider the differences in the way we grew up. In my family, you used the word I very sparingly. It was just impolite, and you didn't do it.

"I remember one time—this may be the most vivid memory of my childhood—we were living in Washington, D.C., maybe ten blocks from the Supreme Court Building, and one night I had a case of the Big 'I', and my grandmother took me outside. It was a summer night, and the sky was full of stars and constellations. She said, 'There are stars up there that have not even been discovered—they are bigger than the Earth and the distances are such that you can't even imagine—and you are going to stand down here and tell me that you are so important.'

"Every time at A&T, when I would get to thinking about my own importance, whenever that began to overshadow a sense of mission and commitment, I would walk outside and remember what my grandmother told me.

"You see, I didn't grow up needing anything. But Jesse came from different circumstances—circumstances in which you had to struggle to say, 'I am somebody.' I don't suppose I'd be very different. Still, the Big I and the little you is the one thing that gets in Jesse's way.

"You hope that people will be somewhat forgiving, because the thing is, Jesse really does care about people. And he has some terrific ideas. Because of his campaign, you hear people talking about politics who never discussed it before. It opens up a new horizon, a new day, for blacks who were naive, lazy or indifferent about voting. I honestly don't believe there is another black person—or another person, period —who could stimulate the interest that Jesse has."

There is undoubtedly a lot of truth in McCain's assessment. But there are other people who, even if they agree, are far more inclined to emphasize the negative.

The telephone rings at the *Chicago Tribune,* and columnist Mike Royko picks it up. His hello if gruff and his reply is to the point: "I don't want to talk to people about Jesse Jackson. There are other people who can and will. I won't."

But Royko has written a great deal about Jackson, dubbing him

"Jesse Jetstream," maintaining that he's mostly ego and hot air. There are others in Chicago who have equally strong opinions, for that is where Jackson has spent most of the last 20 years, and he has not been a leader who inspires neutrality.

He arrived as a student at Chicago Theological Seminary, his intensity now aimed at the issue of civil rights. John Hope Franklin, the great black historian, now at Duke, but then at the University of Chicago, remembers early morning walks in the direction of campus, down 58th Street beneath the elms of Hyde Park.

"I lived on the corner of Blackstone and fifty-eighth, and Jesse lived a little further up, (at 58th and Kimbark)," said Franklin. "I'd be walking along, and I'd hear this voice: 'Hey Doc, wait on me.' We'd walk together and talk about civil rights—how you improve the lot of blacks. Jesse was very interested, intense, but I didn't find him brash. He was always humble with me. Now he clowns around about it—puts one knee on the floor when he greets me, and so forth. He is very close to his past. History means something to him."

Alvin Pitcher, who taught Jackson in a theology course at the University of Chicago, remembers him in much the same way—recalls him poring over the writings of Reinhold Niebuhr and Paul Tillich.

"Once Jesse got hold of an idea or conception," say Pitcher, "it became so alive within him. It was grist for the way he operated and thought. Ideas were not playthings to Jesse."

Despite his seriousness, however, Jackson was impatient with school, and when the forces of justice in Selma, Alabama, swarmed down from the summit of the Edmund Pettus Bridge, bludgeoning a group of blacks who intended to march to Montgomery, and when Martin Luther King arrived in Selma to organize a follow-up march, Jackson headed south to join the movement.

He made the trek to Montgomery and listened wide-eyed as King delivered his most powerful oration since *I Have A Dream*: "I come to say to you this afternoon that however difficult the moment, however frustrating the hour, it will not be long, because truth pressed to earth will rise again...."

That was March 25, 1965. In July, the movement headed north, as King led a march of 30,000 in Chicago. Organizing the demonstration was Jesse Jackson's theology professor, Alvin Pitcher, and Jackson himself became increasingly visible. He signed on with King's organization, the Southern Christian Leadership Conference, and soon jockeyed for position with King's older hands.

Jackson was there when King was murdered in Memphis in 1968. But his handling of the tragedy was not the high point of his life. Within hours, he was on national television wearing a bloodstained shirt, explaining that he was at King's side at the moment of death and was the last human being with whom King spoke. He repeated the story the next day before the Chicago City Council.

The impression for the public was that the mantel had been passed. But others, especially some of those who loved King most, were appalled and even shocked: Jesse Jackson, as they saw it, was using one of the most horrible moments in American history—the assassination of a mentor and a friend—to promote his own fortunes.

Some in Chicago who have watched Jackson closely believe shameless self-promotion is a fundamental trademark. Perhaps the most biting indictment came from Barbara Reynolds, formerly a black reporter at the *Chicago Tribune*, and author of a biography, *Jesse Jackson—The Man, The Movement, The Myth*. Reynolds maintained that Jackson "is not an invention of the media, as is often charged. He invented himself, his own opportunity, his own moment of glory."

Still, it is difficult to deny Jackson's record of accomplishment. First as head of SCLC's Operation Breadbasket, and later as director of Operation PUSH, Jackson emerged as the preeminent black leader in Chicago, manipulating the media with his boldness and charisma. He served, in effect, as a kind of interpreter of events, a semi-official black spokesman, and an all-important backer of black political candidates.

He was an undisputed force in the election of Harold Washington as Chicago's first black mayor, (though some, including Washington, resented Jackson's tendency to dominate the headlines).

More tangibly, Jackson negotiated a series of "covenants" with corporate America, persuading companies ranging from Coca-Cola to Quaker Oats to hire and promote more blacks, and to offer more distributorships to black businessmen. Jackson says the covenants are worth nearly $2 billion.

Nathaniel Clay, a former PUSH staff member and later the editor of a Chicago weekly, offers this summary of Jackson and his accomplishments: "Jesse came to Chicago making a splash. At first, I watched him from a distance. I was a guy on the fringe. I didn't get involved until late sixty-nine or seventy, when I started going to Saturday morning PUSH meetings, and helped picket supermarkets that were selling rotten food or refusing to carry products that blacks had made.

"Jesse would picket the stores and demand that they save shelf space for black merchandise. He led the picketing himself with his bullhorn and chants, urging shoppers not to go in. We would turn around a lot of people.

"On a personal level," Clay continued, "Jesse has such polar qualities. He's very bright and quick and compassionate on the one hand. But he can be very abrupt and harsh on the other. He is short-tempered at times, and impatient with people who are not as quick, or as willing to work, as he is.

"He'll dress down a staff member in front of everybody, instead of taking him off to the side. I've seen him do it a number of times. And yet I've seen him show such sensitivity.

"I went with him to the Middle East in nineteen seventy-nine, and we visited several Palestinian refugee camps. I remember the squalor in one particular camp in Beirut—the little children with sores on their bodies. I recall Jesse picking up one little kid, and he said, 'I've seen this. I don't have to be told.' There were almost tears in his eyes. That camp, to him, was Greenville, South Carolina, all over again.

"Today, of course, Jesse isn't poor. But the truth is, money doesn't interest him a lot. I have seen many times when he would come off the road, his pockets stuffed with cash and checks he'd been given. He'd just hand it over to the secretary. Money is not what motivates Jesse. He has a nice house on the south shore (that he shares with his wife and five children), but he drives a ten-year-old station wagon.

"Jesse's interest—and also his need—is making a difference."

Manly High School is a desolate place, lost in the middle of a Chicago slum, where buildings collapse into piles of mere rubble, and the wind blows garbage among the shotgun houses.

In recent years, Jesse Jackson has been a regular in Manly's hallways—urging students to turn off their televisions at night, to stay away from drugs and take responsibility for their bodies and their minds. Manly is the target for Jackson's PUSH Excel, a federally-funded project, which seeks, in effect, to take the strengths of Greenville's Sterling High School in the 1950s and apply them to ghetto schools around the country.

It is one more indication that Jackson's identity is still shaped by the lessons of his youth. His ambitions are inseparable from those of his constituency, and with his candidacy he embodies the truth of his message: He is a black man rising from the most humble origins, running credibly for the presidency of the United States.

That at least was how it seemed until the Hymie controversy, when he stumbled badly and did damage to the cause. He was genuinely stung by the outrage of Jews, for he is not a man who likes to be despised. But worse than that, he provided the whole country with a reason not to listen.

So he brooded for awhile at the Manchester Sheraton, but within a few days he had picked himself up—and when his campaign headed south, dipping into his homestate of South Carolina, the old fire had returned. He made overtures to the Jewish community: "We need a new trialogue among blacks, Arabs and Jews. We need to export the American experience to the Middle East, not import the divisions from there to here."

And then he arrived at South Carolina State College in the little town of Orangeburg, where black protestors were gunned down by police in 1968. He gazed out across the overflow crowd, grinning and teasing in conversational tones, the buttons unlocked on his double-breasted blazer.

"How many of y'all are not registered to vote here in Orangeburg?" he asked. "Don't be 'shamed. Be proud you are able to vote. We got some registrars here in the front of the room. So come on down, now. Come on down." And when they came forward by the hundreds, as if in a peculiar variation of a Billy Graham altar call, he grinned again and said: "How many of y'all are gonna vote for me?"

But then his mood turned deadly serious. He paid homage to the martyrs of the civil rights movement: Goodman, Cheney, Reeb, Luizzo —a Jew, a black, a Unitarian, an Italian—and his rhetoric took flight:

"There are times," he said, "when you have to stand in the face of judgment. We are not perfect servants. We are public servants. We've made some mistakes, and we'll make some more.

"But we're winning today. When new voters step forward to register, we're winning. When our spirits are revived, we're winning. When our people put down the bottle or stay away from the needle, we're winning. When little children have false notions of inferiority removed from their minds, and they say 'I can go where I want to go and be what I want to be,' we're winning.

"Who knows but what in some child's mind—born out of wedlock, locked into welfare—might be the cure for cancer? Who knows but what in the mind of some child born in the slums might be the equation for world peace?

"Today, there are five million more people in poverty, and most of them are not black. They are mostly white—infants and women, children and old people. I intend to be the conscience of our party, the conscience of this nation. If we can feel the pain and hurt, we can do something about it."

John Hope Franklin argues that Jackson's declarations "raised the level of discourse in the presidential campaign to a level it would not have reached in his absence. It was a dull and uninteresting campaign except for the remarkable, charismatic power of this young man."

But it was also true that in the end, Jackson's vision was rejected, as a very different mandate prevailed at the polls. On November 6, 1984, Ronald Reagan was reelected by an overwhelming majority, and black Americans—and the poor of all races—began to grapple with a new sense of isolation.

Jackson, however, remained philosophical.

"Change comes slowly," he said, "but it does come and we need to keep it going. I want to keep repeating what my mother and grandmother instilled in me—that we are God's children, and God has defeated the impossible."

It is a simple Christian message, Jackson added. And it is just as true on either side of an election.

A Tale of Two Cities

Before the 1988 Democratic Convention in Atlanta, I was assigned to do a profile of that city, where all all of the progress and problems that exist in the South could be seen at one time. The story was written as Atlanta was braced for a scrutiny more intense than it had ever known.

The Charlotte Observer
1988

Andy Young seems to love those black-tie occasions, standing there at the dais, with the tables spread before him in the great banquet halls, silver clinking discreetly over the last remnants of the meal, and then not a sound except his own voice.

In cities from Tokyo to Charlotte, Young, the eloquent and energetic mayor of Atlanta, has used such opportunities to tell the story of his city. It is a story he is likely to repeat again and again in the next week, as Atlanta braces itself for the Democratic National Convention. By the opening gavel on July 18, more than 35,000 people are expected in town—including 15,000 in the international media—and in the minds of Young and other leaders in Atlanta, there is no way to put a price tag on that kind of exposure.

They are convinced the city can withstand the scrutiny—that by the time the reporters leave town, Atlanta will be established, even more firmly than it already is, as a city of vision: a place of opportunity, where progress is rooted in the greatest moral triumph the nation has known.

"We have dealt head-on with the issue of race," Young said recently. "If you look at other places—places like South Africa, the Middle East or Northern Ireland—that by all logic is the way that we should be. But we have defied logic in our part of the country. In the city of Atlanta, we have learned to live together, black and white, and in so doing we have created a climate where progress is possible."

Young is convincing when he says such things. He is handsome and self-assured at the age of 56, with an angular face, flecks of gray adding dignity to his neatly cropped hair, and his style at the podium is modern and cool—much more cerebral than that of his mentor, Dr. Martin Luther King Jr. There also is a great deal of truth to his words. Atlanta has made progress, becoming, in the past 30 years, the political and economic capital of the South: an area of 2.5 million people, with 375,000 new jobs and more than 860 new companies coming in since 1983.

Its airport is one of the world's busiest, with an average of 65,000 passengers a day; its freeways have recently been expanded to 10 lanes; and its mass transit system, approved by voters in 1971, is the final key ingredient of an efficient infrastructure.

But there is another side to Atlanta's personality, another index of its character and health: It is a city of stark and sometimes terrifying poverty. Perry Ginn, executive director of the Christian Council of Metropolitan Atlanta, an interfaith organization that tries to deal with human need, estimates that Atlanta has as many as 10,000 homeless people, many of them passing their nights in makeshift shelters scattered around town.

There is a particular grimness about those scenes—the crowded rows of cots in church auditoriums, the stares that range from vacant to hostile—and it is all a contrast to the glitter of downtown, the towering glass monuments to the city's success.

But the symptoms of poverty are far more pervasive than shelters for the homeless. Michael Lomax, chairman of the Fulton County Commission, a slender and articulate black man who is the resident intellectual of Atlanta's leadership, puts the issue this way:

"We have developed a large black middle class in Atlanta, and we have a strong black power elite, which is largely political, secondarily economic. But what we also have—what Atlanta attracts, but doesn't necessarily nurture—is a large poor class, representing thity-five per cent of our black population."

For Lomax and others, that underclass, with its predictable problems of drugs, gang violence and teen-age pregnancy, represents a crisis—an affront to the city's official image of itself. The national media have already taken notice, and the realities of poverty have begun to raise a question: What kind of city, really, is Atlanta?

Is it the Democratic Mecca in the rhetoric of Andy Young, the great and shining city on a hill, built on the ashes of defeated racism? Or is it a place of poverty and despair, the third most violent city in the country,

104

where the cycles of destruction are only getting worse?

The truth, of course, is that Atlanta is both. But people like Lomax see that fact not so much as an admission of schizophrenia but as evidence of an evolution not yet complete.

"This has always been the kind of town," he says, "that bellied up to the bar, that did the things it had to do, when the times required it. And these are the issues we now have to face."

Lomax believes Atlanta will come to terms with its latest challenge, the burgeoning problems of the poor. But to understand how and why that is likely to happen, he says, it's important to understand the city's rich history.

There is a startling picture on Ivan Allen's wall. He is standing on the hood of an Atlanta police car, facing a mob of angry black people. One man in particular has stepped to the front, the rage taking over his middle-aged face, and 20 years later, there is still something chilling about the scene: the raw hatred frozen by the blink of a camera.

But if anything, the look on Allen's face is even more striking. There isn't any anger and, from all appearances, not even a lot of fear in his bespectacled, white-haired countenance—just an earnest attempt to reason, to listen, to buy a little time.

From 1961 to 1969, Allen was the mayor of Atlanta, a lifelong resident who understood the stakes. It was a time, he knew, of promise and prosperity, a time when Atlantans had built a new airport and were about to add to it, when they were making the transition to major-league sports and when business showed signs of a continuing boom.

Given such promise, white people like Allen—keen businessmen who had a sense of what was coming—had a simple objective: They were determined to keep their city from exploding.

They could see the alternative in other places in the South, in cities like Birmingham, which seemed to be dying—caught up not only in the bombings and random violence of the Klan, but also in a kind of official terror that left the nation repulsed: fire hoses turned on peaceful demonstrators, police dogs tearing at the flesh of black children.

In Atlanta, city leaders vowed, never would their image suffer such a stain. And when the moments of shock and terror did come—when, for example a Jewish temple was bombed in 1958, a retribution for the civil rights pronouncements of its rabbi, Jacob Rothschild—there was a widespread cry of revulsion. More than 300 clergymen signed a manifesto, adding their voices to that of the rabbi, and Editor Ralph McGill thundered on the front page of The Atlanta Constitution: "This is the harvest. It is the crop of things sown."

McGill was far from a radical in Atlanta. Indeed, his basic sensibilities—his understanding of the destructive costs of segregation, both practical and moral—were shared by much of the city's leadership.

"A city too busy to hate." That was the slogan coined by Ivan Allen's predecessor, Mayor William Hartsfield, a balding, sometimes hot-tempered man of quick wit and strong will.

Hartsfield was first elected mayor in 1937 and didn't give up the post until 1961. During that time, his mission was to create a climate in which business could flourish—an agenda that included not only such projects as airports and roads, but also attention to the issue of race. He met regularly with such black leaders as William Holmes Borders and the Rev. Martin Luther King Sr. and took such steps in the 1940s as desegregating the city's police force. And when it came to Ivan Allen to seize the baton—to try, if anything, to step up the pace that Hartsfield had set—he was grateful for the counsel of the city's black leaders.

"We were blessed," he remembers with a sigh. "It would have been hard to get along without the Kings, the Borders, people like that." That kind of black leadership first began to emerge just after the Civil War. Atlanta was young, less than 30 years old—and in the opinion of some who have studied its history, there was a brashness about it, an absence of nostalgia for the days before the war.

"The Rhetts and Scarlets won out," Michael Lomax says. "Ever since the end of the Civil War era, Atlanta has been a city on the make." For blacks, that was good. As Lomax puts it, a kind of "enlightened paternalism" developed in the city—a feeling that good race relations were good for business—and in that climate, important black institutions began to emerge. Atlanta University was born in 1865, Morehouse College two years later and Spellman College in 1881. They were the cornerstones of a black university complex that would later include six schools, and by the turn of the century they had not only nurtured a black middle class, but had also made Atlanta a center (some say *the* center) of black intellectual life in America.

W.E.B. DuBois was there, and then Benjamin Mays, the South Carolinian who had risen from a sharecropping boyhood to become president of Morehouse and mentor to several generations of black leaders, including Dr. Martin Luther King Jr.

Thus it was no surprise in the 1960s when Atlanta became the center of the civil rights movement—although even then it was hard to imagine that, in less than 20 years, one of King's chief lieutenants, Andrew Young, would be mayor of the city. Or that his son, Martin Luther King III, would be a county commissioner. Or that John Lewis, a founder and president of the Student Nonviolent Coordinating Committee, one of the most militant black organizations of the day, would be elected to Congress, with the margin of victory provided by whites.

But if all of those things were well hidden in the future, it was clear by the early 1970s that monumental change was just around the corner. Blacks were rapidly becoming a majority (they now make up 67 percent of the city's population), and that had important political implications.

"The business community recognized that we were going to see a black mayor elected very soon," says Dan Sweat, former director of a downtown alliance called Central Atlanta Progress. "These leaders knew we were entering a time of black political control and white economic control and that if they were going to retain power, they had to share power in a whole different way."

Sweat's organization had already produced a study of the city's needs—"a blueprint for economic stability," Sweat called it—and it included such items as widened interstates, a mass transit system and major expansions of the airport.

Many white executives feared that Atlanta would change course when blacks took power. But much to the relief of the business community, many things remained the same after the election of Mayor Maynard Jackson in 1973. Roads were built. Mass transit began. The skyline gleamed with new glass towers. Atlanta's white leaders soon discovered, in fact, that their power-sharing arrangement—that inescapable accommodation with the city's black majority—was one of the greatest selling points the town had ever known.

Particularly with the election of Andrew Young, who will complete his second four-year term next year and who, by most accounts, has carried the mantle of his office with charisma, Atlanta appears to be competing more effectively than ever, luring new investment, laying claim to new status as an international city.

According to Chamber of Commerce figures, between 1983-88, 188 foreign companies set up operations in Atlanta, and with aggressive recruitment by Young and others, the total keeps rising. "The mayor is our clean-up hitter," says chamber President Gerald Bartels. "He is such an eloquent speaker, and he has an outstanding grasp of worldwide economics. The white business community didn't support him when he first ran for office. But after he was elected, he was not the least bit vindictive. He made overtures to the business leadership, and it's been a love affair ever since."

And so it is that the Democrats are convening at a time of fierce pride in Atlanta—when leaders like Bartels have vowed "to sell this city like no other city has ever been sold." They don't deny the problems. But when controversies emerge, they say, that's when the city is really at its best.

Bartels, for example, cites a recent series of articles in *The Atlanta Constitution* detailing the reluctance of Atlanta's banks to make loans available in black neighborhoods. The revelations were followed by a flurry of meetings—tough negotiating sessions, most participants say—and soon the banks had fashioned a response. Not only would they change their policies, they also would establish a $65 million loan fund especially for neglected parts of town.

Bartels maintains that it was vintage Atlanta, pragmatic, effective: "people of good will, sitting down, airing their views, trying to find the way to solve a problem." Andy Young, too, is a champion of that spirit. "Nothing happens in Atlanta," he says proudly, "that government and business don't work together on."

And yet it also has to be said that there is a great deal of unfinished business in Atlanta—bitter disputes about encroaching development and thousands of people cut off from the prosperity and the harmony of Andy Young's city.

"Atlanta has its problems," concedes Rep. John Lewis, whose district includes downtown Atlanta, part of a core city that ranks as the second-poorest in the nation. To get a sense of what the problems are, it helps to start in Inman Park, a neighborhood not far from downtown, with Victorian houses and broad streets winding through canopies of oak. It is a peaceful place, prosperous and quiet, but there is anger these days in Inman Park, and it has spread to Druid Hills, Candler Park and other residential areas that share a common grievance. They are all in the path of a proposed four-lane expressway intended, among other things, to improve access to the Jimmy Carter Presidential Center.

To neighborhood activists like Ruth Wall and Gale Walldorff, the expressway represents a looming disaster—a threat to the livability of historic neighborhoods and one more symptom of the fundamental problem confronting Atlanta. "There is a whole pervasive feeling in the city," Walldorff says. "All the neighborhoods close in, not just ours, feel threatened by development. If you lose the trees, the greenery, you lose a lot of what makes the city so wonderful. It's crucial to balance progress and preservation, and the Atlanta leadership has not been sensitive."

Others point out that development has also worsened the city's housing problem. Perry Ginn and Neal Ponder, for example, officials at the Christian Council of Metropolitan Atlanta, say acres of small houses have been razed to make way for parking lots at Atlanta-Fulton County

Stadium. Ginn and Ponder don't argue that the houses were any good; many were substandard, but at least they were there. "With development," Ginn says, "a lot of little houses have been torn down and replaced by apartments where the rent is high. The result has been a tremendous, growing need for low-income housing—especially since people are getting scared to live in public housing because of the drugs."

Louise Watley says she's not afraid. For more than 30 years, she has lived in a sprawling project known as Carver Homes—more than 100 acres of rambling, red brick buildings, some with the windows now boarded up and garbage scattered on unkempt lawns.

But if fear isn't her style, Watley, longtime head of the Carver Homes Tenants Association, says life has changed in Atlanta's public housing —with conditions now resembling what she used to associate with big cities of the North. "Detroit, New York, places like that," she says. "With the drug problem, and with the gangs and violence and the whole attitude of kids, it's not like it was," Watley continues. "Seems like we've turned back the hands of the clock in a way. There are no more role models in poor black communities. They have all moved away."

Increasingly, that isolation of the black underclass and the worsening problems that have gone along with it are a matter of concern to Atlanta's leadership. "We have a tendency to forget what we don't see," Michael Lomax says. "But in this case, we can't. Too big a percentage of the next generation is at risk."

Earlier this month, Economic Opportunity Atlanta, an anti-poverty agency, released a study indicating that about a fourth of Atlanta's population is poor. The study also cited an increase in "the severity and magnitude of poverty," including "widespread drug abuse...and an increase in organized crime in housing projects and low-income communities."

That reality, Dan Sweat says, was one of the reasons he decided to leave his job at Central Atlanta Progress and take over the presidency of the CF Foundation, which has been set up to help launch an attack on poverty. In the past, Sweat says, city leaders, black and white, have done a brilliant job of planning for the future. They have understood the need for airports, subways, a good road system, good race relations to keep business healthy. "But when it comes to inner-city poverty," Sweat says, "we have been trapped for too long in the shelter mentality. We have got to get beyond it."

For his own part, Michael Lomax remains optimistic. "We'll see these problems addressed," he says, "when the business community understands the total cost."

•   •   •

So how, in the end, do you make sense of Atlanta? What is the city all about, and what sort of future is it likely to face?

One person who has considered such questions is Manuel Maloof, the 64-year-old county commission chairman in neighboring DeKalb, where the suburbs sprawl from Atlanta's city limits, testament to a history of prosperity and growth.

Maloof is a powerful figure in the metro area, known and respected for his outspoken opinions. He is proud of Atlanta, proud of its handsome black mayor who represents it so well in the marketplaces of the world. In a way, he says, Andy Young embodies Atlanta's evolution, its spirit of inclusiveness and shining opportunity. For most of his life, Maloof has seen that spirit get stronger—ever since his boyhood, when, as the Catholic son of a Lebanese immigrant, he was afraid to venture into the county where he is now an official. "DeKalb was Klan country," he says.

But times change. And if there are people, as there surely are, who remain untouched by Atlanta's prosperity, Maloof simply views it as a problem to be addressed. "Atlanta has always been a place of vision," he says, "and the basic vision didn't change with the transfer of power. It's simply been expanded to include more people."

And if that circle has kept getting wider, Maloof says he sees no reason why that should ever change.

The South According to Hugh McColl

From the Civil War forward, many of the visions of rebuilding the South had to do with economic power. In the late 20th century, Hugh McColl has been an ardent proponent of that economic vision, and so has his competitor, Ed Crutchfield. The two of them are bankers in Charlotte—CEOs who have managed to build their institutions into giants: two of the biggest banks anywhere in the country. This is their story, and its implications for the region they serve.

Charlotte Magazine
1996

There's an element of parody about Hugh McColl—the glass hand grenade that sits on his desk, the stock certificates from a string of conquered banks that hang like mounted trophies on the wall. The chairman and CEO of NationsBank, the country's fourth largest, is proud of all that he has accomplished. He has managed to channel his Marine Corps aggression into the task of transforming his medium-sized bank—creating a powerhouse based in the South. No longer, he says, must the business leaders in his part of the country go hat in hand to the money center banks—the Chase Manhattans and all the rest who seem to regard the Southern states with disdain. McColl himself has felt that sting, and it pleases him now that those days are gone. In the first three months of 1996, NationsBank earned $590 million, with total assets of nearly $200 billion.

Those kinds of numbers have helped to transform the city of Charlotte, the place where McColl has spent his career, making it the third largest banking center in the country. But McColl will be the first to tell you that he has not accomplished that feat by himself. Just up the street from his own headquarters, in a glass office tower that's not quite as tall, his grey-haired competitor, Ed Crutchfield, is much the same kind of visionary maverick—a small-town Southerner delighted by the fact that his region can hold its own with anybody. His bank, First Union, ranks sixth in the country in total assets, first in the number of branches nationwide, and its total earnings in 1995 were well over $1.4 billion. Corporate profits of that magnitude are rare in the history of the American economy.

"I don't think twenty companies have done it," says Frank Dunn, a former First Union executive who teaches now at the Center for Banking Studies at University of North Carolina at Charlotte. "And the amazing thing is, two of those companies are now in Charlotte."

This is the story of how they emerged—two megabanks and the city where they thrive. It is a story of brashness and heart and a little bit of luck, which begins as the story of Hugh McColl—a smallish man of five-feet-seven, now turning grey at the age of 61. He still has an impish twinkle in his eyes, and he can wear his confidence sometimes on his sleeve, telling an interviewer not long ago, "when I walk in a room, I think that I own it."

But there are people who say there's another side to his character —a compassion that provides a ballast for his ego, and a deep sense of loyalty to the people around him. It's a trait, friends say, that's been in his family since the 19th century, tracing back eventually to his great-grandfather, a Confederate veteran who came home from the war and set about the task of rebuilding his county.

Duncan D. McColl, as the old man was known, set up a mill and a bank and a strip of railroad with the ambitious name of South Carolina and Pacific, even though it never left the state. He understood the needs of the community around him and how they tied in nicely with his need to prosper. The understanding survived through the Great Depression, when McColl's own father kept the family bank open, while financial institutions were failing all around.

Hugh McColl has that same kind of drive—that same understanding that his own company's fortunes are tied to his place. "It's as natural to him as washing his hands," says his rival, Ed Crutchfield, and Crutchfield has every reason to know. Many people say he's not that different—"better loved," says McColl, but if that is true it's just a matter of style. As one banker put it, "Ed is a little bit more 'aw shucks.'" Beneath that genial veneer, however, Crutchfield seems to be just as driven. Like McColl, he loves buying banks, having done it now some 65 times, and his ambition is fueled at least in part by the pride of the underdog from the South.

"Like Hugh," he says, "I have this feeling. We got beat once and this whole region was decapitalized. Everything went north. At the start

112

of our careers, we saw the New York crowd and others smugly dominate this business. For the first time now, we are sure as hell at least even."

Crutchfield smiles when you ask how it happened, considering it a little ungraceful to boast. He talks instead about the favorable conditions—the banking laws in North Carolina, which have permitted branch banking for most of this century—making it possible for banks to grow statewide. (The law, at first, was silent on the subject, then confirmed a practice already in place.) In addition to that, the economy in Charlotte has mostly been good—"a kind of economic saline solution," as Crutchfield puts it, that has allowed local banks to prosper and expand.

But there is another ingredient that's even more important—at least in the eyes of Crutchfield and McColl. They both came of age in a corporate culture every bit as aggressive as their own personalities. Both First Union and NationsBank's, or NCNB as it was known earlier, have been buying other banks for nearly 30 years.

"It was second nature to us," Crutchfield concludes. "From the time we started, we had them lined up—like airplanes waiting for their turn to take off."

It's hard to say who began that trend, but it was already in place by the time Hugh McColl hit the ground in Charlotte. That was 1959. He was a graduate of the University of North Carolina—and perhaps more importantly, of the U.S. Marines. Authors Howard Covington and Marion Ellis, in their book on the history of NationsBank, argue that in the case of McColl, the Marines served essentially as his school of management. He was almost killed in a training exercise, when he jumped from a helicopter into the sea and his scuba tank struck him in the back of the head. He was drifting unconscious, sinking slowly from the weight of the tank, when a sergeant followed the trail of his blood and pulled him to the surface. That episode, along with others in the Corps, left him with a sense of interdependence—a loyalty to those who were on the same team—and it was a quality he found at NCNB under the leadership of Addison Reese, the CEO when McColl first arrived.

Reese was a quiet but competetive man, engaged in his own private war with Wachovia, the largest bank in North Carolina. Based in Winston-Salem, with branches scattered all across the Piedmont, Wachovia was the aristocrat of Carolinas banks—and Addison Reese, with his horn-rimmed glasses and soft-spoken style, was the improbable renegade from Charlotte, working every day to dethrone it.

There were essentially two ways to accomplish that goal. You could make more loans to more different customers, and increase your revenues that way, or you could buy other banks. The latter course was a great deal faster, particularly if you managed to pick good targets, and Reese had the knack. Surrounded by a cadre of bright young men, recruited from schools all over the South (and a few from the Ivy Leagues as well), he criss-crossed North Carolina making deals. By the time he retired in 1974, his bank was a rival in size to Wachovia.

First Union, meanwhile, was not far behind. Operating comfortably in the underdog role, Reese's counterpart was C.C. Cameron, tall and erect, a Southern gentleman in his manners and his style, who had his own legions of ambitious men. One of those in the 1960s was Ed Crutchfield, a former football player at Davidson, who went on for his Masters at the University of Pennsylvania—an Ivy Leaguer from a small Southern town. Crutchfield learned a lot in college, but his values and character were shaped in Albemarle, N.C., where there didn't seem to be any room for pretension.

"Growing up in a town of 15,000, you have to become self-aware," he says, "because everybody knows everything."

The rest of his education came at the bank, where he learned from his mentor, C.C. Cameron, that building a business was not that different from putting in a crop. Preparation was the key. You had to have good people, putting in thousands of hours every year just tilling the soil—getting to know bankers from every part of the state.

"That's the way you consumate deals," said Cameron. "You get to know people—the CEOs, the board members—and get them sold on what you can do together. It's a very time-consuming process."

For First Union, however, it was time well-spent, and by January of 1985, when Cameron retired and passed the chairmanship to Crutchfield, the bank was ready to take the next step. In the spring, it merged with Northwestern Bank, which was then the fourth-largest in North Carolina, and with that deal First Union suddenly had the resources to compete—to test itself against any bank in the South.

The problem was, there were laws against banking across state lines. People like Cameron and Ed Crutchfield had predicted for years that the laws would change—that the day of interstate banking was at hand—and more and more, they were feeling claustrophobic in North Carolina. That was especially true because NCNB had managed to escape. It was led in the '70s by Thomas I. Storrs, the intellectual successor to Addison Reese, who had his Ph.D. from Harvard. It was easy for Storrs to envision the day when the red and white signs of NCNB would be posted on banks all over the South. He set up a task force to make that happen, and one of its members, a young vice president by the name of Joe Martin, traveled across North Carolina and beyond with a slide show for politicians and bankers and anybody else who wanted to see it, trying to build support for interstate banking.

The results for the first few years were mixed. There seemed to be a lot of timidity and doubt, for bankers as a group were never very bold. But a breakthrough came in 1981, and it took a form that no one expected. Paul Polking, a corporate lawyer at NCNB, was studying the laws and regulations of Florida, searching for ways to get into that state. As Martin remembers it, everyone assumed that the laws would have to change, but Polking came in one morning and declared: "I think we are in."

What Polking discovered was that before the legislature of Florida had passed a prohibition against out-of-state banks—chiefly as a barrier to those from the North—NCNB under Addison Reese had bought a small trust company in Orlando. It was not very profitable, had no deposits, and offered only limited financial services. But as Polking read it, it was enough to secure for NCNB a place in the banking business of Florida. Under the law, he concluded, they were grandfathered in.

Back at First Union, the news was alarming. NCNB now had an advantage, moving unfettered into one of the most lucrative markets in the country, while everyone else was still shut out. It underscored a resolve among Crutchfield and others to secure new laws about interstate banking—particularly in the South, where economists argued that a regional compact, a common market of sorts among the key Southern states, could add to the economic power of the region. As the '80s wore on, the argument prevailed. In state legislatures all over the South, new laws were passed and tested in the courts, and early in the summer of 1985, the U.S. Supreme Court gave its assent. The barriers to interstate banking were dead.

Ed Crutchfield's secretary brought him the news, a tearsheet ripped from the Dow business wire, and Crutchfield immediately picked up the phone. He called Billy Walker, the CEO of Atlantic BankCorp, one of the prominent financial institutions in Florida. They met the next day at a beach resort outside of Jacksonville, and hammered out a deal. Walker had been thinking about a merger for awhile, and Crutchfield's bank, which had been too small, was now in the running because of its earlier purchase of Northwestern.

The stakes were daunting in this game of buying banks. In Crutchfield's mind, it was grow or die—and it was clear by now that he was one of the survivors, chasing Hugh McColl across the marketplace of Florida.

It was nip and tuck for the first few years. They both established a presence in the state and began to look at other markets as well—

Georgia, South Carolina, Texas. The opportunities were endless for a company with the vision, and the bankers from Charlotte were sure that they had it. McColl had taken over as chairman when Tom Storrs retired in 1983, and while he knew First Union was a formidable competitor, he was more and more convinced as the decade progressed that his own bank—which now had a little bit of swagger in its step—would be the first to break really big. The capital and the talent were already in place. Now he was simply waiting for the chance.

It came in Texas in 1988. The economy was troubled in that part of the country. Marion Ellis, co-author of *The Story of NationsBank*, says the financial structure of Texas amounted essentially a house of cards that teetered with a drop in the price of oil. The banks were left in a vulnerable position, and one of those most affected was First Republic Bank of Dallas. It had long been a large and healthy institution, with assets totaling more than $32 billion. Now, however, it was in deep trouble—"doomed" in the words of William Seidman, chairman of the Federal Deposit Insurance Corporation. To Seidman, that was a matter of grave concern. His agency was established in 1933 to assure public confidence in America's banks, and in the 1980s, it accomplished that goal by insuring deposits up to $100,000. Estimates were that if First Republic went down—and it was clearly unable to rescue itself—it would cost Seidman's agency more than $10 billion.

That was when Hugh McColl stepped in. He proposed to Seidman that NCNB and the FDIC form a partnership to manage First Republic. NCNB would handle the good loans, sharing the profits with the FDIC, and the agency, in turn, would manage the bad ones—as it would anyway if First Republic failed. Within a few years, when the ship was righted, NCNB would buy out its partner, the FDIC, becoming sole owner of the biggest bank in Texas.

It was a complicated, self-serving proposal. But it seemed just novel enough to work—brilliantly innovative, in fact, a way to head off the catastrophic collapse of one of the biggest banks in the United States.

The question was whether Hugh McColl could pull it off. His bank, after all, was a little bit smaller than the one he was now proposing to save—a preposterous competitor to Citicorp and others who were bidding also for control of First Republic.

With the bank sinking deeper into debt every day, it was up to Seidman and the three-member board of the FDIC to decide on a savior. That was where Hugh McColl got lucky. One of the board members was C.C. Hope, a banker from Charlotte that McColl knew well. For years, he had worked up the street at First Union, where he was a leading strategist in the war over mergers. From all of those struggles, the thing Hope knew about Hugh McColl was that he generally accomplished what he set out to do.

That information was the critical piece, off-setting the inevitable fears about size, and to the astonishment of reporters in the national media, who didn't even have Hugh McColl on the screen, NCNB won the prize. There was plenty of nasty work still ahead—foreclosures on loans and dealing with stockholders left in the cold—but with a single transaction, McColl had doubled the size of his bank, and he wasn't finished yet.

The following year, 1989, he set his sights on Atlanta. His target this time was Citizens and Southern—C&S, as everybody called it—a healthy bank with total assets of $21 billion. McColl wrote the chairman, Bennett Brown, proposing that the two of them talk about a merger. When Brown said no, McColl picked up the phone and called, announcing his plans for a hostile takeover.

"I've got to launch my missiles," he said, and Brown, a warm and genteel man, who regarded Hugh McColl as the opposite, braced himself for a fight. He knew that under the laws of banking, he was required to take any reasonable offer to his board. The board, however, didn't have to accept it, and Brown intended to make sure they didn't. He launched a public relations barrage, depicting McColl as a corporate raider who had used a "government assistance program"—the partnership with the FDIC—to get his toe into Texas, and now was trying to muscle into Georgia.

As further protection against that possibility, or some other marauder who might come later, Brown found another partner for a merger —Sovran Financial Corporation in Virginia. The two banks came together in September, but the deal, in the end, did not go well. The banks agreed to dual headquarters, one in Atlanta, the other in Norfolk, which was always awkward, and they discovered soon after the merger was official that Sovran brought with it a pile of bad loans. They came from the real estate market in Washington, and with the problem getting worse, C&S Sovran was a bank in trouble.

Under the circumstances, McColl decided on another run at Bennett Brown. He wanted to do it right this time, and in *The Story of NationsBank*, Howard Covington and Marion Ellis recount how McColl sought the advice of his staff. He turned to Chuck Cooley, his chief of personnel, and Joe Martin, an executive vice president known for his candor as well as his tact. The two of them knew, and told McColl, that Brown was put off by his military metaphors. He was a man who valued civility and warmth, and he hadn't found much of that in McColl. Martin, however, understood that it was there. His boss could be a hard-charger at times, but in Martin's eyes he was decent and loyal, a man of his word. The challenge was to communicate that to Bennett Brown. They began a series of role-playing sessions—mock negotiations with Cooley or Martin standing in as Brown, while McColl struggled mightily to soften his style.

In the end, it worked. In a series of talks, which began at the beach in South Carolina and shifted from there to New York City, Brown and McColl were able to make a deal. On January 1, 1992, NationsBank was born. With the merged assets of C&S and NCNB, it was, at the time, the third largest bank in the United States.

Not since the Civil War, said McColl, had there been such a powerful bank in the South. "But NationsBank," he declared with a flourish, "sends out the signal that the region is back...."

Ed Crutchfield couldn't help but be impressed. His rival up the street was clearly on a roll, but Crutchfield had never been one to back away. He and Billy Walker, the CEO of his Florida operation, were continuing their march across that state, and they were also well-established in Georgia. But Crutchfield was hungry for a coup of his own, and in 1992, shortly after NationsBank came into being, he began a courtship with First Fidelity, a New Jersey bank with $35 billion in assets and branches scattered from Pennsylvania to Connecticut.

He was talking regularly with Anthony Terracciano, First Fidelity's silver-haired CEO, a handsome, dark-eyed man who was not an easy sell. But there was a personal chemistry that sprang up between them, and Crutchfield patiently began to make his case. Together, he said, the banks would cover the whole East Coast with a line of products and a level of technology that First Fidelity did not yet have. In addition to that, a major league bank in the 1990s had to have assets of $100 billion—and with First Union now at $85 billion, the two banks together could exceed that goal.

Terracciano knew that it all made sense, but as the months went by he continued to resist. "He made me sweat," Crutchfield remembers. But eventually his logic, plus $5 billion in First Union stock, were enough to make a deal. In late '95, the two banks merged with Terracciano as president and Crutchfield as chairman and CEO. At the time it happened, it was the largest bank merger in the history of the country, and back in Charlotte, the headquarters city, the implications were profound.

In the words of Tony Plath, director of the Center for Banking Studies, Charlotte was suddenly "the center of the bulls-eye." There were still huge banks in New York City, but two of the biggest were now in Charlotte, and they were drawing to the city some of the brightest people in the business. Ed Crutchfield was happy about that. There was a vibrancy now in the life of his community—a continuing increase in the level of talent that had implications far beyond the economy.

The city at the end of the 20th century was more urbane, more noticed nationwide. Among its selling points were the NBA and the NFL and a performing arts center in the heart of downtown, and the banks were involved in all of those things. They provided the capital and the expertise, the economic muscle to make it all happen.

But their sense of duty went deeper than that, for the story in the end was more complicated. There was a dark underside to the glimmer and the shine, the New South skyline so full of promise. As Hugh McColl put it not long ago, "...our region's growth has brought with it a high cost...urban ills that our neighbors to the north have known for decades."

In the several dozen speeches that he makes every year, McColl talks often about those themes—the downside of growth, and the struggles and the problems of the people left behind. His instincts are those of a Southern Democrat, and his definition of his bank's self-interest includes the creation of a healthy community—a place where people understand the common ground, and where powerful institutions like his own invest in the parts of town that need it most.

Among other things, NationsBank, in a four-year span across the South, has poured $13.4 billion into low and moderate income neighborhoods, and spent at least 15% of its procurement dollars—money for buildings, office furnishings, etc.—with minority enterprises.

There are many people, particularly in Charlotte, who are not surprised by those kinds of investments. Ron Leeper is one. For years in the '80s he was a respected member of the Charlotte city council—a young black man with a huge Afro and an easy smile, who represented the interests of his own part of town, and also emerged as one of the statesmen. He was admired by leaders all over the city, and in the election of 1988, he decided to leave the safety of his district and submit himself to the voters citywide. To the astonishment of many observers, he lost—his years of service overtaken by his race—and there were people who were deeply embarrassed by his fate.

One of those, apparently, was Hugh McColl who telephoned Leeper soon after the election and invited him to lunch. "It was his way of apologizing" Leeper says today. "He smiled and said, 'to hell with politics, let's make some money.'"

At that lunch and later, they began to talk about the fate of black business—how urban renewal in the 1960s had destroyed the line of business succession, uprooting dozens of family enterprises and cre-

119

ating a break in the chain of business knowledge. It was time, Leeper said, to deal with the problem, but black business people still needed some help.

A few months later, McColl responded with an offer that was startling. He said if Leeper wanted to get into construction—a business where minority contractors were needed—NationsBank would pay half his salary at a company in Charlotte called F.N. Thompson, a successful corporation that could teach him the ropes. When he felt he was ready to step out on his own, the bank would extend him a line of credit and give him some work. In return, they hoped he would share what he learned with other minority entrepreneurs and guide at least a few of them to the bank.

Both Leeper and McColl have done their parts. The R.J. Leeper Company is thriving. One of its most important projects has been the transporation center in uptown Charlotte, which it has helped to build on assignment from the bank. Leeper, meanwhile, says he meets once a month with other minority entrepreneurs, and those he has sent in the direction of the bank have most often gotten the backing that they need.

None of that surprises Susan Sewell, who believes in the conscience of Hugh McColl. For five hectic years, beginning in 1987, she was executive director of the Charlotte affiliate of Habitat for Humanity, the most active Habitat group in the country. She first met McColl on a Habitat site. For the sake of publicity, they were building five houses in 24 hours, and McColl had agreed to be a part of it. He had returned that day from a trip to Japan, bleary-eyed and exhausted, and Sewell assumed he would work an hour or two at the most. Instead, he decided to work all night.

"There are a lot of executives who talk it," she says. "Hugh is one who wants to make a difference."

McColl says it's true, though it's not just his conscience that comes into play. It is, somehow, the flipside of his ego, for he wants to be remembered for a different kind of vision—for something more substantial than the size of his bank. "You look at the people who make a difference," he says. "They are usually artists or writers, a few politicians. Business people don't usually do that. There's something inside of me that wants to."

Ed Crutchfield understands the feeling, and he says it's as natural almost as breathing. Both he and McColl grew up in a culture where an executive was measured by what he gave back. C.C. Cameron set the tone at First Union. He was a passionate supporter of the United Way and the Charlotte branch of the university system, and that spirit con-

120

tinues in the civic work of First Union.

The public schools have emerged as a focus—partly as a matter of enlightened self-interest. Every bank needs an educated workforce, and good public schools are essential to recruiting. But there's also another, more personal ingredient. Crutchfield's mother was a public school teacher. Whatever the reasons, says Judy Allison, director of corporate giving at the bank, education is first on the list of priorities.

Among other things, First Union wants workers to donate their time, paying them for up to four hours a month to get involved in their own children's schools, or to volunteer as tutors wherever they they can. Last year in Charlotte more than 900 people took advantage of the program, and company-wide there were 4,000 more, donating a total of 162,000 hours. In addition to that, the bank offers cash and scholarship awards to outstanding educators and students, and in the fall of 1995, corporate executives helped run a bond campaign in Charlotte —raising $190 million for building new schools and renovating others.

Crutchfield, meanwhile, was a supporter of John Murphy, the controversial school superintendent in Charlotte who resigned in 1995 after four intensive years of reform. Crutchfield says he will play the same role for Murphy's successor, offering whatever support he can. He does the same for John Tate, a First Union executive who serves on the school board, and Tate says he's grateful for Crutchfield's backing.

"The company's involvement in public education is something I'm proud of," Tate declares. "The corporate world is not a warm and fuzzy gentle giant anymore."

Some people say it never has been. Jane Burts, director of the Charlotte Organizing Project, a non-profit group that and has been a persistent critic of the banks, is a veteran of skirmishes going back to the '80s. Her organization challenged both banks—NCNB for investing in segregated South Africa, and First Union for red-lining black neighborhoods in Charlotte.

She says more than 94% of First Union's home loans were made outside of black census tracts, and NationsBank "was not much better." On that basis in 1989, she and other activists challenged a First Union merger in Florida, and things, she says, have been better since then.

"There are," Burts admits, "some very fine people in both of these banks who want to do the right thing. But the primary energy has gone into mergers."

Burts undoubtedly is right about that. There are some powerful egos at the heart of the story, and there have been for years. From Addison Reese and C.C. Cameron to Hugh McColl and Ed Crutchfield, these are ambitious men, obsessed with growth and the possibility that beckons somewhere in the distance that one of them, one day, will be number one.

"Whenever you climb a mountain," says McColl, who once reached the summit of Kilamanjaro, "you want it to be the tallest one around."

But it's also true that in addition to naked ambition and drive the banks have made an investment in Charlotte, staking their claims to the city's success. Some critics say that they should have done more, or that they acted only after being embarrassed. But the banks' leaders say they will stand on their record. They have invested in schools and inner city communities, supported the arts and minority business, paved the way for sports franchises and new arenas in the heart of downtown.

All of those things, says Ed Crutchfield, are simply a part of the corporate personality, an area in which he and McColl, so fiercely competitive so much of the time, have a permanent truce. "We agreed a long time ago," he says, "that we would compete like hell when it came to business. But when it came to the city and civic affairs, we were going to be partners."

That commitment seems to serve as a balance, the gentler side to a split personality, for when it comes to the matter of mergers and growth —accomplishments in which they both take pride—there's an institutional indifference to the pain. There has to be. Most mergers are accomplished with the loss of jobs, cost-cutting economies, at least initially, that play well in the stock market but not in the lives of the people let go. It is the brutal underside of success.

It remains to be seen, for both megabanks, whether such mergers will continue to define them. There are hints that First Union is finished for awhile.

"We are now the sixth largest bank in the United States," Crutchfield said in a recent interview. "That's probably big enough. The competition now has to do with the technology for delivering more services— trying to stay on the front of that curve. I feel good about the possibilities. Both banks have done the right thing so far. But it's not written anywhere that we're also entitled to stay on top."

Hugh McColl sounds a little bit different. He also talks about technology and service, "running the company we've built," as he said in one speech. But at the age of 61, he is only four years away from retirement—an event that will occur in the year 2000. As he leads his bank toward the end of one century and the beginning of another, he is

122

proud of all that has happened so far—the emergence of economic power in the South, the growth of Charlotte, the opportunity to make his city more humane. But it is clear that he yearns for one more rush —one more moment of adrenalin and triumph—and his sense of drama is so well-defined that it would almost have to be the biggest so far.

A merger, perhaps, with a bank in New York? San Francisco? Something even bigger?

He refuses to speculate about specifics, but his eyes light up when you ask if there's a crowning moment yet to come.

"One doesn't know," he says with a smile. "But one would hope."

To his friends in the company, and those who have battled with him down through the years, it's a signal at least for the rest of the banking world to stay tuned.

An American President

Of all the people I've met who are determined to make a difference in the world, none stands out more than Jimmy Carter. I've written about him on several occasions—first in 1985 when I was assigned by the Charlotte Observer *to do a retrospective on his presidency—a series that eventually became a book called* The Unfinished Presidency. *Ten years later, I wrote another book, this time on Habitat for Humanity, one of Carter's most cherished causes. The piece that follows is taken mostly from the final chapter of* The Unfinished Presidency, *which deals with Carter's life after he lost to Ronald Reagan in 1980. The section on Habitat has been expanded.*

The Unfinished Presidency
1986

Bitterness is the black beast that stalks politicians. I have observed but few who managed to escape it. When you find an exception, almost always it's a religious person.
　　　　　—Ray Jenkins, former Carter aide

It is a Norman Rockwell scene on a Baptist Sunday morning:

The church is nestled in a grove of pecan trees, and the cars, many of them symbols of small-town affluence, are parked beneath the shade, filling the parking lot and spilling onto the lawn.

Across the road is a John Deere tractor, standing idle in a field of corn, its tires stained red, the chunks of Georgia clay still clinging to the treads.

The Rev. Dan Ariail arrives at 9:30. He is the minister at Maranatha Baptist, and he looks the part—stocky, red-haired, with an easy smile and a generous disposition, greeting the visitors and trying to make them feel at home.

Yes, he says, President Carter is scheduled to teach his class that morning, and yes, of course, everyone is welcome. And when the question comes, as it inevitably does—what is it like to have a president in your church?—Ariail replies with a practiced sincerity:

"Oh, it's fine, you know. To us around here, he's just Jimmy."

In fact, that assessment is only partly true. Carter may be an active participant in the church, he may teach his Sunday school class every weekend he isn't traveling, and he and Rosalynn may dust and vacuum the sanctuary when their turn rolls around.

But Jimmy Carter is not simply one of the boys down in Plains, for the other boys don't have Secret Service agents consistently at their elbows; they don't jet off now and again to Damascus, Bangkok, Buenos Aires or Cairo; and none of them has ever greeted a group of former hostages at a West German hospital, or matched wills simultaneously with Menachem Begin and Anwar Sadat.

Those things and other memories separate Carter inevitably and profoundly from the place of his origins. And yet it is more than a matter of sentiment when he declares that Plains is home. There is probably no other place where nuances of his personality, or the subtlety of his values, are sketched with greater clarity.

Carter is fully capable of impatience and coldness, and those who have worked for him—Hamilton Jordan, Jerry Rafshoon, among many others—have all come to dread the arctic chill of his displeasure.

But as a matter of principle as well as inclination, Carter is more often friendly and unpretentious, quietly at ease with the richness of his memories and the vigorous challenges he has mapped for his future.

That contentment comes as a surprise to many people. Interviewers often search for the bits and pieces of his bitterness: the anger at his critics, the doubts about the things that didn't work out, the frustrations from an agenda only partially complete.

And there are, of course, times when Carter is angry, when he wonders what might have happened if Edward Kennedy's challenge in the Democratic primaries of 1980 hadn't lasted so long, or if there had been no crisis in the international price of oil, or if the helicopters had functioned in the deserts of Iran and the hostage crisis had ended much sooner.

But Carter is also disdainful of living in the past. More than that, he is essentially incapable of it, for it is a violation of his values, as well as his nature. While his Christianity may offer a measure of reassurance, a bedrock of certainty in a time of rapid change, it serves also as an affront to satisfaction.

"The theologian Paul Tillich...," Carter explains, pausing beside the lectern in his Sunday school classroom, looking thoroughly at ease in his navy blazer and pale gray slacks, "Paul Tillich wrote that religion is the search for the truth about our existence, our relationship with God, our relationship with others.

"It raises major questions that undermine our complacency: What is truth? What is wisdom, what is the nature of life, the essence of reward and punishment? What should we seek from God? What is the purpose of prayer? How much should we be concerned about ourselves?

"One preeminent theme in the teachings of Jesus is a warning against pride. Pride keeps our minds from being stretched, and when we think we know it all and are satisfied with what we have accomplished in the eyes of God, we are already far from God. Unless we are attempting things that might fail, we have too little faith—in ourselves or in God."

For some people, all of that has the ring of mere homily—the tidy predictability of a Baptist Sunday school. For Carter, however, it is precisely what he thinks, and the proof seems to be in the current vigor of his life.

Professionally, his primary focus is the Carter Center at Emory University in suburban Atlanta—a public policy institute that brings together international convocations of scholars, diplomats, politicians and other thinkers to discuss such subjects as the arms race, the Middle East or the revolution in health care.

At two of the largest conferences—on the Middle East and the arms race—Carter acted as cohost with former President Gerald Ford, a once-bitter rival who has become a friend, and their collaboration, implicitly, was a statement about America: that the things that unite it transcend the divisions, and that there are issues too important for the luxury of being partisan.

In addition, Carter lectures when he chooses—at Emory and other universities—and he has written several books since leaving office. The first was his memoir, *Keeping Faith*, and shortly afterward, *The Blood Of Abraham*, a kind of layman's primer on Middle Eastern strife.

But perhaps the most noted and celebrated of Carter's post-presidential activities has been his affiliation with Habitat for Humanity, a non-profit enterprise out of Americus, Ga., dedicated to providing decent housing for the poor. Habitat is the ambitious undertaking of Millard Fuller, a tall and energetic transplanted Alabamian, who gave away his multi-million dollar financial empire back in the 1960s because, he said, the pressures had become a threat to his integrity and his marriage.

126

In 1965, Fuller and his family paid a visit to Koinonia Farm, an interracial commune down the road from Americus, founded by a preacher by the name of Clarence Jordan. Jordan was a kind of renegade Baptist who had a peculiar and haunting understanding of Christianity—a radical literalism in his interpretation of the Bible.

Once, for example, during Fuller's affiliation with Koinonia, a minister friend of Jordan's came calling with a problem: The janitor at the minister's church—a hard-working man with a wife and eight children —was compelled to subsist on $80 a week.

"It's wrong," the minister said. "I have pleaded with the deacons to raise his salary to a reasonable level, but they say we can't afford to; there's not enough money in the budget. What can I do?"

Jordan mused over the dilemma for a moment, then offered a solution. Swap salaries with the janitor, he offered matter-of-factly, and he pointed out that such a move wouldn't affect the size of the church budget and that the minister—with only two children instead of eight, and with a comfortable place to live provided by the church could subsist on $80 more easily than the janitor.

Then, sensing the minister's discomfort, Jordan demanded gently: "What's wrong, John? What's wrong with that solution? Is it contrary to Christian teaching?"

Jimmy Carter, already aware of Koinonia Farm and serious enough in his own odysseys of the faith, was intrigued by the legends of Clarence Jordan—and especially by the story of Habitat for Humanity. It began in discussions between Jordan and Fuller—long, prayerful musings on Exodus 22:25: "If you lend money to any of my people who are poor, do not act like a moneylender and require him to pay interest."

Applying the notion to low-income housing, Jordan and Fuller decided to build livable homes near Americus, relying on volunteeer labor and—to cover the initial costs—donations and loans from the friends of Koinonia. The point was not to offer houses as an act of charity, but to sell them to the poor for exactly what they cost—no interest, no profit— and then to use the house payments to begin new construction.

Millard Fuller called it "the economics of Jesus," and in Jimmy Carter he found a willing disciple to the Habitat idea. First, it was a way to break the cycle of poverty—a concrete improvement in the lives of poor people, but one that they could take pride in earning. In addition to that, in dozens of cities and third world countries where Habitat began to operate, it was a way to involve the affluent and the comfortable in a sacrificial gesture of Christian partnership.

Carter's own deep involvement in the Habitat mission began in

January 1984, when Millard Fuller, having called for an appointment, drove the short distance from Americus to Plains and rang the doorbell at the Carters' brick house. Carter himself greeted Fuller at the door, and led him to a sitting room inside.

Rosalynn Carter was also there, cordial as always, but Millard says the small-talk ended quickly. He thanked the Carters for the words of support they had offered in the past, then wondered if they were willing to do even more.

"Are you interested in Habitat for Humanity?" he said. "Or are you very interested?"

Carter smiled at the brashness, then answered after only a moment's hesitation, "We're very interested."

They agreed that Fuller would write him a letter listing all the ways that Carter might help. "Don't be bashful," the President suggested, and Fuller was not. In a letter that he mailed on February 8, he suggested that Carter could serve on the Habitat board, make media contacts, help raise money and serve on a construction crew for a day.

Fuller made 15 proposals in all, hoping that Carter might agree to one or two. Incredibly, the President agreed to them all. "We think," he said in a followup meeting, "we can help in most of the ways you suggest."

He was especially intrigued by the notion of working on a house, and a short time later, on a speaking trip to New York, he says he was jogging in lower Manhattan, and he stopped at a building that Habitat had acquired. The building was a mess, and the restoration of it was taking some time.

"Maybe Rosalynn and I can help," he said, and almost before he knew it, it was set. He would come back to Manhattan the following September, leading a group of volunteers from Habitat. They would travel together by Trailways bus and sleep in the bunks of an inner-city church, and Carter would work every day for a week.

It quickly became a Habitat tradition—Carter leading his army of volunteers every summer to Indian reservations and big city ghettoes and dozens of other places in between. It was a task that he seemed to approach with some relish, for in the years since the end of is presidency, Carter has settled into the role of moral leader, a part that he never quite mastered as president, but one he plays today without the contaminating nuisance of day-to-day politics.

"It's not a bad life," Carter affirms with a smile; and indeed, it doesn't seem to be.

In 1985, on a rainy afternoon in Plains, he settled into a couch in what used to be his late mother's house—an unobtrusive brick building he now uses for an office—and in a manner as casual as his striped work shirt and his faded blue jeans, he talked about his life at the age of 60:

"I did my best," he said of his presidency, "and I think tangibly speaking we accomplished some good things. The standards that we set I think will be permanent. So I feel at ease with myself.

"The main thing now is for me to look to the future. Rosalynn and I are both relatively young (Rosalynn, 57), and I'm now carving out a career that I hope will be as significant perhaps as my time at the White House.

"The Carter Center is where we will devote the rest of our active lives. We'll work on matters that are not surprising: peace throughout the world, the resolution of crises or disputes, the enhancement of human rights, arms control, environmental quality, health care, improvement in educational processes; trying to bridge the gap between ourselves and developing nations."

Carter sees his own agenda as essentially the antithesis of President Ronald Reagan's. His successor, he says, "has abandoned and even opposed the civil rights movement in this country—and abandoned the human rights movement abroad. I think he had, in the first four years, no intention of reaching an arms agreement with the Soviets.

"There is obviously the ability of a president—particularly one as effective in the media as Reagan—to strengthen certain inclinations on the part of the American people. He makes it acceptable for those of us who are white, secure, prosperous and independent to assume that we're that way because we're especially worthy, or blessed by God—and that people who don't measure up to those standards are somehow inferior. It's their own fault that they're not as successful as we are.

"That's been the very attractive contribution of Reagan to the sociological conceptions of our people. How long that can prevail, I don't know. It seems that for the first three or four months of his second term, it's begun to come apart. Whether that's just wishful thinking on my part, or whether it's actually taking place, I don't know."

Carter says he understands that he and Reagan will inevitably be compared—as presidents, certainly, and perhaps in the roles that they played after that—and he seems content to let history be the judge.

As Rosalynn Carter puts it, a little wistfully perhaps, "Jimmy is secure in the fact that he did a good job. We assume that the record will be there for people to see—someday."

If the judgments so far still seem to be mixed, James David Barber, the presidential scholar at Duke University, believes that Carter's undeniable strengths have come more clearly into focus because of his work since he left the White House. In addition, says Barber, Carter's record as president can be measured not only by his achievements—Camp David, SALT II and all the rest—but also by the tragedies that did not happen.

As Barber puts it, "when a president leaves office with the Constitution more or less intact, and without a lot of dead American boys scattered around the planet, we ought to give him a medal."

The King of Hearts

Among the journalists I've known through the years, there are few I've admired as much as Kays Gary, a long-time columnist at the Charlotte Observer. *He was, and is, a man who understands the tragedies of life, but pursues the good news— "the shining moment," as he likes to call it—with as much tenacity as anybody in the business.*

Southern Voices
1991

It was one of those chilly March nights with intermittent drizzles giving way to a few fluffs of clouds and a full moon overhead. The big blue Ford with its V-8 humming, its driver lounging comfortably in a padded bucket seat, topped a rise in the road and suddenly slowed to a halt.

There, in a little hollow at the bottom of a hill, was a collection of flashing lights and a crowd gathering around and a policeman directing traffic past a lump near the median. The lump, it turned out, was a corpse, covered discreetly by a rumpled white sheet.

The man in the Ford got out of his car, for he was a newspaperman, and somehow it just wasn't in him to pass up such a scene. He didn't really know what there might be to write, but ever since his reporting and sports writing days at the *Shelby Daily Star*, Kays Gary always breathed a little quicker, always puffed a little harder on his Pall Mall cigarettes, in the presence of natural or man-made disasters.

Like all reporters, he was part voyeur—cursed with the insatiable curiosity of his calling, a certain morbidity even, that led him to stick his nose into other people's business. He did it very well, of course. Like many good reporters, he seemed smaller than life—rumpled and mumbling and semi-articulate, the kind of person who could enter a crowded room and attract absolutely no attention.

Gary knew very well from more than 20 years experience that charisma is not the stuff of which reporters are made. So he mumbled his questions and blended with the crowd, and usually, before it was over, he had the story in his pad.

But on this particular night, March 19, 1965 there wasn't much of a story. A 90-year-old Shelby man named Wattie Jeeter had started across the highway as the dusk began to fall and had hobbled squarely into the path of a shiny station wagon. He dented the grill and shattered the windshield and by the time he landed nearly a hundred yards away, he was dead.

There wasn't much to say about Wattie Jeeter's life, and even his death was a matter of routine. The policemen measured the distance of his fatal flight, marveling at the dimensions of it as they cleaned the debris and directed traffic around the scene. Jeeter, they said, was old and strange, living in a shack on an old truck bed.

Gary listened to what they said and took a few notes. Then he drove away. But the next day, when he reported to work at *The Charlotte Observer*, where he was an award-winning columnist and—then, as now—easily the most famous newsman in the state, he couldn't seem to shove Wattie Jeeter from his mind.

Throughout his time at *The Observer*, Gary had been the consistent champion of the state's dispossessed, raising thousands of dollars for innumerable good causes, but more than anything else, celebrating the ordinary people of his region—telling the human stories that kept tugging at his conscience.

"In the case of Jeeter," he remembered much later, "I just kept thinking from the way everyone was acting, it could have been anything out there on that road. I mean anything—not even a person. It made me wonder about this guy. He must have done something, sometime. He had lived at least. So I talked to his wife, Mary, and since there was nothing else in my head, I wound up writing about it. There was nothing else, and I was trying to get it out. A lot of times, I'm afraid that's what I do—just write to get it out, so I can move on to something else."

Whatever the motivations and internal chemistries of Kays Gary's mind, whatever the impurities in his sentimental compassion, this is what he wrote about the death of Wattie Jeeter:

Down there on the Big Road in the night with red lights flashing and officers measuring with their tape, somebody wondered if the biggest dent Wattie Jeeter had made on this world had been that ugly place in front of the station wagon.

132

No, Mary said. No.

He'd sired five sons and four daughters and there were 30 grand-children and that was the truth.

Most of them would come to the funeral in the New Ellis Baptist Church, too.

But nobody had asked questions like that in the night with the red lights flashing. There wasn't time and there wasn't any need to ask questions like that. You have to get things measured and cleaned up and cleared out and it happened like that in about an hour.

Then the traffic could roll and it did roll.

The moon was just a little higher and it was a nice night with the radio playing softly and the black rubber spinning and the purring engine winging you westward while you lounged in the bucket seat just like the rocking chair at home.

You can really blow it out on the Big Road.

They told me about Kays Gary, who is now 64, as soon as I got to Charlotte. They said that as a writer he takes a lot of risks, and sometimes he misses. But when he hits, they said, when the overflow of his emotions is appropriate to his subject, or when he holds the reins a little tighter on his blank-verse prose, well, on those occasions, hang onto your heart.

As it happened, the people who knew him best seemed to rave about him most. His friend Jim Bishop, the nationally syndicated columnist, called him "the St. Jude of journalism" and said his writing, at its best, "would draw red corpuscles from a rock."

And Associate Editor Ed Williams of the *Charlotte Observer*, a journalist from a younger and more cynical generation, says, "When Kays is telling a story, it's as though the writer is not even there between you and what is going on. He is so skillful and so clean and sharp and direct, you don't get the feeling you are reading writing: you feel that you are having an experience. That's the kind of writing that can make you cry."

Those were the sorts of things I had heard over and over—and all of it about a man who had been doing a column at least three times a week, and usually five, since 1956—churning out sob stories and innumerable bleeding heart celebrations of triumph, raising money for orphans or giving away bikes to poor kids at Christmas.

I knew all of that, and I expected to be impressed, and I felt startled and guilty when at first I wasn't. That was the early summer of 1972, and the hard truth was that Gary was in a slump. He had left the *Observer* briefly in 1968, lured into public relations work by the doubling of his salary. But he was never quite happy at it, and in 1971 he returned to the paper. His editors splattered the city with KAYS IS BACK billboards, and everywhere around him the hype was very thick. He seemed to freeze from the pressures of it all, and his problems grew worse in July of '71 when tragedy struck his life: His wife was killed in a fire at his home. Gary was out of town when it happened, and just before he left, they had had quite a fight—a serious verbal collision that left him frustrated and angry. Then suddenly, she was gone, and he thought for awhile that the guilt and anguish might drive him insane.

"I was in a real tailspin," he says. "I didn't know much of what was going on for the next year or so."

But a year later he remarried, and his life settled down, and his writing once again resumed its old cycles.

"I probably overwrite three out of four times," he admits today, swiping at the temple of his frumpy gray hair. "Maybe even four out of five. One of my great faults is that I never rewrite anything, and I should. But I have some kind of weird feeling that if I started tampering with what I'd written, I'd be fouling up the legitimacy somehow. I know that's not true, but that's how it feels.

"I guess I let myself be vulnerable. I don't ever sweat over a way to say something—building sentences, or whatever. Whatever comes out is no contrivance. It's what I felt at the time. Now, the next day I might feel different. I read some columns the next day, and they're so saccharine and overripe that I can barely stand it.

"The object of this thing is to communicate, and you have a great number of people who don't get it when you strip something down to the bare bones. Still, those are the columns that I always like the best —those that are written with restraint, when the writer doesn't stand between the reader and the subject."

The first Kays column I remember like that—the first, at least, after my arrival in Charlotte—came late in 1972. He had interviewed a young Charlotte woman named Caroline Elliott, a volunteer on a Quaker team working in the hospitals of Vietnam. She was precise and apolitical in her descriptions of the war, seeing the horror of it in simple human terms. Gary captured her feelings in a powerful piece of writing that was, I thought, the most effective anti-war document I had ever read.

I began to read through his old columns after that, going back in the clip files to the 1960s, becoming more absorbed in what he was doing. I read the column on Wattie Jeeter and a few dozen like it, and although the bad ones were almost as abundant, the good ones sparkled and went straight to the heart.

Then I began to watch him, with his baggy gray slacks and faded

134

turtlenecks, his mumbled conversations and disheveled amblings through the *Observer* newsroom, and I wondered how a man with such anti-charisma, such an understated and ineffectual Columbo exterior, could be the possessor of such extravagant emotions. Finally, years later, I decided to ask him, and the answer turned out to be fairly simple.

"My father," he said, "was really very important. My mother, too. They had to be. I was an only child."

As he warmed to the subject, he was sitting at the dining room table in his modest frame house in one of Charlotte's working class neighborhoods. He lived there alone, and the house was neatly painted; the remodeling gave him something to do during the bleak weeks and months in 1982, after his second marriage fell apart.

The breakup deepened his acute sense of tragedy. But it also reinforced the lessons that his parents left him with: that life is noble and heroic as much as it is brutal, and that even the worst of human foibles are fit objects for compassion.

"My father," says Gary, "was the principal of the school in Fallston, up in Cleveland County. My mother was the first-grade teacher. The school served grades one through eleven, and those were the Depression years. Probably seventy per cent of the families were tenant farmers.

"My father was a little guy, about five-feet-six and one-hundred twenty-eight pounds, but he was fiery and explosive, and he commanded the respect of some pretty rough people. He had a ready smile and a ready temper, and you never had to guess what he was thinking or feeling. My mother was the stabilizer. She handled him with quietness and patience; they complemented each other well.

"We had an oil stove in the kitchen and there was always a big pot of soup. In those days, kids brought their lunches and they kept them in the cloak room. My mother would regularly invade their privacy— looking through the lunches to find those with just a biscuit or just a sweet potato. Then around lunch time, she would ask those kids to help her carry something up to the house, which wasn't three hundred yards from the school, and while she was there she would offer them some soup.

"Later, this coalition of women began to do it. They would bring meals of hot soup for the kids who needed it. There were no rules that I can remember, no eligibility requirements, but not everybody got the soup—only those that would have been hungry.

"My father knew every student who went in and out of that school —every student and why he was like he was. I'd talk about some bully or crud-type person, and he would slam his hand down on the table

135

and say, 'Now wait a minute. Where do you get off judging?' And he'd take me with him when he went to visit the families in the school. We'd go to some of those little tobacco road shacks, and there'd be two-inch cracks in the floor, and chickens inside, and no diapers on the kids.

"He knew everybody and what their lives were like, and yet he wasn't a gossip. He was proudest of the kids who wound up being anything—a foreman or whatever. He took some hope and delight in that—a lot more, of course, than he would from a doctor's son who grew up to be a doctor."

As Gary rambles on, you get the feeling he may have idealized the lessons of his youth, may have purified and enlarged them as the years have slipped away. But whether he did or not, there is no doubt that he absorbed them and took them along with him when he left the nest in Fallston.

He went away to college in 1937—first to Mars Hill, where, at 5-feet-7, he was a hot shot guard on the basketball team. Later, he transferred to the University of North Carolina and played a year of basketball there as a deep reserve (scoring, he remembers with a strange flicker of pride, a single free throw in a game that was nearly over).

He got a degree in journalism in 1942, spent three years in the Army as a military policeman, then took a job in the Cleveland County town of Shelby at the *Daily Star*. He was a sports editor, columnist and courthouse reporter, a stringer for the *Charlotte Observer* and a radio announcer. He worked seven days and nights a week, and from all accounts, he loved every minute of it.

He moved full time to the *Observer* in 1951, and by 1956 he was established as a columnist. But as much as anything, he was a splendid reporter, mumbling his way to some legendary scoops.

Jack Claiborne, a long-time Gary colleague and later an associate editor at the *Observer*, remembers a train wreck in Clemson in the early 1960s. Claiborne and photographer-reporter Jimmy Dumbell hopped aboard a small plane and flew to the scene, combing the area for survivors and witnesses. Eventually, Claiborne made his way to the hospital, walking and hitchhiking, and camped himself proudly outside the operating room, waiting for the doctors to supply more details. Finally, they emerged, and there among them, stripping away his gauze mask and pale green gown, was Gary—his pad in his pocket and the whole story in his head.

But if Gary had a knack for being near the action, his real genius lay in what he did with the facts. He let his emotions run free, and his readers responded in astonishing ways. In 1960, for example, he wrote the story of a baby with serious birth defects. More than $100,000 poured

136

in to establish Holy Angels Nursery, a facility Gary still helps support, to provide a home for such children. Twenty years after the founding of Holy Angels, he raised more than $100,000 to endow the Children's Medical Fund in Charlotte. And, in between, he raised $20,000 for surgery for Virgilio Pinto, a Bolivian peasant boy with a face disfigured by life-threatening tumors.

His appeals were often gimmicky, as well as sentimental. In the case of Pinto, he published a picture of the Bolivian boy's face—the good and untumored side of it—promising a picture of the whole face when the tumors were removed. But the gimmicks are submerged in something much stronger—an irrepressible compassion that causes his friend Ed Williams to say:

"Kays has emerged as the somebody we mean when we say, 'Somebody ought to help those kids,' or 'Somebody should do something to help those old people.' He ought to have a big 'S' on his chest for 'Somebody.'"

There are times, however, when Gary gets sick of the role—when the phone keeps ringing, and the callback messages pile up on his desk, and everybody seems to want another piece of his time. Eventually, there isn't any time—not for his hobbies, like reading and remodeling old houses, or for his four children and four grandchildren, who occasionally stop by to visit, or for his hopeless addiction to televised sports.

Years ago he turned to alcohol to get away from such pressures. But even after he defeated that particular demon, he would still find himself every now and then at 5 p.m., his deadline looming and not a word written down, and he would lurch off to the bathroom to throw up and pray.

"Yeah," he says, "I resent it sometimes. I don't know why I resent it, because it's what I do. But you get put in the role of playing God, and I resent that because I got no right. There are stories that are appealing and easy to tell, because the people involved are so appealing. But what about the people who are obnoxious and a pain in the rear, but whose needs are just as great? How do you tell their story, and how do you decide? Yeah, every now and then it has to get to you, and I screw up sometimes and get impatient when I shouldn't."

One of those occasions came in 1981. It was the Christmas season, and the phone, it seemed, was even busier than usual. Then the call came from a Charlotte woman who had no money and a baby with crossed eyes who needed an operation. She had been from one agency to the next and nobody would help her, and finally a social worker told her to call Gary.

Maybe the call was just one too many, or maybe it came a little too close to deadline. Whatever the reason, Gary exploded, demanding to know what the woman expected him to do. Then he caught himself, apologized bleakly, and decided to write a column about the whole episode.

"I exploded," he wrote, "because everybody keeps shifting responsibility. 'Somebody' is supposed to help the baby with crossed eyes. 'Somebody else.'...But the outrage, the frustration, the blaming, a belly boiling at politicians who think that what is wrong with this country is food stamps—all of that stuff is sound and fury signifying nothing.

"The bottom line is a baby with crossed eyes."

In 1981, writers Dot Jackson, Ed Williams, Jack Claiborne and some of Gary's other friends began working with Sally McMillan of East Woods Press, a North Carolina publishing company, to put together a book called *Kays Gary: Columnist*, a kind of greatest hits collection of his most moving columns. The first entry was short, and it went like this:

He was scrawny for a 10-year-old but he sat on the front row bench of Domestic Relations Court and tried to look like a man.

There were six other people in the room besides the judge who sat behind a desk 'way up high.

There was a lady in a blue suit who sat beside the boy and patted him on the shoulder.

Behind a table to his right sat a man and woman with whom he'd lived a long, long time.

Yes, he had said, he loved them. He sure did. He was all they had. They didn't have any kids of their own.

And facing him, in a chair on a platform, was a third woman in the room.

She was the modern Magdalene. She'd had two husbands at the same time and many boyfriends. She also had three children and the eldest and scrawniest of these she had tossed to the man and woman who now sat behind the table.

Now the husbands were gone and the boyfriends were gone. The days were long and the nights were longer and, she vowed with shuddering sobs, now she was changed. She wanted her son.

Ten-year-old eyes never left her as she poured out her soul on the witness stand.

The return of custody on a temporary, trial basis, said the judge, was largely dependent on the wishes of the child.

They waited for the verdict. The boy looked long at the man and the woman behind the table.

Then he walked toward the Magdalene. She threw herself into his bony arms. Her eyes were fountains of tears. His were deep wells of mercy.

Even as they left, his arm around her, he walked very straight...for that is the way a man of responsibility must walk...when he becomes head of the family.

I recently asked Gary to talk about the column. I said it was very moving, of course, and that it touched something deep about blood relations and the triumphs of caring. But I also told him of the cynic inside me, the nagging voice of skepticism that kept whispering the question: Ah yes, but what happened next? How do we know that the mother really changed?

Gary smiled at the question, for he understood it completely.

"The hardest thing about this kind of writing," he said, "when you are dealing in vignettes, is that you have to leave them there. In even the most beautiful situations, if you pursue them to the end, corruptive influences will begin to creep in.

"Sometimes you write that. But other times you leave it at the moment of triumph. Why? I don't know. Except that we need to know that the shining moment is there—the hope of it is there—for everybody. You have to celebrate the little victories because, God knows, there are enough defeats."

For more than 30 years, that has been his calling, and today as much as ever it borders on obsession. It is difficult for Gary to cease being Gary even at age 64, when his health could blow at any seam, and when the self-imposed pressures of his work add stoop to his shoulders and labor to his gait.

"Gary," concludes Jack Claiborne, "is the kind of guy who walks around the world with a magnifying glass. He sees all the pain and the hurt and the brutalities of life. But he also sees the beauty and the heroism and courage that escape the normal eye. That's a gift that he has, and it's something the rest of us should be grateful for."

As this book goes to press, more than 10 years after this article was written, Kays Gary is retired and his health is shaky. But he still breaks down every now and then and writes another column. He still has the gift.

Shooting at Elvis

One of the most poignant stories I have ever covered was the funeral of Elvis Presley. Because of that experience, and because I once saw him perform on stage, I was offended in the fall of 1981 by some sensationalized attempts to tear at Presley's legacy. His story, I suppose, was tragic in the end, but this article was intended to affirm his importance—exploring the elements that made up his appeal, including his radical fusion of white and black music, perhaps the most natural form of integration, out of which emerged the beat of rock 'n' roll.

Race, Rock & Relgion
1982

A toxicologist testified Monday that he had never found so many drugs in a body as he discovered in the remains of Elvis Presley.
    —United Press International, October 20, 1981.

He could be the Pillsbury Doughboy, so fat and puffy and pillow-stuffed does he appear...When he faces front, or worse, turns profile, the effect is appalling.
    —From *Elvis* by Albert Goldman, copyright 1981 McGraw-Hill.

First we create them.

We build them into something much larger than life, then grow weary of admiration and begin to tear at their flaws. Hank Williams was a drunk. Martin Luther King and John Kennedy both cheated on their wives, and Mickey Mantle was rude to the fans that adored him.

So now, it seems, it's Elvis Presley's turn. Newspapers have been filled with headlines from Memphis—how his doctor, George Nichopoulos, shot him full of drugs, presiding over his pathetic deterioration as an addict.

140

Simultaneously, a heralded biography—proclaimed by its publisher to be a "definitive" piece of work—is excerpted by *Rolling Stone* and riddled with revelations that are intended to be sensational: "Like all junkies," writes author Albert Goldman, "Elvis suffers from a paralyzed colon. Opiates immobilize the striate muscles that produce defecation.

"The abnormally large doses of laxatives that he must take to rouse his numbed gut force his body to the opposite extreme. Sometimes, he loses control of his bowels completely. Many a morning, it is necessary to strip the bed before the housekeeper arrives, lest the gossip spread through the hotel that 'Elvis Presley shits in his bed.'"

I find such passages remarkably depressing. The reason, I suppose, is that I saw Presley twice, and that was all it took to evoke a certain sympathy—a respect for his talent, and a fascination for his place in American culture.

The first time I saw him was in 1977—February 20, a breezy, cold night at the Charlotte Coliseum. His fans began arriving a little after 7, streaming across the parking lot and crowding toward the doors.

Elvis himself did not appear until 10. He seemed a little thick around the mid-section and puffy about the cheeks, but splendid nevertheless, with his glittery white costume and gold chains around his neck.

For the first half hour, he mostly fooled around—posing for the flashbulbs and kissing the women who made it past the cops. But after a while, the music took hold of him. It happened on a song called "How Great Thou Art," an old hymn he used to hear as a boy. He sounded like Mario Lanza with soul, bending over the mike as the sweat dripped from his face, cutting loose the notes that would send chills up your spine.

You listened to that and suddenly you understood if you had never known before: Despite all the hype, the carnival hoopla generated deliberately—even perversely—by his manager, Tom Parker, Elvis Presley was no fluke.

Part of his appeal was simply his charisma—his moves and sneers and punky air of rebellion. But above all that, it was his feeling for the music, his instinctive understanding of the emotions it contained. And there were few people better at putting the feeling across.

The second time I saw him, the circumstances were different. It was six months later, and I was in a line of people that stretched for half a mile—10 or 20 abreast on a cloudy Memphis day. The line inched its way through the entrance to Graceland Mansion, up an oak-lined drive and past a lawn decked with wreaths.

There, in the doorway of his columned, brick mansion, his body lay in state, looking pale and waxen with a blue shirt, white suit and stiffly

combed black hair. Women burst into tears as they passed by the casket. A few of them fainted or staggered to iron benches outside.

And the striking thing about the scene was that the grief was very
real. For every gawker who was there, several thousand genuine mourners had assembled to pay their respects, and the poignance was of a
sort that you don't soon forget.

Somehow, you know how his death must have happened—that he
had destroyed himself in slow, painful increments—and the tragedy of
the destruction added sadness to the occasion.

I guess that's what's missing from the headlines and stories out of
Memphis today: a sense of perspective and empathy and poignance.
Albert Goldman's biography certainly has none. The deeper you plunge
into the sordid revelations, the more you are struck by a certain furtive
meanness—a quality beyond voyeurism, shading into contempt.

You can find it in almost any sentence you choose. Goldman contends, for example, that Elvis emerged from "hillbilly" stock—"people
incapable of...improving their own lot." And after a chapter called
"Redneck Roots" (Would he have called it "Nigger Roots" if Presley
had been black?), Goldman offers a description of Presley's high school:

"Of all the dumb activities in this dumb working-class school about
the dumbest was shop: Elvis Presley's major." And he referred to one
of the Presley's high school friends as "a tough, aggressive, football-
playing poor boy, whose ribs are visibly deformed from rickets, a disease produced by not having enough money or enough brains to eat
right."

All of that is intended to destroy the Elvis myth. But the effect, of
course, is precisely the reverse. For it was a reaction and a rebellion
against that kind of condescension that has always been at the heart
of the Presley phenomenon.

Back in 1954, he wandered into Sun Records in Memphis, an unimposing brick building on Union Street, which, at the time of his death,
had become an auto body shop. In the '50s, however, it pulsated with
the rhythms of that part of America—the kinds of sounds you could
hear on the radio in northern Mississippi or in the Memphis housing
project where Elvis spent his youth.

It was class music—country, blues and gospel—the rhythms of the
Southern poor and near poor, which Presley melded into the beat of
rock'n'roll. In 1956, sipping afternoon coffee at the Piedmont Grill, a
Charlotte greasy spoon with formica-topped tables and a line of booths
near the window, he told *Charlotte Observer* columnist Kays Gary:

"Colored folks been singing and playing this music for more years
'n anybody knows. They played it in the shanties all 'round Tupelo,

Mississippi, where I got it from them, and nobody paid 'tention till I goose it up. I remember old Arthur Crudup. He'd bang the box the way I do now and I usta think if I could feel what ol' Arthur felt I'd be a music-maker like nobody ever saw!"

Presley seemed distracted for much of the interview. He was barely more than a kid, 21 years old, and remarkably ordinary in his priorities for the day. He grinned at the waitress and fingered the hem of her slip, then left to play pool with one of his Mississippi cousins.

But before he did, he had a few words for some critics who had panned his recent show in New York.

"Debra Paget," he said, "was on the same show. She wore a tight thing with feathers on the behind where they wiggle most. Sex? Man, she bumped and pooshed out all over the place. I'm like Little Boy Blue. And who do they say is obscene? Me! Them critics don't like to see nobody win doing any kind of music they don't know nothing about "

And, of course, he was right. The critics were shocked when he would saunter toward the mike, a waterfall of hair hanging toward his eyes and his pelvis wiggling to the screams of the crowd. But the disapproval was essential, for it helped make him a rebel—a sensational cult hero with at least two followings: the nation's young, and the people who came from his own economic background.

Youth and class. Both ingredients defined his career, and both could be felt when it ended—in the mood of the crowd that assembled for his funeral. It was a peculiar mood, one that seemed to mingle both triumph and grief.

At 11:30, for example, on the night before the service, some 2,000 people were huddled in the rain, keeping resolute vigil outside of Graceland. Suddenly, Caroline Kennedy—the daughter of the late president—emerged from the mansion. With TV cameramen in hot pursuit, she made a dash for her car.

She was in town to cover the story for a New York paper, but the crowd didn't care what her reasons were. For those who swarmed around her, her presence was symbolic. And as she unlocked her car—her fingers trembling with the anxiety of the moment—a white Memphis teenager and his black companion exchanged rebel yells and soul brother handslaps.

"OOO-eee," they exclaimed. "Caroline Kennedy!"

The implication seemed clear enough. For whatever reasons, a member of one of the world's richest families had come to pay tribute to one of their own.

All that is heady stuff, but there was one final ingredient in the Presley phenomenon. It was the promotional genius of Col. Tom Parker, a frumpy carnival huckster who set about in 1955 to transform Elvis from a promising young singer to an American institution.

"I didn't tell him what to record, and he didn't tell me how to promote," says Parker. "He'd say, 'The Colonel will let 'em know I'm coming.'"

And so Parker did. He took all the talent, as well as the charisma and rebellion, and after Presley moved from Sun Records to RCA, he got him on TV and negotiated rich contracts for a string of movies.

But as the money poured in and the fame began to mount, Presley was trapped under the weight of it all. In the end, of course, it crushed him. He was, at his core, a rather ordinary person—not especially well-equipped to handle his own genius, much less the excesses that it began to produce.

"Sure it got to him," says his friend Joe Moscheo, now a Nashville music executive. "There's an old Indian saying, 'Walk a mile in my shoes.' He had a lot of problems, but you just can't take his accomplishments away...."

The Ghost of Hank Williams

*So much of American music evolved in the South—coun-
try, blues, jazz, rock 'n' roll—that it should come as no surprise
at all that many of our heroes have emerged from that realm.
After Elvis Presley, the second most famous was probably Hank
Williams, another flawed genius who died too young—slipping
away in the back seat of his car in the early morning hours in
rural West Virginia. This is the story of Hank and the place
where he died—a town that has struggled for more than 40
years to come to grips with its footnote to history. Finally, in
1993, it began to make some progress.*

Creative Loafing
1993

It was a Friday night at the Skyline Drive-In. The parking lot was full, with cars spilling out along the shoulders of the road, and inside the building the juke box was cranked. George Hamilton IV, long-time veteran of the Grand Ole Opry, was huddled with some friends in a booth near the back. To Hamilton, the Skyline Drive-In is a shrine, which seems a little strange to some of the regulars. To normal people in Oak Hill, West Virginia, the Skyline is nothing special at all—just a cement block tavern on the south end of town, where the beer is cheap and the food is pretty good, and the crowds are friendly on a weekend night. But legend has it that on New Year's morning more than 40 years ago, a blue Cadillac pulled up to the door, and the driver got out to take a break. He glanced at his passenger who was sprawled in the back, and suddenly he noticed there was no sign of life. Frightened now, the driver, Charles Carr, rushed into town and asked directions at the Pure Oil station. "The hospital," he said. But he could see already that he was too late. Hank Williams was dead in the back seat of the car.

For the better part of four decades, this was an awkward bit of history for the town of Oak Hill. To be known as the place where Hank Williams died, or at least where the fact of his death was discovered, and where the autopsy showed that whiskey had killed him, was not a distinction that most people relished. Slowly, however, that feeling has changed, and by the summer of 1993, the town was celebrating its footnote to history—holding its first Hank Williams festival.

George Hamilton IV was delighted by that. He knew he had played a role in the change, and he let himself feel a measure of pride. Hamilton is a North Carolinian by birth, a native of suburban Winston-Salem who spent a good part of his life in Charlotte. Despite his city-boy roots, he was drawn to the music of the back-country South, and few singers moved him as much as Hank Williams. There was something about that raw, wailing voice—echoes of the blues that Williams had learned in Georgiana, Ala. He had studied the techniques of Rufus Payne, a black street singer who worked the corners of Georgiana and Greenville, performing under the name Tee-Tot. Williams could project the same kind of pain, but there was something more—a compassion and hope that sprang from his faith and gave a gospel flavor to many of his songs.

That, at least, was Hamilton's view, and he found some people in Oak Hill who shared it. Working with Jack Pennington and Roger Seay, two life-long residents, Hamilton helped organize the Hank Williams festival. He agreed to appear, but rejected top billing. That distinction, he said, should go to Jett Williams, a 40-year-old singer, who learned at the age of 21 that she was probably Hank Williams' illegitimate daughter. Hamilton had followed the Jett Williams story—how she had battled in court to prove her identity, and finally won—and now in Oak Hill, he had heard her sing.

It was hard to harbor any doubts after that. She had her father's features—the high cheek bones and wideset eyes—and she had his mannerisms onstage. The tilt of her head, the phrasing of her songs—all those things were familiar somehow, and when the concert was over, Hamilton and Pennnington and Roger Seay decided to head down the Skyline Drive-In for a midnight cup of coffee and a toast. The more they talked the more they agreed: They were living in the middle of a pretty good story.

It began on an ugly winter's night in Montgomery. Hank Williams' career had hit the skids. He had been fired from the Grand Ole Opry in August of 1952, and in those days the Opry was the pinnacle of country music. Hank had been a regular for nearly three years, and he was easily the most popular performer on the cast. He had such presence

146

when he stepped on stage, and there was so much power in the lyrics of his songs. "Cold, Cold Heart" and "I'm So Lonesome I Could Cry" had set new standards for country song-writing, and the songs came alive with the tear in his voice. But Hank was also drinking pretty hard. It had been a problem for most of his life—binges that sometimes lasted for days, though there were also stretches when he didn't drink at all.

"Hank was an alcoholic," says his friend, Jerry Rivers, the fiddle player in his band, the Drifting Cowboys. "When he produced and wrote songs and made a little money and was feeling successful, he managed to control it. But sooner or later, he'd be drinking again, and Hank couldn't write his name when he was drunk. He couldn't crawl onstage, and the people at the Opry just lost patience with him."

The final year of his life was the worst—partly because of his own lost loves. His troubled first marriage had ended officially on May 29, and many of his friends, including Jerry Rivers, were convinced that Hank had never gotten over it. Nevertheless, he took a new wife, Billie Jean Eshliman, in the middle of October—and in between his marriages he had an affair. His mistress, Bobbie Jett, was a pretty young woman from Nashville, who lived with her uncle and spent her days taking care of her grandmother. She met Hank Williams in 1951, and by the following April she was pregnant. They continued to see each other through the summer, but Hank had also met Billie Jean.

Something had to give, and in October they came to a curious resolution. Three days before Hank's marriage to Billie Jean, he and Bobbie signed a written agreement, duly notarized in Montgomery. He acknowledged that he was probably the father of her child, and he agreed to support it. In the meantime, Bobbie would move in with his mother, and when the baby was born, Bobbie would leave and the baby would stay. Hank and his mother would take over custody.

That was the plan, but Hank Williams never saw his child, a little girl born on January 6, 1953. He left Montgomery on December 30, heading for a show in Canton, Ohio. It was a major performance in a large auditorium, and Hank was hoping it would resurrect his career. Nevertheless, he was drinking hard as his young driver, Charles Carr, an 18-year-old freshman at Auburn, headed north on Highway 31. They spent the first night in Birmingham, then started fresh on New Year's Eve. The weather was terrible—snowing all the way from Montgomery to Canton—and they decided to take a break in Knoxville. They found a motel, where Hank was so sluggish that Carr called a doctor. According to Williams' biographer, George William Koon, the doctor gave Hank a couple of shots—vitamin B-12 with a quarter grain of morphine to kill a persistent pain in his back. After a three-hour rest, Carr and Williams

147

headed north again through the mountains.

It was nearly dawn when they arrived in Oak Hill, still bitterly cold when Carr stopped to rest, then rushed into town in search of a hospital. Within a few hours, the word was slowly beginning to spread. There was a big Cadillac at the Pure Oil station, and they had found Hank Williams dead in the back. People said whiskey had torn up his heart.

Jack Pennington heard the news the following day, and immediately his mind began to drift back. He remembered the night from a few years earlier, June 11, 1949, when Hank made his first appearance on the Opry. Jack was only a boy at the time, but he knew he was listening to somebody special. Hank only sang one song that night, "Lovesick Blues," but as soon as he finished, the crowd at the Ryman Auditorium in Nashville was clapping so loud that he felt like he had to sing it again. It happened six times—six different encores, with that same old yodeling moan in the chorus—and the applause was so deafening on Jack Pennington's radio that it sounded at first like a wave of static.

Pennington was a fan from that moment on, and in the years that followed, he found himself thinking that there should be some remembrance—something dignified, befitting the memory of a man like Hank, who had lived with pain of his own creation, but had brought such solace to the people who heard him. He knew a handful of people who agreed, but the years went by and nothing much happened—not until 1989, when George Hamilton IV came to town for a concert. Hamilton sang his own string of hits—"Abilene," "Break My Mind"—but he was much more excited about the business just ahead. He had never been to Oak Hill before—had never seen the places he had read about for years. His friend, Vic Gabany, a native West Virginian and an engineer at the Opry, had told him about Pennington and Roger Seay, two employees of the city of Oak Hill who shared Hamilton's own admiration for Hank.

On the morning after his concert appearance, Hamilton met Pennington at the Holiday Inn, and they set out together on a tour of Oak Hill. The first stop they made was the Pure Oil station. It had changed a little in the intervening years. It was now a Union 76, and the old owner, Pete Burdette, was dead. But most of the people at the station remembered what Hamilton was now calling "the last stop on the last tour of Hank Williams." The new owner, Wilbur Toney, said his uncle was a Justice of the Peace in the '50s, and held a four-day inquest into Hank's death. Another gas station regular, Shirley Blake, said he was working in a dairy barn nearby when his friend, William Rogers, rushed in with the news.

Rogers is a black man, known to most people in Oak Hill as Razz.

He served as the chauffeur for the town's richest man, Herbert Jones, who owned a coal mine among other things. Before Jones died a few years back, he made arrangements for Rogers to live in his mansion —two-story brick with ivy-covered columns and a view of the mountains rolling off in the distance. Now pushing 80, Rogers is a man who loves a good story, and he told George Hamilton how Hank Williams' Cadillac sat in the service bay of the station. There were a couple of cowboy hats in the car, and the station's owner, Pete Burdette, took to wearing them around until he started going bald. Then one day a few years later, Burdette decided to take his own life. It was a messy suicide, accomplished with a shotgun, and some people said it was the ghost of Hank Williams that drove him to it. But Rogers didn't put a lot of stock in that. He said Burdette was having health problems, and he simply got tired of living with the pain.

George Hamilton smiled at the stream of old stories. The more he listened, the clearer it became that the death of Hank Williams was already part of the identity of Oak Hill—part of its lore. And there was something else as well. Oak Hill in the '80s was beginning to change. It had been a coal camp back in the '50s, its fortunes rising and falling with the mines—mostly falling as automation started putting miners out of work. Now, however, there were new possibilities. Tourists were flocking to the New River Gorge, which cut through the mountains a few miles away, and it was beginning to occur to the city fathers that tourism was a lot more promising than coal.

In this new climate, Hamilton and Pennnington and Roger Seay, along with Vic Gabany at the Grand Ole Opry, began to talk about a memorial to Hank. They began with a plaque, tastefully modest, on the lawn across the street from the service station, then started thinking about a Hank Williams festival. Mayor Eugene Larrick of Oak Hill was interested. So was Jim Murdock, the mayor of Fayetteville six miles away. Grant Turner, the venerated voice of the Grand Ole Opry, endorsed the idea on his radio show, and by early 1993 everything was in place. Hamilton agreed to be the opening act, and they signed Eddie Wayne, a veteran gospel singer from Ohio, who had filled in for Hank on the day of his death. But they were most excited about the headline performer—Hank Williams' own daughter, the girl he never saw, whose identity was hidden for so many years.

Jett Williams was happy to accept the invitation. She had never been to Oak Hill, and it seemed like a missing piece in her story. She had tried many times to picture what it looked like—a main street lined with flat-roofed buildings, a tiny post office with a flag on the lawn. So many things were like that in her life. She knew they were real, but couldn't see them clearly. For 21 years, she had no clue about her past. She grew up simply as Cathy Deupree, the adopted daughter of Wayne and Louise, in the frayed aristocracy of Mobile, Ala. Her father was kind, though sometimes remote, while her mother was temperamental—an alcoholic given to sudden swings in mood.

The Deuprees discouraged Cathy's curiosity about her birth, but when she turned 21 she learned she'd inherited $2,000 from the estate of Lillian Stone in Montgomery. Lillian Stone was Hank Williams' mother. It was startling, of course, and for more than a decade after that, Cathy kept searching for absolute proof. Could it really be true that Hank Williams was her father? Why else would his family have left her the money?

The answers started coming in 1984, when she hired Keith Adkinson, a handsome and energetic lawyer from Washington, who encouraged her to pursue a singing career while he followed the paper trail of her life. They already knew that Bobbie Jett was her mother. The birth certificate made that clear. Then in 1985, Adkinson found the files surrounding her adoption. Among the documents was the written agreement between Bobbie and Hank, notarized, in which Hank made it clear that he was the father. There were other documents that were even more conclusive, and for the first time in her life, Cathy felt a calmness about her identity.

Things began to happen quickly after that. For one thing, she and Keith fell in love and were married. They also began a long legal battle to secure her share of the Hank Williams estate. It was a bitter fight, with suits and countersuits against Hank Williams Jr. and a handful of others, who denied her claim to the song-writing fortune. But the battle ended well for Cathy Deupree. In addition to securing her share of the money, the amount undisclosed, she also won something else in the courts—a clear-cut judgment that she was, in fact, the lost daughter of Hank.

Her singing career, meanwhile, moved slowly. The powers in Nashville treated her with caution. In 1989, however, she started performing under the name Jett Williams—a tribute to both her parents—and she hired her father's old band to back her. The Drifting Cowboys were anchored as always by Jerry Rivers and Don Helms, whose fiddles and pedal steel guitars had provided the heart of the Hank Williams sound. Rivers says they were skeptical at first.

"Don and I kept saying, 'If Hank had a daughter, why didn't we know?' So we asked Ray Price, who was rooming with him around the time of his divorce. Ray just smiled. He said, 'Of course I know about that baby.'"

If there were any doubts left, they disappeared onstage. There was something undeniable about Jett's presence when she was performing her father's songs or her own. Her voice was plain, but expressive, and she had that confident stride toward the mike—mannerisms that had to come from her genes. That, at least, was Jerry Rivers' view, and the impression grew stronger every time they performed. They played state fairs and one-night stands, and some of the crowds along the way were huge.

Oak Hill was modest—maybe 1,000 people in a stuffy auditorium where the seats were uncomfortable and the acoustics were worse. But nobody seemed to mind, certainly not Jett Williams, who told the crowd, "It is an honor to stand here as a representative of my father. His spirit is here and always will be."

George Hamilton was pleased when he heard those words. Like Jett Williams, he had played to bigger crowds—and some perhaps that were even more lively, particularly when he played for his friends at the Opry. But it was hard to top this night in Oak Hill. The discovery of Hank's death had been so ugly—the alcohol in his blood, the memories of the pills and the morphine shots—and all of it coming with a baby on the way.

Now, however, the symbolism was changed. Oak Hill was a place of resolution and triumph, and later that night at the Skyline Drive-In, with the juke box blasting and the cold beer flowing and the crowd spilling out into the gravel parking lot, Hamilton smiled and said to his friends, "Maybe there is some justice somewhere."

The Heart and Soul of Emmylou Harris

Ever since the days of Hank Williams, country music has been an art form rich in tradition, and in the past 20 years, Williams' fellow Alabamian, Emmylou Harris, has done her part to see that the art and the tradition survive. I caught up with her in 1994, just before she went on tour, and in this brief essay, I tried to capture her feeling for the music—falling short, of course, for words alone are a little too pale.

Creative Loafing
1994

She's on the road now to promote her latest labor of love. They are all that way for Emmylou Harris—these albums she has crafted for the past 20 years. Her most recent, *Cowgirl's Prayer*, was nearly 18 months in the making, and the critics agree that it's one of her best—a heart-rending mixture of pure country ballads, with a little bit of cajun and gospel and rock 'n' roll. She has never been one to worry about the boundaries, and lately that may be part of her problem. For as Emmylou Harris makes her way across the country, she has reached a curious point in her career.

Her place in country music is secure. There is probably nobody in the past 20 years who has done more than she has to keep it alive, to nourish the heart and soul of that tradition. She has been a student as well as an artist, finding threads of continuity in disparate performers, from the Louvin Brothers to Bruce Springsteen. She has recorded their songs and made them her own, paying more attention to art than demographics, and the result is an impressive body of work. But lately, there's a problem. For nearly five years, despite her energy and the widely acknowledged quality of her work, she's found it hard to get her songs on the radio.

Commercially at least, she doesn't have to worry; her sales are steady enough to make a living. "I'm luckier than most," she says to-day. "My audience doesn't live or die by the radio."

Still, there's a pain that goes with rejection, and she feels it most when she thinks of the songs—the creations of composers like Leonard Cohen, who wrote the title cut for *Cowgirl's Prayer.* Cohen is a writer of stunning finesse, and the beauty of his words—the story of a girl and her runaway horse—is crystalized in the voice of Emmylou. She says she falls in love with good songs, and perhaps with Cohen's even more than most. Linda Ronstadt sent it to her in the mail, a haunting rendition by the pop singer, Jennifer Warnes, and Emmylou was deeply affected from the start.

"It's the kind of music that enriches my life," she says, "and it's a shame that these songs that say so much are less and less likely to be on records. Certainly, they're not played on the radio, which is becoming so caricaturish and shallow. Until we get a different kind of format, I'm concerned where country music is going."

The anger flashes for a moment in her voice, but it seems to subside when she talks about herself. "I'm not really sure," she says with resignation, "that country music and I, right now, are compatible."

If that is true, her producer, Allen Reynolds, says he understands why. "For Emmy," he explains, "music is more than a matter of commerce." For the past 20 years, it has been the defining love of her life, and at a time when radio is becoming more cautious, more predictable and narrow and indifferent to art, she refuses to bend with the demographic winds.

It hasn't always been that way, for Emmylou Harris came late to country music—to those heart-breaking harmonies with the voices intertwined and lyrics so clear and honest and real. There was a time, she says, when she couldn't quite hear it. She came from an upper middle class family, born in Birmingham, Alabama, and she later studied drama at the University of North Carolina at Greensboro. But she left the school after three semesters, having already started to sing, and she began to play little clubs in Washington, doing folk music mostly—the songs of Joni Mitchell and Dylan and Baez. By then, she was dabbling in the old stuff too, developing an ear for Bill Monroe, and maybe on nights when the crowds were small, which seemed to happen a lot in those days, she might do a ballad from Kitty Wells. But she says she never really listened to the music, never really felt it deep in her bones, until the night in 1971 when she met Gram Parsons.

Parsons was a rebellious refugee from Harvard University and Waycross, Georgia. He had been a rock 'n' roller for most of his life—a lead singer with the Byrds, and later with the Flying Burrito Brothers—but a piece of his heart still belonged to country music. It was the music he knew in small-town Georgia, the songs of Merle Haggard and Kitty Wells, and by the early 1970s, when he met Emmylou, he was determined to cut his own country album. He took some delight in the shock value of it, a shaggy-haired rock 'n' roller like himself sounding just as raw as Haggard and the rest. He was looking for a girl to sing some duets when he met Emmylou in a bar called Clyde's. It was a singles club in the heart of Georgetown, and she played there a lot. On the night when Parsons came in to hear her, she says there were maybe three people in the place, but Parsons seemed impressed with what he heard, and on one of her breaks, the two of them headed off to the basement. They began to work up some songs, sitting there together on the kegs of beer, and for Emmylou, it was magic. There was something inexplicable in the blend of their voices. Gram's was flawed, cracking sometimes as he strained for the notes, but it was also strong and full of heart, and when Emmylou sang the harmonies for him, she knew it didn't get any better than that.

They made a couple of albums together, the second of which, *Grievous Angel*, was widely hailed by the critics as a breakthrough record—one of the greatest country albums ever made. But Gram had a wild and self-destructive streak, and in 1973 he died—apparently from the effect of too many drugs. For Emmylou, there have been other moments of tragedy and pain—broken hearts and marriages that didn't work out—but few things have hit her with the force of that death. Not long afterward, she sat down and wrote a tribute to him, a soul-wrenching ballad called "Boulder to Birmingham," in which she sang about the longing just to see his face.

She has said many times in the years since then that she loved Gram Parsons as a musician and friend—but perhaps even more, she treasured the gift of music that he left her. She built her career on the strength of that gift, and by 1975 her solo records were beginning to take off—to the sound of rave reviews all around. "Listening to her sing," said Nashville songwriter Marshall Chapman, "is kind of like getting a sneak preview of heaven." But there were others who argued that her choice of material was even more distinctive and important than her voice. She found country songs in the strangest of places—from the urban rock 'n' roll of Bruce Springsteen (she said he reminded her a lot of Hank Williams) to the old-fashioned ballads of Stephen Foster.

Historian John Rumble of the Country Music Foundation says he used to see her often in the musty stacks of the foundation's library, searching out the history of assorted country songs. But she also admired the contemporary writers, and many's the time, says Allen Reynolds, when a group of them would gather to play at her house.

"Emmy is so tuned in," he says. "She keeps up with new artists, and goes way out of her way to help them. I've seen her do it time and time again."

Reynolds and many others in Nashville maintain that Harris has become a symbol of country music artistry. But even as her status has grown more secure, her commercial standing in the industry has slipped. She never has Number One records anymore, and it's been a few years since she's cracked the top 40. Partly, it's a matter of her own indifference, for when she formed a new band in 1990 and asked Allen Reynolds to be her producer, their first major project was a live country album. Live albums rarely get a lot of airplay, but Harris was determined to do it anyway.

She wanted to perform at the Ryman Auditorium, legendary home of the Grand Ole Opry before it moved to its slick new quarters. There was something mysterious about the building, she said, something in the feel of the hillbilly dust, and she was a little awestruck when she first took the stage. She knew that Hank Williams had once played there, and Roy Acuff and Bill Monroe, and it was an eerie feeling as she gazed through the lights at the stained-glass windows and the benches that still resembled old pews. She knew she was taking a chance with this one—doing an album of songs she had never performed, and doing it live with no time to rehearse. But she also cherished the feeling of fear, the feeling that she was pushing the music to its limits.

In the end, the album won her a Grammy, but was totally ignored by country music radio.

The same fate seems likely for *Cowgirl's Prayer*, which hit the stores in the fall of 1994. It's already winning its share of acclaim, while the radio programmers look the other way.

On the surface, their indifference is hard to understand, for most of the album is clearly in the mainstream. There's a hard country-rocker called "High Powered Love" and a heartbreak ballad called "Lovin' You Again." But there are also some songs that plow new ground. Many of the arrangements are folky and spare, and the lyrics on occasion even shade toward gospel—an unpredictable mixture overall, with a feeling of coherence that's a mystery to Emmylou.

"The more records I do, the less I know about it," she says. "You just respect what an album seems to be becoming. Allen Reynolds and (co-producer) Richard Bennett have a good feel for that. They respect the mystery of the whole process, which is the thing that makes them so good to work with.

"Allen is a very song-oriented producer, and my career progresses one song at a time. I'm always drawn to the lyrics first. People know how hard life is. They need music that will give words and expression to the feelings they have. That's what country music is about. It has to be more than entertainment or escape."

And what if the radio won't play it?

Emmylou says it bothers her some, but she also knows she's not alone. Waylon Jennings, Willie Nelson, Merle Haggard, Johnny Cash —all of them known for their integrity and substance—have joined her in the ranks of the radio rejects. Maybe it's simply a matter of image— too many gray hairs for the "young country" playlists. Whatever the reason, Harris and the others say they try not to worry.

"It frustrated me for awhile," she admits, "but it's a natural thing that happens in a long career. You compete with yourself and your own oldies. I really don't give it a lot of thought anymore. The important thing is to be passionate about the music."

That's the good news for Emmylou Harris. Even when her voice is fragile and tired, hoarse from the string of one-night stands, she whirls and dances in the soft blue lights, and the old lover's fire still burns inside her. You can see it in her smile, hear it in the aching beauty of her songs. When it comes to the music that's defined her life, nobody feels more passion than she does.

Sweeter With The Years

The next two chapters are about songwriters, the people who do as much as anybody to keep Southern music alive— and also connected to the people who listen. Many of them live more intensely than the rest of us, and that is certainly true of Marshall Chapman, a country-rocker who lives in Nashville, having taken her Vanderbilt education just a few blocks south to Music Row. I caught up with her in 1995 at the beginning of a national tour with Jimmy Buffett. She said she is feeling better these days.

Creative Loafing
1995

There are two different versions of the Elvis story.

According to the first, Marshall Chapman was seven years old, growing up in Spartanburg, South Carolina, when Elvis Presley came to town. He was playing on a package show out of Nashville, an opening act on a tour of country stars, but already the word was beginning to spread.

The Chapman family's baby-sitter and maid, Lula Mae Moore, took little Marshall by the hand, and led her down to the Carolina Theater. They climbed the back stairs to the all-colored balcony, steamy and packed, to catch a glimpse of this picker from Memphis who sang country music as if he were black.

"When he came on, it was like an explosion," Marshall said years later. "The whole place just shook."

The story, undoubtedly, will ring pretty true for people who have seen Marshall Chapman on stage. At the age of 46, she has built a cult following in the past 20 years as one of Nashville's cutting-edge performers.

She has a new album in 1995, recorded live at the Tennessee

Prison for Women—and when she appears next week in Charlotte, the opening act for her friend, Jimmy Buffett, nobody will doubt there's rock 'n' roll in her soul.

But in terms of her earliest inspiration, there's another whole version of the Elvis story, which is offered these days by some of her friends. It's different in detail from the one in her press kit, but in its own way it's at least as revealing.

In this one, too, she was seven years old. It was a Spartanburg Sunday, and the family was gathered around the television set. Her mother was knitting, and her father was hidden behind his Sunday newspaper, when Elvis Presley flickered on the screen. Mrs. Chapman tried to say something nice. She talked about young singer's eyes and the emotion that shimmered in his Mississippi voice.

"But those sideburns," she said with a frown.

Marshall, meanwhile, was simply transfixed, and at the age of seven, she dove headlong into the first great wave of rock 'n' roll. It wasn't just Elvis. As a teenager she was drawn to the black singers, too—Jackie Wilson, Maurice Williams and all the rest. She bought their records, and saw them whenever they came to town—joining other whites, in the latter days of segregation, in the sweltering balcony of the Carolina Theater.

Eventually, she began to think about performing, but first came college. She left Spartanburg for Vanderbilt University, where she majored in French. But the Vanderbilt campus was just a few blocks from Music Row, a part of Nashville that began more and more to command her attention.

She was already a closet country music fan, having listened as a kid to the Arthur Smith Show as it beamed out of Charlotte. It was easy to make fun of the cornpone humor, but the music was real, and in songs like Arthur's "Guitar Boogie," she could hear the antecedents of rock 'n' roll.

When she graduated in 1971, she took her Vanderbilt degree and went to work as a waitress at the Red Dog Saloon, a basement bar on the fringe of the campus, where she bided her time, waiting to begin her career as a singer.

It was not exactly what her family had in mind.

Her father, James Chapman, was a textile magnate, the president of Spartanburg's Inman Mills, and he expected great things from his impressive young daughter. She was six feet tall with soft blond hair and a winning smile, and she was smart enough to hold her own with anybody.

"He thought I would get the music business out of my system," says Marshall today. But then in 1976, she signed with Epic Records, and her debut album, *Me, I'm Feelin' Free*, was a hit with critics all across the country.

It was about that time that the crowds grew larger at the Exit Inn and all the other watering holes around Nashville whenever Marshall Chapman showed up to play. But there were warning signs even from the start. Her record label didn't really believe. They saw her as rock 'n' roll, not country, and in a business where everybody has to have a niche, she simply didn't fit.

"Marshall Chapman was too cool and real for Nashville in the Seventies," writes Alana Nash, a nationally known music critic and author. "Not to mention too bluesy, too irreverent, too original, too powerhouse and too tall...."

After only three albums, the label cut her loose, and it marked the beginning of a difficult time. Her career was on the skids. Her father died, and there was also a suicide in her band.

Marshall, meanwhile, was living wild, perhaps in a flight from too much pain—or maybe, she says, she was just trying to be what people expected: a rock 'n' roller on the edge. Whatever the reason, there were too many boyfriends and too much booze, but it's the blessing and the curse of a songwriter's life that hard times often make good lyrics.

It was true for Marshall in the 1980s. She wrote her songs of disillusionment and hurt, tempered most often with irony and humor. Soon other singers began to take notice, and her songs were recorded by a whole host of artists, from Joe Cocker and Dion DiMucci to Conway Twitty and Emmylou Harris.

By the end of the '80s she was making good money—BMW money, as one friend put it—and she also discovered that her life was growing calm. She found a good man, a Nashville doctor by the name of Chris Fletcher, and she was recording again on her own record label.

It was about that time that the letter arrived.

The warden at the Tennessee Prison for Women, Eileen Hosking, had long been a fan, having heard Chapman play at the Bluebird Cafe, a songwriters' mecca on the south side of Nashville.

After one of those performances, in March of 1989, the warden wrote Chapman and asked her to do a show at the prison. Marshall read the letter and put it aside, and there it sat for the next three years. It wasn't the fact that the prison couldn't pay. She was used to that in a town where benefit concerts are common.

But there was a line near the bottom that left her queasy. "Quite frankly," the warden felt compelled to admit, "I have no idea how you

159

would be received."

For Marshall at the moment, the possibility of being hooted from the stage by a room full of prisoners was a little too daunting for her to confront. And yet somehow, she couldn't dismiss it—couldn't make herself throw the letter away.

Finally, she paid a visit to the prison. She went to the cells and talked to the women, then went to the gym where they wanted her to play. It was musty and old, but when she snapped her fingers the acoustics seemed right.

"I thought, Wow, we ought to record it."

And so they did, and the album may well be the best she has done. It has its raw and ragged moments, as live albums do, unless they've been sanitized later on. But there is something electric as Chapman rocks her way through the set.

Predictably enough, there are hard-living songs of love gone bad and boyfriends hanging around like a debt. But the most haunting moments on the album are the soft ones—the winsome ballads of childhood memories and the passage of time, and feelings that only grow sweeter with the years.

That's the way it is for Chapman these days. Songs once born in rebellion and pain now seem to come from a different source. The title of her album, released on Buffett's Margaritaville label, is *It's About Time...* a reference, in part, to the Tennessee prison. But it's also a reference to her own frame of mind.

On the final cut, she sings of a time when "every night was now or never, and the road just seemed to go on forever." She says today that it isn't really so. She's still in love with the rock 'n' roll life. But after 40 years of it, she says she's learning to take it as it comes.

Vince

There have been a lot of great songwriters to come through Nashville—Mickey Newbury, Guy Clark, Kris Kristofferson, Hugh Moffatt, Bob McDill and many, many more. But of all of those, I think my favorite may have been Vince Matthews, who was the subject of a chapter in Watermelon Wine, *a country music book that I wrote in the '70s. As that chapter makes clear, there have been some writers with more talent than Vince, but not very many who had a better heart.*

Watermelon Wine
1978

That great speckled bird sang her song in his ear
Whisperin' words of magic that only Vince could hear.
—Larry Wilkerson & Shel Silverstein

It was a rainy Nashville night, the dregs of winter, as Vince Matthews and his Budweiser stumbled down a back-alley stairway and ducked into the automobile of a friend. Vince was entering that happy stage of inebriation in which his tongue is unleashed on a variety of philosophical rampages ranging from the evils of Richard Nixon to the trials and tribulations of writing country songs.

The latter subject is actually most interesting to him, for, like most people, Vince finds himself one of the world's more fascinating topics of conversation. Unlike most people, he is probably right.

He has been knocking around Nashville for a dozen years, writing songs that run the gamut from terrible to poignant, and building (sometimes consciously) a richly deserved reputation as the quintessential crazy, mixed-up, manic depressive, unlucky, when you're-hot-you're-hot, when-you're-not-you're-not kind of songwriter who is still hanging in there and no doubt will be as long as he is breathing.

161

"You gotta live it, man," he said with slurry-tongued sincerity as the car bounced gingerly along the alleyway potholes. And with that he launched into the story of how he once hitchhiked to Chicago with five dollars in his pocket, arrived with only one, and passed three days in a drainage culvert wondering how to spend a lonesome dollar bill.

Eventually he said to hell with it and threw it away. After miraculously failing to starve, he somehow wound up in Nashville again, where he wrote a song about the whole experience. Johnny Cash heard it, recorded it, and before long "Wrinkled, Crinkled, Wadded Dollar Bill" had made it to the top of the country music charts, and Vince became temporarily rich.

"I think," he said, as his mind wandered reluctantly back to the present, "that it's called casting your bread on the water. At least that's what Jesus called it."

The parallels between Jesus and Vince are not overwhelming, however. He has a lot of traits that Jesus no doubt would have admired, but throwing away the dollar was more an offering to art than to religion, and in an odd sort of way it typified Matthew's whole career. There is nothing he loves more than a wallet full of money, but he has steadfastly refused to become a slave to its pursuit. And the refusal has kept him pure—a personification of the uncommercialized side of country music.

Matthews was born in the West Tennessee town of Waverly on May 3, 1942, and spent his teenage years listening to the rockabilly outpourings of Sun Records in Memphis and trying his hand at some amateur songwriting. Some time around his 20th birthday he headed east to Nashville, and he cut a pretty impressive figure when he hit town—a bright and energetic young man with the high Cherokee cheekbones and the jet-black hair of a forgotten Tennessee ancestor.

He had little trouble landing a job in an advertising firm, then later in the office of a commercial artist. But a friend named Bill Brook (who had written a song for Chubby Checker) showed him how to approximate the A, F, and D chords on a guitar, and on the same afternoon Vince sat down and wrote 28 songs. They were terrible. He was hooked, however, and kept on dabbling until finally, in the late winter of 1963, he helped compose a maudlin ballad called "Hobo and a Rose."

"Don Vincent and I wrote it on a Sunday," Vince recalled. "We pitched it to Webb Pierce on Monday, and he cut in on Wednesday. I thought 'Jeez this is the easiest thing I ever did. I think I'll do it every day.' I've been hitting off and on ever since—mostly off, I might add."

The gyrations between high-riding success and abject, starvation-level failure have defined Vince's career, and the capricious pummeling has taken its toll on his ego and all-around psychological functioning. His songs kept getting better and better, but his ratio of success remained frustratingly constant. There were some definite high points: He wrote "Bob" for the Willis Brothers, which was one of the most serious records that they ever did, and along with Jim Casey he wrote a song called "Toast of '45" for Sammi Smith. It told the story of an over-the-hill movie actress, and established Matthews as a writer with a deep-seeded understanding of the human condition.

It established him, that is, among the other artist-types around Nashville—but not among the record-buying public. For the dry spells continued, and the eye-opening fact of the matter was that they had little relationship to anything—to how hard he was working, or how well he was writing or even how deeply he wanted to succeed.

That kind of psychological environment will leave you with a finely honed sense of the absurd, and it may have been for that very reason that Vince fell in so compatibly with Kris Kristofferson. Kristofferson arrived in town several years after Vince had already established a toe hold and like Matthews he found himself bouncing around between his own basic confidence in what he could do and the hard and cold fact that no one was listening. So the two of them took what comfort they could in a loose confederation of other Young Turks, a sort of artistic cabal consisting of Mickey Newbury, Townes Van Zandt, Billy Swann, and a few dozen more—sharing songs, joints, and good times, and boosting one another's creative instincts.

Vince was (and still is) genuinely stunned by Kristofferson's ability with words and during the lean years when the Music Row decision-makers weren't paying much attention, Kris would bring over his latest compositions and lay his ego on the line for a Matthews critique. Sometimes he listened to what Vince had to say and other times, fortunately, he didn't. Once, for example, Kristofferson brought over a brand new ballad called "Me and Bobby McGee," and Vince told him it was great except for the line about freedom being just another word for nothing left to lose.

"Doesn't fit," Vince insisted. "Disrupts the story line."

Matthews will tell the story on himself with considerable delight these days—laughing in his semimaniacal way about how Kristofferson's words have become a sure bet for any updated versions of Bartlett's *Familiar Quotations*. Then, with another slurp at his Budweiser, he will turn suddenly serious and affirm with a sheepish nod of his head that "there was actually a time when I thought I was as smart as ole Kris."

It's a revealing confession, an unintended testimonial to the fact that his friendship with Kristofferson has been a double-edged reality. On the one hand it has certainly helped him, for Kristofferson has pushed his songs, plugged him on National TV, and even, on occasion, shoved him onstage for concert appearances. But on the other hand Kris became famous and Vince never did, and that's a tough one to take no matter how well you and your ego get along. In Matthews' case, the relationship with his self esteem has always been a little bit turbulent, and he has spent more hours than he cares to remember wondering why he wasn't born a genius.

Actually, however, that may be the wrong question, for at his best Vince can write songs with anybody. Johnny Cash once maintained that a Matthews composition called "Melva's Wine" was "the best contemporary folk song in American music." And "On Susan's Floor"—recorded in equally moving versions by Gordon Lightfoot and Hank Williams, Jr.—has its own minicult following among country musicians.

So the barrier between Vince and stardom is not really his brain. But it is something equally basic: it's his voice. He can't sing a lick. Some people would argue, of course, that Kristofferson can't either, but Vince is to Kristofferson as Kristofferson is to Mario Lanza; and to understand the full weight of that reality, you had only to accompany Vince one night a few years back to an Exit Inn appearance by Mickey Newbury.

Newbury is one of the more magnificent vocalists on the country scene with a voice that is mellow and strong and throbbing with emotion. When he turns it loose on his own compositions—songs like "Heaven Help the Child" and "An American Trilogy"—jaws will drop in the crowd, eyes will become riveted to the front of the room, and all other sounds will dry up with the kind of awe and deference that the occasion demands.

At least that's what usually happens. But if Vince is along you never quite know what to expect and on this particular night he was so far on his way toward chemical alteration that he couldn't contain himself. He began to sing along from his back-row seat, softly at first, but soon with all the power and sincerity of a wounded dog or a cow in labor.

Through it all, he retained a sort of boozy and beatific tolerance toward the stares of hatred and disbelief that were being cast in his direction. However, when a waiter began taking whispered orders for drinks during one particularly moving number, Vince lurched up to him and demanded that he please show respect for an artist of Mickey Newbury's caliber.

But that, as people around Nashville are fond of saying, is just Vince. He has a fierce and unshakable loyalty toward people he respects, and the feeling is very often mutual. When he decided a few years back, for example, that he wanted to cut an album, Kris Kristofferson and Shel Silvertein agreed to produce it, and Johnny Cash wrote some liner notes and even whistled background on one of the cuts. And surprisingly enough, given Vince's limitations in front of a microphone, most people who heard it thought it was a pretty good record, especially in its content. It was a concept album titled *Kingston Springs Suite* and telling the story of Kingston Springs, Tennessee, a tiny, hill country town that you could plunk down with equal validity almost anywhere in middle America.

Matthews lived in Kingston Springs for seven years, developing a strong affection for its people and he brought that feeling alive with songs about an old man dying, a young girl leaving (because she believed erroneously, that no one cared about her), and a village blacksmith who was also a dispenser of down home wisdom.

Counting the time he spent writing the songs, Vince worked on the album off and on for more than five years. He couldn't find a record label to back the project, but it developed into an obsession with him and he went into the studio anyway. He says he spent $50,000 of his own money (actually money that he didn't really have yet) buying studio time, paying musicians, and even having half a dozen records pressed in order to try to sell the finished product to a major label.

But even with the intercession of his well-connected friends, nobody was interested, and Vince found himself financially and spiritually in considerable debt—especially since he wasn't getting any songs cut by other artists. The year 1974 came and went before he had earned a penny, and the prospects didn't appear too much better in the early months of 1975. So Vince said good-bye to Kinston Springs and Nashville and headed for New York, hoping desperately that greener pastures might be waiting somehow amid the concrete canyons. They weren't.

But then, in one of those unexplainable quirks that have characterized Vince's flirtations with country music, a pair of newcomers named Gene Watson and Crystal Gayle decided to record some songs that he had written several years earlier. Watson's version of "Love in the Hot Afternoon" went to the top of the charts and Miss Gayle (who is Loretta Lynn's little sister) did almost as well with "This is My Year for Mexico"—the story of a housewife trapped by habit and dreaming of the places she would go if her spirit were only a little bit freer.

Charley Pride soon cut a masculine version of Crystal Gayle's hit; Hank Williams, Jr. went into the studio with "On Susan's Floor," and suddenly—13 years after he'd first breezed into Nashville—Vince

Matthews was hot commercial property. He signed a writing contract with Peer-Southern, a prestigious company headed by Ralph Peer, Jr., whose father, Ralph Sr., of Okeh records, had wandered down from New York in the '20s to record such ambitious hillbillies as Pop Stoneman, Jimmie Rogers, and The Carter Family.

One of the first songs Vince wrote after his deal with Peer was titled "Who was Bradley Kincaid?"—an ode of sorts to the college-educated Kentucky guitarist who had headed north in the early twenties to become a star on the WLS Barn Dance. All of that was symbolic to Vince, for he is, among other things, a student of the country tradition, and captivated by the notion that his own niche is being carved, somehow, by an inscrutable destiny—carrying with it the inevitable dose of artistic suffering.

All of that may be simple presumption or conceit, but then again it may not. For Vince has lived and embodied all the things that give country music its power. He has known the sting of failure and the whiffs of occasional prosperity. He has been drunk, lonesome, lovesick, and hungry, and through it all he has clung to the basic sensitivity and human compassion that have always been the cornerstone of good country music.

"I like Vince a lot," says Johnny Cash, with a nod of somber finality. "He's probably one of the greatest writers this business has ever had. I sure would like to see him make it."

Personally, I don't think it will make a whole lot of difference to Vince, for he is equally at home cruising around Nashville in a Cadillac he can't afford or selling the damn thing and hitching a ride with a friend. Which is what he did a little while back, and as we rumbled down the alleyway toward a sleazy little tavern where the pickers gather for pinball and beer, he began to talk about the deal he had struck with Peer.

"I got two songs on the charts, I got a good deal with a publisher, hell I just might make it this time. But then," he said, opening the door and pausing half in and half out for an eloquent summation, "I s'pose I've said that before...."

As he grinned and went trudging off into the Nashville rain, humming off-key and wobbling toward the fog shrouded honky-tonk, you had the feeling, somehow, that country music just might survive.

Though the hits have been sparse in recent years, Vince Matthews is still writing songs and taking care of his elderly mother in Camden, Tennessee.

166

The Fall of Davey Allison

Stock car racing is, in many ways, the most Southern of sports, tracing its roots to the moonshining days in the hills of Carolina. It has changed, of course, in the past 30 years, but some of the old traditions survive. For one thing, there's a genuine accessibility among the drivers who refuse to set themselves apart from the fans. Ordinarily, that's good. But when tragedies strike, as they sometimes do, the pain becomes even more intense. In 1993, I was covering the sport, finishing a book about third-generation driver Kyle Petty, when one of his friends and competitors, Davey Allison, made a mistake in trying to land his helicopter. This is a column I wrote on that occasion.

Creative Loafing
1993

A friend called on Monday with the news, and it was almost unbelievable at first. Davey Allison's helicopter had crashed, and they had rushed him unconscious to an Alabama hospital. From the early reports, it looked pretty bad.

Still, you had to believe there was hope, for how much pain could one family stand? It had been a year since the last round of tragedy— Davey's car flipping wildly in a race at Pocono, 11 times in a four-second span, the sheet metal flying as if a bomb had exploded inside.

Miraculously, enough, Davey survived with a broken wrist and a few other injuries that barely slowed him down. But it was a terrible scare for his mother, Judy Allison, who loved her sons and suffered with the dangers that went with their sport.

Four years earlier, her husband, Bobby, one of the greatest drivers of all time, had nearly died at the same racetrack, and in a way he was the luckiest member of the family. He had forgotten the terror of the

167

bedside vigil.

But the scares at Pocono were overshadowed in August of 1992, when Davey's younger brother, Clifford, was getting set to race at the Michigan Speedway. In an early round of practice, he lost control of his car and hit the wall.

His father was there and hurried to the scene, and he knew in an instant that his son was dead. He could tell it by the way he was slumped in the seat.

Judy Allison had to get away after that. In her grief, she retreated to Florida for awhile, leaving the family home in Alabama and the sport that had suddenly turned so cruel. But in 1993, she was back, trying to be brave, and it was simply inconceivable that she could lose another son.

Even when you saw the TV footage—Davey unconscious when they loaded the ambulance, the hospital spokesmen offering little hope —you found yourself half expecting a miracle.

"Davey's a fighter," one crew member said, and a TV reporter used the word "optimistic."

You had to feel that way for Judy's sake.

But the script this time had a terrible ending, and when Davey died from his massive head injuries, you found yourself praying for the passage of time—praying tor the moment somwhere in the future when the pain will give way to the memories of life.

For now, however, the Allisons' grief is incomprehensible.

It's true, of course, that they don't grieve alone. I don't mean to be trivial here, to compare the feelings of the public to those of the family. But everywhere I went those first few days, it was the only thing anybody wanted to talk about.

I think we shouldn't be surprised by that. There is something unusual about the sport of racing. One of the television commentators last week, in an effort to reduce the world to cliches, called it a family.

In this particular case, the commentator was right. One of the most touching realities of racing is the remarkable accessibility of the drivers. Most are very much like the fans—small-town people, mostly Southern, sharing a bond that seems to be instinctive.

As Richard Petty once put it, "We've never really gotten above our raisin'—and thank goodness for that."

What this means is that many of the fans who mourned the death of Davey Allison felt as if they knew him. They had met him at autograph sessions, or in traffic jams outside the track, or maybe having lunch at a local restaurant. They had talked to him, touched him, shaken his hand—and on most of those occasions it was easy to like him.

168

He seemed much younger than 32. His grin was bashful, and there was a little-boy shyness sometimes in his eyes, and a decency, I thought, that went with his talent.

After the death of his brother and his own wreck at Pocono, he told an interviewer that the Allisons were not unique in their pain. There were thousands, maybe millions, of people in the world whose suffering and grief were simply more anonymous.

"We shouldn't forget them either," he said.

I suppose all of that is still true today—but the Allisons' tragedies are more poignant than most, and the terrible thing is, they just keep coming. You think of Judy, and Davey's wife, Liz, and his two small children so full of life.

The first time I ever did an interview with him, his kids were there, squirming and climbing on the couch where I sat. One of them finally settled in my lap, and Liz Allison asked if they were driving me crazy.

When I told her no, she smiled and said, "You must have kids." Davey seemed to loosen up after that. If I liked his children, I was OK with him.

I think about those children today, and the consolations are pretty hard to find. The Allisons are deeply religious people. Maybe they'll find the strength to make it through.

But the story this time has the wrong kind of ending. This is just about as brutal as it gets.

The Rise and Fall of David Thompson

Another star-crossed hero from the realm of athletics, David Thompson was a basketball star in the 1970s, who helped change the way the game was played. He lead North Carolina State to a national championship, and in the NBA, became the highest-paid player in the history of the league. But there was also an aura of tragedy about him. On March 16, 1974, he crashed to the floor of the Reynolds Coliseum in Raleigh, landing on his head and triggering a wave of fear through his fans. His friends often recall that fall, seeing it as a kind of metaphor for his life, one that foreshadowed a devastating fall from greatness, a fall into a life dominated by drugs—but a fall, they hoped, that would end with recovery.

Southern Voices
1991

The horror of it was hard to forget: the sudden and unintended cartwheel, the sickening thud on the hardwood floor and then the young body lying silent and still.

The moment had begun like so many others—an elegant blur of motion and grace. Here was David Thompson, the basketball star at N.C. State, lifting off to block a shot—hanging there in the air as only he could, so gifted and confident, so completely in control. But then his foot caught the shoulder of one of his teammates, a six-eight forward by the name of Phil Spence, and Thompson was suddenly revealed to be mortal. He flipped and landed on the back of his head, and for the next four minutes—a time of dead silence in the Raleigh arena—he did not move.

"I thought he was dead," Spence said at the time.

In fact, however, Thompson recovered quickly from that first fall. He had a concussion, and a gash that had to be stitched shut. But he returned to Reynolds Coliseum before the end of the game, a 100-72 victory over the University of Pittsburgh. His head was now wrapped in a heavy gauze turban, but he was smiling, and it seemed for a while the cheers would never end.

Thompson had already emerged as one of the biggest sports heroes his state had ever known, and as the applause made clear on this March afternoon in 1974, the fall only served to elevate his stature, adding a certain urgency to the warm feelings of his fans.

"It made me feel good," Thompson remembered much later. "It made me feel like people really cared."

Indeed, they did. It was easy back then. By the end of his junior year at N.C. State, the team had built a record of 57-1. They won the national championship that season, and Thompson had established himself as one of the best players in the country. But the dimensions of his fame went beyond his talent, which, however dazzling, was tempered and enhanced by a humility and simple niceness that prompted one Charlotte columnist to write: "There has always been a sensitivity about him, a mark of infinite gentlemanly grace...that has produced a genuine hero for us at a hero-thirsting time."

In retrospect, there is a terrible irony in such words of praise, for there was a darker side to young David Thompson—a tragic, parallel track in his life that would produce another fall, one far more devastating than any that occurred on a basketball court. Within a few years, after he had left N.C. State and become the highest paid basketball player in the world, he would find himself addicted to cocaine—mired in a life of paranoia and deceit, squandering gifts and opportunities that most young Americans could only dream of.

"I had a chance to be one of the greatest players in the history of the game," he recently admitted, "and I blew it."

But the story continues, and Thompson is trying to put his life back together. He has stopped using drugs, and he has a good job with the Charlotte Hornets, an expansion team in the NBA. The team hired him, among other things, to talk to youth groups, warning against the temptations he failed to resist.

"It's good therapy," Thompson declares.

His friends, meanwhile, are cautiously optimistic. But they know the odds against an addict's full recovery, and they know that in the past—despite his awesome talent and an air of gentle goodness that made people love him—you could never really tell about David Thompson. Somehow, despite his strengths, he had drifted so passively in the direction of disaster.

"Maybe David was just too nice for his own good," says Monte

Towe, a former teammate at N.C. State. "Sometimes, I think, he just had trouble telling people no."

He came from rural Cleveland County, North Carolina, the youngest of 11 children. His father, Vellie Thompson, drove a truck and served as a deacon in the Maple Springs Baptist Church, and for the first 14 years of David Thompson's life, the family lived in a run-down tenant house nestled in the woods. In the yard, there was a basketball goal near a patch of bare earth, and David took up the game when he was five.

Over the years, basketball quietly became his obsession, offering a satisfaction unmatched by any other pursuit. He played it hard, and worked to improve—not to build his ego, for there was never even the vaguest hint of arrogance about him, but to push his skills to the next highest level.

"David," remembers his high school coach Ed Peeler, "never opened his mouth on the court. He never showed a temper, or argued with the referee. He was very coachable and unselfish as a player. I think people liked that."

In Peeler's view, Thompson's qualities as an athlete and a person were extremely important to Crest High School, which opened as a totally integrated facility in 1967, the same year Thompson arrived as a ninth grader.

"I think David helped soothe the transition," says Peeler, "he and that group of athletes. It was an integrated team, and David was the star. He got along super with the white kids on the team...and people came from everywhere to see him play."

Still, there were times when Peeler was concerned about Thompson—when he found himself in an odd and ironic position for a coach, worried that a player had become too dedicated.

"I never saw David take any other interest except basketball," Peeler remembers. "He was just constantly playing....You've got to do something else to make your life more meaningful."

But in retrospect, the most serious warning sign of the problems that lay ahead may have come late in Thompson's senior year. Thompson, says Peeler, had been heavily recruited by colleges across the country, and even after he had committed to N.C. State he still continued talking to other schools.

"That's the biggest part of his problem," says the coach. "David just wanted to please everybody."

The odd thing was, for the next several years Thompson almost did. At N.C. State, he averaged nearly 40 points a game on the freshman team. As a sophomore, in 1972-73, he led the varsity to an undefeated season (though State was on probation and couldn't compete for the national title until the next year.)

But it wasn't just the wins. At six-feet-four and 190 pounds Thompson played the game with an exuberance and grace that began to transform it, to suggest new possibilities to a generation of young players then coming of age on America's playgrounds.

"He was the original skywalker," says Bobby Jones, a former opponent from the University of North Carolina, and later a teammate in the NBA.

With his 42-inch vertical leap, Thompson always seemed to be soaring above the rim, and though he did it with a joyful confidence, there was never any trace of the hot dog about him. He was part of a team, and that became another key ingredient in the David Thompson myth.

There was a special chemistry and friendship among Thompson and the others, especially with Tommy Burleson, the team's seven-foot-four center, and Monte Towe, a five-foot-seven point guard. Thompson is black, and Towe and Burleson are white.

"I was just being myself," says Thompson. "I was taught not to be prejudiced."

If that was his simple and straight-forward reasoning, there were many fans who endowed it with a heroic sort of wisdom.

"A quick intelligence, a certain princely manner fleshed with fellowed warmth," *Charlotte Observer* columnist Kays Gary once wrote, and he was not alone in that perception. This was the South of the 1970s, when racial prejudice was beginning to crumble, and Thompson became a symbol of the change.

Monte Towe says he worried about it. He had a deep respect for Thompson's sensitivity and kindness, but he saw them enlarged to epic proportions by fans, and the myth, he says, may have been a burden for the real David Thompson.

"I think it's something he had trouble dealing with," says Towe. "I'm not so sure it didn't contribute to his problems."

In any case, the myth didn't square with another piece of reality: whatever his good points, Thompson was also an ordinary, hard-partying college athlete, fast developing an affinity for alcohol.

He had his first brush with the bottle when he was in high school. He was on a recruiting trip to Columbia, and there were some players and girls drinking wine at a lake house. "I got really sick," he says. "I told my parents I had the flu, and it was awhile before I wanted to drink

173

after that."

At State, however, he quickly grew accustomed to parties at the frat houses and pitchers of beer virtually every night, and though he never really saw it as a problem, there was one particular episode that caused him alarm. He says he was driving home from a party one night —fast, down a back road that led to his dorm, his tape deck blaring with the Isley Brothers and Stevie Wonder. He was feeling relaxed from an evening's worth of drinking, when he saw an oncoming car that had crossed the center line. Thompson swerved to avoid a collision. His wheels hit some loose pavement on the side of the road, and he slammed his Grand Prix into a tree.

"I don't really remember it too clearly after that," he says, "but somehow I walked back to my dorm and reported a stolen car. I knew if I didn't I'd be charged with DWI."

The deception worked, but it also became one more piece of David Thompson's looming tragedy. He had begun to develop a sense of invulnerability—a feeling, buttressed by his fame and his success on the court, that he was immune to the consequences of irresponsibility.

It was a devastating lesson to take with him to the pros.

Carl Scheer remembers how hard they recruited him. It was 1975, and Scheer was general manager of the Denver Nuggets, one of the strongest teams in the American Basketball Association, an upstart rival of the NBA.

Thompson had been the Number One draft pick in both leagues, and the Nuggets were in a bidding war with the Atlanta Hawks. Scheer was determined to win, for he saw David Thompson as the future of the franchise. He signed Monte Towe, Thompson's closest friend at N.C. State, and then flew Thompson to Denver for a playoff game with the Indiana Pacers.

"It was at the old downtown auditorium," says Scheer. "There were sixty-nine-hundred people, a full house, and when we introduced David, there was a tremendous, thunderous standing ovation. Looking back, we recruited him pretty much the way you would a college player. We made sure he felt comfortable, that he saw what a young and vibrant community Denver was. It was yuppie before that was a word, and David liked that—obviously, he liked it a lot as things turned out.

"Denver was into the drug culture, partying. We didn't really know the extent of it at the time—I was as ignorant about drugs as anyone could be—but we exposed David to all that."

Thompson's career was brilliant at first. He was named rookie of the year in 1975-76, was an NBA all-star in his second season (after the two leagues had merged), and after his third, when he once scored 73 points in a single game, he signed an unprecedented contract.

"Four million dollars over five years," he remembers. "The highest contract a basketball player had ever received until that time."

But the seeds of catastrophe were already sown. Three years earlier, during the ABA playoffs in Thompson's first season, when the Nuggets were playing the New York Nets, Thompson and several other players returned to their Long Island hotel. The season had been long —more games than he had played his whole time in college.

"I said to another player, 'I'm mentally and physically tired,'" he remembers. "He said to me, 'I've got just the thing.' He poured out a couple of lines of white powder. I tried it and I liked it. I didn't feel tired anymore.

"That powder was cocaine."

By 1978, Thompson had become a daily user, but he scoffed at the danger.

"I remember," says Tommy Burleson, "the first time he admitted to me he was doing cocaine. It was probably 1978. He said, 'It's no big deal.' He said he would not get hooked. I said, 'Don't let it get out of hand.'"

Gradually, however, people close to Thompson began to notice a change—particularly during his fourth year in Denver, when there were new faces on the team and he was unhappy. Bobby Jones was gone, a quiet and unselfish player who liked Thompson and worked well with him. Jones had been traded for George McGinnis, a flashy, high-scoring forward, and suddenly, there were too many scorers—Thompson, McGinnis, Dan Issel. When Thompson's average began to dip, he says he felt new pressure from his coach, Larry Brown.

"They expected me to score more, but we had more scorers. The team started slow, and I was getting a lot of blame."

All of that added a certain edge to the more generic pressures of the NBA: the seven-month seasons, with four or five games a week and endless afternoons with nothing to do.

In that climate, Thompson says, it wasn't long before drugs began to dominate his life. "I lived to use, and used to live," he remembers. He tried free-basing—smoking cocaine instead of sniffing it—on a 1979 road trip to Portland. Soon, with more and more of the stimulant surging through his system, he began to drink more, relying on alcohol as a chemical ballast to bring himself down.

Carl Scheer began to hear reports that Thompson had a problem, and he remembers at first that he refused to believe it.

"But all the characteristics of drug use were there," he says. "Classic stuff. Erratic behavior. He became very injury-prone, very paranoid, thinking everyone was against him. There were chronic absences from practice. I'd confront him. He would look me square in the eye and deny it. There was never a time when he admitted doing drugs, ever.

"During that time, David hurt me probably as much as any single person. He lied, cheated, all the things that drug abusers do. And yet, through it all, there was something about him—a sense of character and goodness, a kindness that made him different."

Thus it was painful to Scheer when he decided, finally in 1982-83, to trade Thompson to the Seattle Supersonics. For Thompson, the trade left him feeling alone and cut off from his friends in the game—"I'm not that outgoing anyway," he says—and his drug use escalated.

Frequently, he remembers, he would go to a hotel room alone, "and I would use drugs until I got enough." He says he was spending $2,000 a week on his habit.

Thompson had a family by then—a wife and two young daughters he began to neglect. Cathy Thompson, whom he had met in Raleigh and married in Denver, tried with increasing desperation to get him into treatment.

In 1983, he succumbed to her pleadings. But even though he stopped using cocaine for a while, he continued to drink.

"A drug is a drug is a drug," he says today.

A few months later, the Seattle Supersonics took a road trip east, and after losing four straight games, Thompson and several of his teammates took a bus one night from Philadelphia. They wound up at Studio 54, a dark and cavernous disco in midtown Manhattan. As Thompson remembers it, he was talking to a woman about 4:30 a.m., when a man he didn't know came up and shoved him. In the scuffle that followed, they fell down a flight of stairs and the man's weight landed on Thompson's left knee, tearing the ligaments.

"It was a career-ending injury," he says. "I went into a deep depression—and back into drugs."

Problems soon followed with the IRS, and the tension grew at home. Finally, one day in the spring of 1986, Thompson and his wife began to argue, and in a moment he regrets as much as any in his life, he hit her.

"When you're on drugs," he says, "you lose your ability to control your emotions.... It's something I have to live with. It happened."

Thompson was charged with simple assault, and sentenced to six months' probation. But he violated the terms, failing to report for counseling sessions, and in 1987, spent four months in a Seattle jail. He began to take stock: he was broke (he had 41 creditors and owed the IRS more than $800,000); his career was over, and his marriage in ruins.

A lot of people gave up on him then, and even those who didn't were discouraged. His high school coach, Ed Peeler, remembers writing letters that went unanswered, and some of his closest friends worried that the tragedy was irreversible—that a handsome young hero, decent and flawed, had fallen so completely that the wreckage of his life was beyond all repair.

One exception was Tommy Burleson, who told one reporter in 1987: "David will be all right if he just comes home to North Carolina. We love him here. He needs to come back to where people care...."

He did come back, at Christmas of 1987. He returned to live with his parents in Shelby, taking a room in a house he had built them, and gradually he began to feel a new sense of purpose. His father pointed out passages in the Book of Job, stories about suffering, and urged him to look for a basketball job.

David was beginning his search when Carl Scheer called. There were still some wounds left over from Denver, but Scheer was now general manager of the new Charlotte Hornets, and somehow he couldn't get Thompson off his mind.

"When you love someone fiercely," he said, "you can be disappointed. But we go way back. We have a lot invested."

So they met for lunch in the summer of 1988, and after a cordial conversation, Scheer promised to talk to Hornets principal owner George Shinn. Shinn was skeptical. He was an image-conscious, self-made millionaire, not quite accepted by Charlotte's elite, and he worried about the response to Thompson's problems. Nevertheless, at Sheer's urging, he invited Thompson to sit with him at a pre-season game.

He was astonished at the public reaction.

"People lined up for autographs," Shinn remembers. "Parents sent their kids down. It was amazing, a real confidence builder for me, because I had been bogged down in the negatives. So we met again and talked about his problems. I was blunt and open. I asked him how he got started with drugs. I asked him about his wife.

"I told him I wouldn't create a job for him, but I wanted somebody to speak to young people, to encourage them to stay in school and stay away from drugs....

"I said, 'David, if I knew that you would never use drugs again,

177

ever, even though I've never heard you speak, I would hire you today.' He told me he knew it could be a last chance for him, and then he said, 'Mr. Shinn, I won't let you down.'"

So Shinn decided to take a risk, though he knew there would be pressures in Thompson's new public role—the hero-worship beginning once again. And that's how it's been. At appearance after appearance, people have risen to declare: "We are fortunate to have David's courage in our community. He has been a hero for fifteen years and still counting."

The adulation is true as far as it goes. There is courage involved in David Thompson's recovery. But it's also true that however honest the telling of his story, and however beneficial to the people who hear it, he is still a young man on a desperate mission. At the age of 34, he is trying to save his own life. Death or insanity, he says, are the only alternatives to staying free of drugs.

Nevertheless, there are times when Thompson's friends worry. On October 1, 1988, he was involved in an early morning incident in his hometown of Shelby. He told police he had been hanging out with friends when he became involved in an argument, and someone—he said he didn't know who—approached him from behind and hit him with a stick on the side of the left eye.

There was no indication that drugs were involved, but Hornets officials were concerned—particularly by the time the incident occurred, which police reports listed as 3:15 a.m.

"It scared me to death," Shinn says.

A few weeks later, Thompson went back into treatment—not for drugs this time, but because he had developed a new craving for beer. Soon, however, he returned to his job—more committed than ever, he said, to recovery.

But he knows the pressure comes in many forms—the weight of the latest version of the David Thompson myth, the strains of a continuing separation from his wife, the hectic pace of his job and the monotony of telling his story again and again.

"But I'm stronger today," he declares. "I know what I have to do....This job is a start, a foot in the door. It's helping me. Still, I'd like to get more into the basketball end. I still love to get out there and play. At least I'd like to do a little scouting, maybe some assistant coaching down the road."

Shinn is aware of those ambitions, but he is also determined not to move too fast. "We'll take it one step at a time," he says.

But Shinn is nothing if not a dreamer himself, and he has thought about the symbolism of the David Thompson story—the terrible fall, for

example, at the Reynolds Coliseum, and how Thompson picked himself up and returned in triumph, weeping quietly while the fans stood
and cheered.

That, says Shinn, is how it could be in the rest of Thompson's life.
His story is now a warning, a parable of failure. But the day could come
when it's something much more: a reminder that after all the pain we
inflict, on ourselves and other people, the best that's within us can
somehow survive.

The choice, Shinn knows, is up to David Thompson.

*As this book goes to press, in 1996, Thompson is still work-
ing for George Shinn and the Charlotte Hornets, and from all
accounts is still free of drugs. He has been elected to the Basketball Hall of Fame.*

A Moment of Hope

In 1988, I covered the Democrat National Convention in Atlanta, and one of the real pleasures was writing about the Congressman who served as the host. John Lewis was a pupil of Martin Luther King's, shaped forever by the civil rights movement, proud of the things they had managed to achieve, but worried in the climate of the 1980s that something precious was about to be lost. Lewis said he was looking for hope, and he found a glimmer in the 1988 meeting of his party—a foreshadowing, perhaps, of better days ahead.

The Charlotte Observer
1988

The carriage made its way slowly through the oak-lined streets, past the great Victorian houses, with their spreading front porches and carefully trimmed lawns, and on this particular day, so full of promise and so full of dread, Congressman John Lewis couldn't help but smile.

There he was in his gleaming white suit, waving at the people who had turned out to see him—and these were white people, cheering as he passed, clapping, grinning, shouting out his name.

Sometimes on such occasions, Lewis' mind ranges back to a very different time—to the day in 1961, when he was 21 and a group of white boys in the South Carolina town of Rock Hill knocked him to the ground outside the bus station.

Or he will remember the day in March nearly five years later, when he stood at the foot of the Edmund Pettus Bridge, his hands thrust stoically into the pockets of his coat, while a phalanx of deputies in Selma, Ala., nudged their horses from a trot to a gallop and began to swing their nightsticks at his head.

Lewis was an activist in the 1960s, a young black leader in the sit-in movement, a freedom rider, a founder and chairman of the Student

Non-Violent Coordinating Committee (SNCC). He lacked the charisma of his mentor, Dr. Martin Luther King Jr., but nobody questioned the depth of his courage—or his passionate commitment to the cause of civil rights.

But many things had changed since the 1960s. Now 48, Lewis was balder, plumper, and for the past two years, a member of the U.S. House of Representatives. And on this particular Sunday, July 17, 1988, the Democratic convention was about to begin in his district.

Already, he enjoyed his cheerful duties as host—this parade, for example, through a prosperous neighborhood near downtown Atlanta, where the residents were among his most loyal supporters. But if their affection made him smile, Lewis was also troubled by the week that lay ahead. He believed in the claims of the Democrat Party—that it embodied the promise of a more inclusive nation, one that grew stronger as the dream expanded to make way for more people.

He didn't like to brag, but in many ways, he often thought to himself, his own life embodied that truth. It was a long way from Selma to the U.S. Congress, and as far as he was concerned, the nation was better for it, just as he was.

But Lewis also believed that those kinds of changes—all the racial progress that began in the '50s—had been on hold for the past eight years, stalled by the priorities of the Republicans in power. And if the Democrats now had a chance to retake the White House, Lewis feared the opportunity might suddenly come apart.

The party's standard-bearer, Michael Dukakis, had offended Jesse Jackson and his legions of black followers, not only by choosing Sen. Lloyd Bentsen instead of Jackson to be his running mate, but also by allowing Jackson to learn the news from the press. Lewis had supported Jackson in his run for the presidency, and he could sympathize with the hurt, the feeling of insult. And yet he also believed that the issue was much bigger than one man's pride.

"The election," he said, as the convention was about to open. "That's what's at stake. Jesse and his followers need to understand that. They need to support the decision of Governor Dukakis."

In Lewis' mind, the whole episode was a critical test of the political maturity of black America, or at least of its most visible and charismatic leader—for there was no entitlement in Jesse Jackson's run for higher office. He was simply one more competitor in the field, and that was how it should be. That was the chance they had fought for in the civil rights years.

Jackson had handled himself well in the months of campaigning. But he had also lost, and the time had come to accept the verdict with grace.

Lewis had no way of knowing, for the signals were mixed just before the convention, that within the next several days, Jackson would pass his personal test of leadership. He would find a way to make peace with Michael Dukakis, and four days later, they would all participate in a scene more exciting, more full of promise, than anything they had witnessed in 25 years.

John Lewis was born in Pike County, Alabama, rolling farm country near the little town of Troy. He was the third of 10 children in a deeply religious family, and he still remembers the family picnics at the Macedonia Baptist Church: the uncles and cousins coming in from all over, from Florida or Detroit or Buffalo, N.Y., wherever they had gone in search of opportunity, coming back every summer to the rutted dirt roads of the Alabama black belt. There was something about the place that made it seem like home, despite the racial order of the 1940s.

"It was a community," says Lewis. "We had a hundred and ten acres with a small stream of water. In nineteen-forty-four, my father had bought it for three hundred dollars. We raised cotton and corn and a garden of tomatoes—pounds and pounds that we gave away or sold.

"As for myself, I fell in love with raising chickens. It gave me a sense of caring for living things. When my mother or father wanted to kill one, or sell it, I would protest. I think it was my first non-violent protest. This may sound silly, but I grew up with the idea of becoming a minister, and I would practice my sermons on the chickens. When a chicken would die, we would have a chicken funeral."

Lewis smiles when he tells such stories, but he knows that however strange and out of proportion they sound, those feelings he developed on an Alabama farm—that radicalized reverence for the gift of life —only grew deeper as the years went by.

When he turned 17, he went away to a small black seminary in Nashville, where he began attending workshops on the philosophy of non-violence. Already, his imagination had been stirred by the early skirmishes of the civil rights movement—the Montgomery bus boycott, among others—and he began to sense a different set of possibilities of America.

With his mentors in Nashville—a black Methodist minister by the name of Jim Lawson, a white Southern Baptist by the name of Will Campbell—and later in conversations with Martin Luther King, Lewis began to reflect on a heady idea: The task, he thought, was not simply to destroy the old institutions of segregation, though that destruction

182

was crucial. But the necessity was to build something better in its place, "a beloved community," Lewis liked to say, where people black and white could respect each other as fellow children of God.

"If you accepted that goal," Lewis says today, "you also had to accept the idea that means and ends were inseparable. The methods had to be consistent with the goal, and so there could be no room for bitterness or hate, no matter what the provocation. It was not a struggle against people, but against custom, against tradition, against a system."

The struggle took some nasty turns over the next several years. In 1961, when Lewis joined the Freedom Rides—a series of integrated bus trips through the South—he was attacked by a gang of toughs in Rock Hill, left unconscious by a mob in Montgomery and jailed for approximately a month in Mississippi.

If those occasions were a test of his faith in nonviolence, a test that he found easier and easier to pass, there were other shining moments when his faith was affirmed, when the movement assumed the status of a holy crusade. On Aug. 28, 1963, Lewis was one of the key speakers at the March on Washington—and though he was overshadowed by the eloquence of Martin Luther King, he didn't mind. To hear King's words...I have a dream today...and to see them cheered by 200,000 people—those were experiences he regarded as a gift, a priceless recollection to be carried through the years.

There were times, however, in the next quarter century when he doubted that he would feel such emotions again.

King was murdered only five years later, and with his death the non-violent movement suddenly lost its center. Black power was on the rise, with its intermingled messages of bitterness and pride, and Lewis began to worry about the direction of the country.

And there was something else as well. For the followers of King, the murder in Memphis raised a disconcerting question: What did they do now?

For years, their egos and ambitions had been subservient to King's, and when there were conflicts, King's presence—his unchallenged ability to evoke a sense of mission—made the rivalries much easier to resolve. But now a whole galaxy of bright young leaders, Andrew Young and John Lewis, Jesse Jackson and Julian Bond, faced the necessity and opportunity of charting their own futures.

Many of them, as it happened, lived in Atlanta, a city where blacks began to seize political power in the 1970s, and in the emerging rough and tumble of that expanded opportunity, it was only a matter of time until their ambitions collided.

John Lewis was determined to keep the collisions to a minimum, and he succeeded pretty well through the '70s, when he worked to register black voters in the South and spent a few years in the Carter administration. And even in the early 1980s, when he ran and was elected to the Atlanta city council, he avoided serious conflict with his old friends in the movement.

Many years earlier, he had urged Julian Bond—one of his closest friends from the early days of SNCC—to run for Congress. "After the death of Martin Luther King and Robert Kennedy, you arose as the political leader of many," he wrote to Bond in 1969. "Your presence filled a vacuum...."

But Bond, a reluctant hero at best in those years, ignored such urgings until the congressional election of 1986. By then, Lewis himself had decided to run, and the two old friends squared off.

In many ways, it was a classic confrontation. Bond was the favorite —polished, urbane, articulate, intellectual—while Lewis was the hard-charging underdog, a politician whose subjects and verbs didn't always agree, and whose accents revealed his deep Southern origins.

"A work horse, not a show horse."

That became the slogan of the Lewis campaign, and Julian Bond found it both irritating and cheap. But the most bitter moment came in the runoff, when Bond questioned the propriety of a donation to the Lewis campaign, and Lewis—angry at what he regarded as a slur at his integrity—challenged Bond to take a drug test on the spot.

When Bond refused, citing his right to privacy, his campaign never recovered. Lewis was elected, and a friendship was dead.

It was an ugly campaign, and Lewis has brooded about it in the months since then, wondering sometimes if that's what the movement was about—a chance for blacks to play politics as usual.

For the most part, however, he settled the issue by plunging into his work, doing all the little things that congressmen do, chasing down errant Social Security checks, trying to secure federal grants for his district, and also debating the great issues of the day.

"I love it, really," he said on the eve of the Democrat convention. "I guess I sort of feed on it. You go home every week, attend three or four town meetings. The people sort of keep you going. It's different from leading a march from Selma to Montgomery, or taking a seat near the front of a bus. But to me, I really feel that this is a calling."

Still, he continued to be concerned about the country, about what he saw as a moral malaise, too much greed and shallow patriotism, disconnected from a vision of real national greatness. But then came the presidential campaign of 1988 and the astonishing ability of Jesse

Jackson to shape the debate—to imbue it with the spirit of the civil rights movement. Jackson talked not only about the poor, but about a national feeling of community: America as a quilt of interwoven pieces.

For John Lewis, it recalled the old dreams they had forged back in Nashville, "the beloved community," as he had called it then, and he was pleased and stirred as Michael Dukakis borrowed many of the themes.

There were some days of tension just before the convention, when divisions once again began to threaten the party. But Jackson and Dukakis managed to settle their differences, and Lewis was there that triumphant Thursday night, when Dukakis accepted the presidential nomination and called party leaders forward—black and white—to share in the moment.

Lewis knew that such scenes are political theater, staged inevitably at every convention. But ho couldn't escape the feeling that this one was different.

"I kept thinking about the March on Washington," he said when it was over. "This was a different time, a different setting. But there was the same feeling of coming together, the same solidarity around an idea that is right. For me, the whole convention had a kind of soul. To see the delegations from Mississippi and Alabama, black and white, and to listen to the things that were being said—the feeling that all of us were in it together—it was something I hadn't felt for many years."

He knew, of course, that it was a long march to November, when the odds still favored a Republican victory, a triumph of selfishness and fear, instead of the alternative his own party offered. Somewhere inside, he knew that was true, but perhaps they were seeing the beginnings of a change. At least for now, he admitted to himself, after all the ups and downs of the past quarter century, he couldn't resist the lure of a moment of pure hope.

The Dreams of Gilbert Blue

Of all the grass roots leaders I've known, few have impressed me more than Gilbert Blue, a 20th century chief of the Catawba Indians who succeeded where all of his predecessors failed—leading a crusade to recover lost land.

Creative Loafing
1994

A part of him dreaded the whole enterprise, when the phones would ring and the reporters descended and the doubters and critics seemed to be everywhere. Gilbert Blue is a gentle man, a machinist by trade, not much given to controversy or acclaim. But he has endured his share of both for 20 years, and it pleases him now, in those scattered moments when he's able to think about it, that his ordeal, at last, appears to be at an end.

Blue is chief of the Catawba Indians, a proud and tattered band that has dwindled with the years. But now the Catawbas are full of hope. They have settled a claim for their ancestral lands that goes back nearly to the beginning of the country—a settlement that will bring them $50 million for education, development and the acquisition of land. Their status as a tribe has been reacknowledged, and as many as 3,000 Catawbas, many of them poor, will share in payments of more than $7 million.

To Gilbert Blue it was long overdue—the beginning of the story much more than the end, for now real progress is up to the tribe. But Blue is pleased, for despite his tenth-grade education, and a fear at the start that he was totally unprepared, he is beginning to understand what he's done—maybe more for his people than any other chief, at least in the years since the white man came. He is careful not to take the credit for it. He points to his lawyers and other members of the tribe, and he says that the victory is not his alone. But he will also tell you that the moment is sweet.

In 1973, when Blue became chief of the Catawba Nation, even his title had an ironic ring. The nation consisted of a single square mile—640 acres of pitted clay roads and barren-looking forests, a few mobile homes and some cramped frame houses just south of Rock Hill, South Carolina. It was such a pathetic remnant of the past, when the Catawbas roamed the forests and the broad river banks, raising their crops and hunting buffalo and deer.

They were the Iswa Catawba—the People of the River—and there were 16 towns scattered up and down the banks, sturdy and prosperous when the white man came. But the buffalo died or fled to the west, and the wars and the small pox took their toll, and in 1763 the Catawbas made a treaty. They gave up all but 144,000 acres just south of Charlotte in exchange for guarantees against further encroachment. But the whites kept coming, kept seizing the land, and in 1840 the Catawbas tried again to make a deal. They met at Nations Ford on the banks of their river, sitting down with officials from South Carolina and renouncing their title to 144,000 acres in exchange for the promise of a new reservation. The agreement was never ratified by Congress, and no new reservation was established—just a single square mile within the land they had lost.

There was a time when Gilbert Blue didn't worry about it. He has his own life to lead after all, and what could he do? Since the 1880s, the tribe had battled for a return of the land, and every generation in the struggle had failed. But in the 1960s, Blue came home from a stint in the Navy, having sampled the cultures of China, Australia and the Philippines, and he was beginning to think a little more about his own. He remembered his grandfather, Samuel Taylor Blue, a slender man about 6-foot-1, with high cheekbones and jet black hair. The elder Blue was also a chief and a steadfast believer in Indian identity. He still spoke the language, and he would take his grandson on walks through the woods, talking to him earnestly about the traditions of his people, trying to pass along what it means to be Catawba.

He talked about the land and the feeling for a place, and a sense of being a part of the history of a people. By the time Gilbert Blue returned from the Navy he found himself stirred by the old man's stories, and he was beginning to wear the outward symbols of his pride—a beaded necklace, an Indian-head tatoo on his arm.

He knew that some of the Catawbas were making it. A few at least had gone off to college and were building good lives for themselves and their families. But far too many of the others were drifting, caught in the poverty of the rural South without any sense of identity to sustain them. Blue was determined to do something about it, and in the years immediately after his election as chief, he found himself thinking about a claim to the land.

"Our people," he declared, "would never have been in poverty if we had had our land."

It was about that time that he met Don Miller, a lawyer for the Native American Rights Fund, a public interest firm in Boulder, Colorado. Miller was energetic and capable, and he had helped represent the Penobscot Indians in asserting their claim to two-thirds of Maine—a claim that was settled for $37 million. After studying the issue for the better part of a year, Miller told Blue that the Catawbas had a case.

In 1976, they made an announcement: the tribe would pursue its claim to the land—144,000 acres, much of it prime York County real estate, chunks of cities and subdivisions and farms. Blue did his best to set a tone of moderation. "We are not being radical," he told one reporter. "We are not going to take developed land, shopping centers. That's not our intention. We are not going to get condemnation rights. People who own the land now bought it in good faith. We are not trying to push anybody out.... But the land is rightfully ours, and we are going to negotiate for the best settlement we can get."

Despite Blue's attempts at reassurance, the Catawba claim cast a pall over York County development. Land titles suddenly had "Catawba exceptions"—stipulations, in effect, that the titles might not apply if the Indians won their case.

It was then that the torrent of opposition began. Whites organized to battle the claim, which was no surprise. What stunned Gilbert Blue was that some of the Catawbas began to fight him too. They agreed, to be sure, that the tribe had been wronged, but lacking Blue's interest in identity and land, they simply wanted money as a salve for the wounds. There was logic in their preference, of course. Many of these Catawbas were poor, and they had little patience with the dreams of Gilbert Blue —all his talk about a new reservation and restoring the spiritual identity of a people.

At first, Blue simply defended his position. "I, for one," he said in 1978, "am not going to sell my heritage for any amount. We deserve something as a people, not as individuals. I think the Catawba Nation has been wronged. Not Gilbert Blue individually."

But the anti-Blue forces were gaining momentum, and in the end he was forced to compromise—pledging to seek cash payments to individuals, as well as land for a larger reservation and additional federal money for tribal development.

The Catawbas came together around that position, but almost immediately, their case began to go badly in the courts. It was clear that the federal judge was hostile, and there were times when the tribe seemed likely to lose. Blue grew so discouraged at one point that he told Don Miller he was tempted to quit. The whole ordeal was simply too much. He could see his hair turning gray, and the lines on his face were getting deeper all the time, and his teenaged children were growing up without him. Let somebody else take the heat for awhile.

But in the end, of course, he did not quit. "I kept thinking about my people," he says, and he was bolstered also by his Mormon faith, a conviction that God was not really indifferent. All of it fit with his Indian's sense of time, a belief in the cyclical nature of history. For more than 300 years, his people had been caught on the cycle's down side, their homeland vanishing, their identity slowly beginning to fade. But it's all an eyeblink in the great sweep of history, and Blue was convinced that their time would come again.

Now, apparently, it has, and the turning point came in a curious way—with what appeared at first to be a piece of bad news. U.S. District Judge Joseph Wilson, who seemed to rule against the tribe every chance he got, rejecting their position at nearly every procedural point in the case, ruled in 1991 that the Catawbas were not eligible to file a class action lawsuit. The issue had been hanging for more than a decade, and Wilson's ruling left the Catawbas little choice. To prevail in their claim, they would have to sue every white landowner in the area —all 61,767 of them. Most observers assumed that it couldn't be done, or wouldn't be, for the expense alone was almost prohibitive. But the Catawbas and their lawyers decided to try it.

The word quickly spread around York County. The Catawbas were filing more than 60,000 lawsuits, and as soon as it happened the effect would be chaos—gridlock in the courts and a terrifying freeze in the real estate market. Suddenly, state officials, who had shown little interest in a political settlement, were eager to see if anything could be arranged. Led by U.S. Rep. John Spratt, a team of state and federal negotiators began meeting regularly with the Catawba leadership, and the result in 1994 was a Catawba land settlement. It was a sweeping agreement in which the tribe received much of what it was seeking: an expanded reservation, and modest cash payments for individual Catawbas, and $50 million for development and education. In return, the Indians renounced further claim to the land.

Now Gilbert Blue's imagination could soar. He could picture a museum and a replica of an ancient Catawba village on the river; an industrial park with job possibilities for the Catawbas and their neighbors, and maybe a campground for tourists in the area. Many white

189

leaders, too, are pleased, relieved by the settlement and stirred by the possibilities of tourism and progress.

But whatever happens now, Blue says somebody else will have to do it. He is tired. He plans to step aside before too long, as soon as the tribe has a new constitution. Now 60 years old, he says he wants more time with his family—a luxury he hasn't enjoyed in quite a while.

"My children are all grown up," he explained. "They missed out on a lot. But I don't think I would change it if I could. I was poorly equipped to represent my people, and yet we were trying to do something honorable. Nothing will replace the loss of our lands, but this settlement is a tool. If we make some good economic decisions, I think that our people will be all right."

Pride and Prejudice

One of the most eloquent comentators on the South is a friend and fellow Alabamian, Dr. C. Eric Lincoln. After a long career of brilliant scholarship, he published a novel in 1988, a 30-year labor of love called, The Avenue, Clayton City. *This is the story of a writer and his work.*

Southern Voices
1991

Blind Bates began to caress the strings of his battered old guitar.... This time he was playing for love. Love for a woman he had never seen, but whose love he had known not only through the meals she had fixed for him, or the shirts she had patched, but through the sharing of her time, her wisdom and her compassion.

Tears flowed from beneath the dark glasses covering his sightless eyes as he riffed the steel strings with the glass bottleneck on his little finger and launched into a song he had written in his mind for Mama Lucy. It was a sad, lonesome song.

Train done gone
Train done gone

The funeral scene stays with you for a while. The prose itself is haunting in its rhythms—elegant in its cadence and its vivid word pictures—as C. Eric Lincoln describes the little church, hot and crowded and overflowing with grief.

A leading black citizen has died, a matriarch of tenderness and strength, and her funeral was, as Lincoln writes, "an occasion licensed by the whole community to break down—to scream and to shout, to moan and to weep, to engage in the delirium of temporary relief from sadness, from fear, from hatred and frustration.... All in the name and the presence of God."

Lincoln is a scholar by trade, a professor of religion at Duke University, author of 19 works of nonfiction, but never a novel until 1988. Then, however, with the publication of *The Avenue, Clayton City*, he established his place in the front ranks of black writers.

The book was an alternate selection of the Literary Guild, with a large first printing of about 25,000. Paperback and movie rights were already sold at the time of publication, and critics called it a "masterpiece."

Lincoln says he worked on the novel for more than 30 years, writing a chapter here and there and then putting it aside, and for much longer than that he has carried the stories and the characters in his head—the prototypes of life in the black rural South.

He knows the story firsthand. He was born in Alabama in 1924, coming of age in the little town of Athens, in the cotton country near the Tennessee line. He found bits and pieces of heroism there, traces of nobility during a time of segregation. But mostly what he saw—the enduring image that takes shape in his novel—was the crazy futility of life in those times, the lost and squandered dignity among his neighbors black and white.

Lincoln was raised by his grandparents. His mother went away when he was four. She married a preacher and moved off to Pittsburgh, leaving her son in the care of Less and Mattie Lincoln.

Mattie worked for white families as a cook and a maid, and in many ways, ruled her own family with a kind of ferocious generosity—quick to punish a misbehaving child, but ready to go to war if they were ever abused. "She taught us," Eric Lincoln remembers, "You got to respect everybody respectable"—for that was the only way you could expect the same treatment.

Less Lincoln, meanwhile, was a farmer. He did odd jobs for white people on the side, but his passion—his calling—was tilling his own fields: three acres of cotton behind his wood frame house. He was a gentle man, his grandson remembers, dignified, with iron gray hair that was tight and springy to young Eric's touch, and the two of them were great friends. They would sit around the fire on many a Sunday evening, roasting sweet potatoes on the hearth while Mattie was off at church.

For Lincoln, such memories are mingled with those of deprivation —the six-room house so cold some nights that ice formed on the floor —and also of cruelty, an ever-present possibility in a time of white supremacy.

"My experiences with white people were varied," he says. "I played with white kids and loved some of them. It was not unusual for poor whites and blacks to eat together, to hunt and fish together, whore together.... Yet there was supposed to have been a hatred. I didn't see much of that, but then, I wasn't looking. I do remember one time that I was cheated and kicked in the head, for the reason that I unwittingly challenged a white man.

"I was thirteen or fourteen. My grandfather was on his deathbed. There was no food in the house, no fire in the house, no money in the house. My grandmother and I went out to the fields where the cotton had already been picked, not only our fields but those nearby, and we pulled the only bolls that were left."

That night, he says, they picked the cotton from the bolls and put it in a bag, and the next morning, Eric put it in a wheelbarrow and took it to the gin. It was 7 a.m. when he arrived, and the owner, Mr. Beasley, was sitting on the porch.

"Whatcha got there, boy?" he said.

"Cotton, sir."

"Well, dump it out."

So they put it on the scales, and the weight came to 40 pounds, and young Eric made a quick calculation: At nine cents a pound, that would mean $3.60 for food, firewood and other family necessities. He was startled, therefore, when the white man casually flipped him a quarter.

"Mr. Beasley," he said, after a long hesitation, "I think you made a mistake."

Beasley's face turned red, and he got up abruptly and bolted the door. At first, the boy was merely puzzled. But then he found himself gasping, his lungs suddenly empty from a blow to the midsection, as the white man began to kick him and stomp at his head.

"He was in a frenzy," Lincoln remembers, "and I'll never forget his words: 'Nigger, as long as you live, don't you never try to count behind no white man again!'"

There are times, for Lincoln, when that story comes hard—when he tells it with such emotion that he has to stop for a moment and wipe the tears from his large, expressive eyes.

But there are other stories, too, he says—other experiences with white people of a very different kind. One man, for example, a high school principal named J.T. Wright, praised and encouraged Lincoln's gift as a writer, and lent him $50 so he could go off to college.

"I was fourteen," Lincoln remembers. "I had just graduated from high school in May of nineteen-thirty-nine, and I had an uncle in Rockford, Illinois, who worked at what he called an 'auto laundry'—a car wash, we would call it today. I was going to go there and take a job, and the principal, Mr. Wright, loaned me some money and said, 'C. Eric,

193

while you're up that way, stop on by the University of Chicago.'"

Lincoln did and eventually emerged with a divinity degree. But there were some stops in between his enrollment and graduation—a couple of years in the Navy, several more at a black college in Memphis, and a strange and singular job opportunity one summer that caused him to travel extensively across the South.

He became secretary and road manager to a Negro League baseball team, the Birmingham Black Barons. It was an outstanding collection of talent, he remembers (among its players was an Alabama teenager by the name of Willie Mays), and as Lincoln handled the team's financial affairs, renting stadiums, negotiating with the management of the teams they were playing, he got to know the South in a way that stayed with him.

Every town, it seemed, was remarkably the same. Despite some colorful differences in detail, each had a similar cast of characters: a wise man, a fool, a chief bootlegger, a white patriarch. They were prototypes, and they provided, for Lincoln, the images and building blocks of a novel about the South.

Not right away, however, for his major energies were soon channeled into scholarship. He taught over the next 30 years at Clark College in Atlanta and Fisk University in Nashville, at Columbia University and Union Theological Seminary in New York, before finally coming to Duke in 1976. His best-known books during that time were *The Black Muslims in America* and *The Negro Pilgrimage in America*, which together sold more than a million copies.

But he also worked now and then on his novel, and in 1987 sent the manuscript to his friend Alex Haley, seeking a critique. The response was encouraging:

"C. Eric," Haley wrote back, "you can write your ass off! Ain't nothing wrong with this manuscript except that you wrote it instead of me."

When the book appeared a few months later, Lincoln was braced for mixed reviews. The prose and the passion made it easy to read, but the structure of it was unorthodox. Each of the 10 chapters was a self-contained story, and though some characters appear more than once, the chapters are connected more by theme than plot. They read almost like a collection of short stories that together produce a powerful portrait of a place.

In addition to that departure from the standard form, Lincoln knew the novel might offend. It is as unflinching in its portrayal of blacks as it is of whites, for the people of the Avenue in Lincoln's Clayton City are not always admirable, or even sympathetic.

There are some heroes—Mama Lucy, based loosely on Lincoln's

grandmother, or Roger McClain, a white educator who resembles the real-life principal at Lincoln's high school. But there are also petty criminals and assorted other hustlers whose choices are self-centered and sometimes disastrous, and who only add to the debasement that white supremacy has produced.

Most of the characters, meanwhile, are somewhere in between, well-intentioned sometimes, but fundamentally bewildered, trying to survive the vagaries of the South as it was. And then there are one or two who decide to fight back, to take their own fateful stands against the order of the day.

One of those is Dr. Walter Pinkney Tait, an enigmatic black physician who had a profitable practice, a position of prominence among Clayton City's blacks, and who had even grown accustomed to a certain respect among whites. Still, he hated segregation and the slow death of the spirit it inevitably produced, and he decided one day that he had had enough.

His decision took the form of a simple act of defiance, the refusal to obey the desperate order of a white man—a prominent citizen who was addicted to drugs and who wanted the black doctor to give him a shot. Tait refused, not because what was being asked would violate his principles, but because he was simply tired of the way things were, including his own life.

"If the canvas is rotten to begin with," he thought to himself, "no matter what you paint on it, the colors will run and the texture will blister."

Tait knew his decision, at the least, would cost him his practice and maybe get him killed. But he also knew that the time had come.

All his life he had tried to walk the thin, wavering line between what it took to live in the white man's world and what it took to hold on to some semblance of self-respect, but he had never been so blunt with any white man before.

Often, when his dignity was cornered, he had resorted to professional jargon to say what he would never say in plain speech, but never before had he had the temerity to look a white man—not just some poor cracker, but The Man himself—squarely in the eye and tell him precisely what he wanted him to know. It was a good feeling—a liberating feeling—and he felt no fear except for the fear of not being afraid....

He sat motionless in his swivel chair and watched the evening shadows blot the dying sunlight from the room.

The Last Patriarch

During the period described in the preceding chapter, my paternal grandfather in Mobile, Ala., presided as the patriarch of an old Southern family. Its members, for the most part, were genteel believers in the status quo, and my grandfather especially was eloquent and firm in defending that position. He believed in segregation and all the assumptions that went along with it, and proclaimed those views as often as he could. This is the story of his slow change of heart.

Lessons From The Big House
1994

By the 1950s, the accolades were routine for Palmer Gaillard, coming, it seemed, in every facet of his life. He was an old man now, fast emerging as an institution—an elder statesman in the life of Alabama, and a towering presence among the members of his family. Sometimes, in fact, he could be overwhelming. He lived with his daughters in the house he had purchased in 1903, a gift to Maddie, his wife, and their five young children. Neither Mary nor Flora Gaillard had ever married, choosing instead to remain with their father. Flora certainly had had her chances. She lived for awhile in New York City and had suitors there, which was not surprising. She was pretty enough to work as a model, and she must have been impressed with life in the cultural center of the country—the gaiety of it, and the intellectual zest. Flora was the oldest of the Gaillard siblings, and some people said she was also the brightest. She did well enough at Agnes Scott, then took her degree at Columbia University. She decided, however, to return to Mobile, and it was apparently a wrenching separation from her boyfriends.

"Dear Flora," one of them wrote, "I'm sorry it was to end like this, causing such anguish, but you were the one who refused to leave your father and the house. Forgive me...."

In the end her motivations were a mystery. Was there unspoken pressure from the old man himself, telling her without ever using the words that he wanted her to give up her life for his? Or did he simply allow her to do it? Flora never said. She seldom spoke of her New York days, or the things that might have been, settling instead into a life of routine. At eight every morning for the next 50 years, she made the one-block walk out the back gate of her house and up the narrow dirt lane to the schoolhouse. She was a third-grade teacher, dedicated and stern, and her beauty was now replaced with something else—a ferocious primness, some people said, that left her raging at the changes all around her. Her greatest nightmare was the civil rights movement, especially after September of 1957, when the president sent his soldiers to Little Rock, Arkansas, to oversee the desegregation of the schools. Flora had no sympathy for Elizabeth Eckford and the eight other black students who were threatened by the mobs outside of Central High. She remembered instead her father's bitter stories of Reconstruction and the changes enforced by an occupying army. Little Rock seemed like a deja vu.

She vowed it wouldn't happen in her classroom. If they sent any Negro third-graders to her, she would assign them to seats in the back of the room and never acknowledge their presence again. Sadly enough, the people who knew her understood that she meant it.

Mary was different. As the youngest in the family, she was softer somehow—not as pretty as her sister, though she held her own with her small round face and dangling curls. Later in life, she was short and plump and fond of puttering in the five-acre yard. She, too, was given to outbursts of temper, which subsided as abruptly and unpredictably as they came—and like Flora and her father, she was a fountain of stories about the Gaillard family, a keeper of the myth. Her versions, in fact, were probably the best, for she seemed to have no fear of embellishment. There were tales of Reconstruction and the Civil War, the American Revolution and the Southern frontier. Every account, of course, had a Gaillard hero, for as Mary understood it, the family honor had been steeled in the past—a nobility that only a Southerner could understand.

As she entered middle age, the family had emerged as the great love of her life—not so much the individuals who comprised it, for they were venerated, tolerated or despised, depending on which of her emotions they had earned. But their common ancestry was something to revere. It was a lesson she had learned from her patriarch father, and they spent many hours on the family genealogy—updating, refining, adding bits of commentary to the story.

197

They also worked to keep up the homeplace, which was now at the center of the family universe. The Big House itself had never looked better, with its gleaming white columns, rocking chairs on the porch, and grounds that were also stately and fine. There were grassy avenues leading in from the road, shaded by magnolias and live oak trees, and bamboo hedges growing down by the garden. A grape arbor formed a green shelter in back every spring, surrounded by the stands of blossoming pear trees and nestling figs, and the scent of sweet wisteria wafted from the woods. Mary Gaillard was the master of it all. She tended the grounds in the company of her father, who relished the exercise at the age of 95, and a gentle black man named Robert Croshon, who had worked for the Gaillards for most of his life. Robert seemed to enjoy his calling well enough, finding his peace and satisfaction in the soil, and if the pay was meager—$14 a week when he started—he nevertheless felt a kinship with the family. They had come to Mobile at the same time as his own, though the circumstances, of course, were not the same.

Robert's ancestors were runaway slaves. They had left their Georgia plantation one night, expecting to follow the Drinking Gourd north. But the Big Dipper was obscured by a sudden thunderstorm, and in the confusion they found themselves headed south. The escape was led by Gilbert Fields, Robert's great-grandfather. Gilbert was an African, apparently a proud and restless man, who fled with his wife, two daughters and a grandchild. One daughter was lost in the frantic escape, and never heard from again. But the others found a cave, probably somewhere near the Alabama line, where another runaway had built a house underground. He took them in and fed them, told them they could stay, but they decided to keep pushing south to Mobile, which in a way, was the next best thing to the North. The city was a haven for free Negroes. There were more than 1,000 in 1850, which was half the total for the state of Alabama. Their lives weren't easy. They had to report once a year to renew their papers, and it was a crime for them to congregate on the downtown streets or use "insulting" language toward whites. It was better, however, than being a slave, and Gilbert Fields found work at a church.

A half century later, his granddaughter Rachel, the child he had carried to freedom in the storm, became a cook for the Gaillard family. Her days often lasted for 15 hours, starting with breakfast at six a.m.—bacon and eggs, with grits and hot biscuits—then a midday meal for whoever was at home and another full dinner at six in the evening. Robert Croshon was Rachel's young cousin, and he soon began working for the Gaillards, too. By the 1950s, he was a fixture on the place,

198

working with Palmer in his garden, tilling the soil and putting in the seeds, beating back the invasions of insects and weeds. He knew the old man was a white supremacist, convinced of the superiority of his race, but to Robert at least, it didn't show in his manner. In fact, the old man was kind. There were many days when the chores were all done and they would sit together beside the rows of collards, the big-headed kind that grew knee-high, and they would talk about anything that came to mind—their families maybe, or the garden, or God.

"Robert," the old man told him more than once, speaking gravely in his deep baritone, almost as if he were delivering a speech, "you've been blessed with good ability. Don't let anybody think they are better."

Many years later, Robert told the story with appreciation, and smiled as others came flooding to his mind.

"We'd be working hard in the garden," he remembered, "and I'd be pushing that hand plow fast. Mr. Gaillard would say, 'Robert, take your time. You get there even if you don't hurry.'

"Another time, he asked me if I went to church. I said, 'Yes sir.' He said, 'Good. I don't think much of a man who doesn't go to church.'"

Through all of those years, and all the hard work and conversations, there was never any doubt about who was in charge. But the two sweated side by side, and Robert regarded the old man with affection.

"He was," he concluded, "a good, kind man."

The 1950s, however, were a troubled time in Alabama. Black Americans came home from World War II, having done their part in the fight against tyranny, and they expected a little more freedom for themselves. They had some allies now. When a group of black citizens in South Carolina, not far from the ancestral home of the Gaillards, went to court in the pursuit of better schools, they found some judges who were willing to listen. They asked for an end to segregated schools, and in 1954, having considered their case and four others like it, the U.S. Supreme Court ruled in their favor.

Palmer Gaillard understood the stakes, especially after 1955, when the contagion of hope among black Americans spread to Alabama, and a stubborn black woman named Rosa Parks refused to relinquish her seat on a bus. As Palmer saw clearly, the issue was not the bus system of Montgomery, or even the survival of segregated schools. This was an assault on the whole social order, much like the one he had seen in his youth. Palmer, once again, was determined to resist it. At the astonishing age of 102, he wrote an article for the journal of the Alabama Bar Association, decrying "the spirit of Thaddeus Stevens [which] may force upon us a second Reconstruction...."

He also raised the issue in his church, a forum he regarded as even more important. Palmer was known as a man of deep faith. Every night in the Big House, precisely at nine, he would take his place in the rocking chair by the hearth and thumb through the well-worn pages of his Bible, selecting the verses to be read aloud. The psalms were his favorites, those bits of poetry that were written by kings, but there were others also that were scattered through the Book—the words of the prophets and the Sermon on the Mount.

Palmer was an elder in the Presbyterian church, an office he had held for 65 years. But now in the final decade of his life there were troubling new divisions among the members of his church. Their minister, John Crowell, was a learned young man of stunning eloquence, with the kindest heart the old man had ever known. But he was one of a handful of Mobile ministers who preached a few sermons on the issue of race—calling essentially for an end to segregation. Palmer Gaillard didn't agree. He had grown accustomed to the Southern way of life, which seemed to resemble what God had intended, and many of his fellow church members concurred. And yet they were drawn to this brilliant young preacher, with his spellbinding words and a faith that was clearly a match for their own.

It was a dilemma that Palmer helped settle with grace. He made his own position known, writing a letter to the elders "with the prayer that my church and yours may be spared the results of...integration." He recalled his days as a Sunday School teacher at a church of former slaves, and expressed his pride that in the course of his long career as a lawyer, he had never lost a case "in representing a negro against a white man." But he also expressed his deepening fear that in the South and elsewhere, "a unity of Spirit is endangered in an effort to bring about a unity of the Flesh."

He understood that John Crowell disagreed. The minister regarded segregation as wrong—a patent affront to the dignity of black Americans—and the two of them argued about it some. Their disagreements, however, were civil and discreet. In public, to Crowell's everlasting amazement, the old man chose to back him every time.

Perhaps the most basic issue they faced was what to do on Sunday if a black person came to worship at the church. Would he be made welcome—or, as some in the congregation suggested, turned away in deference to the Southern way of life? To Crowell, of course, the answer was clear, but his stance drew fire from some people in the church, until the day the old man rose to speak. He was an amazing figure at the age of 99, nearly 6-feet-1, if a little bit stooped, with clothes that were beginning to sag on his frame. But his voice was strong, as he cleared his throat and proclaimed once again that the minister was

right. Even in the days of his ancestors, he said, slaves had been allowed to worship in the balconies. Surely today, they would not retreat
from the wisdom and generosity of their fathers. But more than that,
they should also remember that "our Lord looks not on the color of
skin, but on the quality of a man's heart and his character and soul."

It was a powerful performance, as it usually was when the old man
spoke—as if his words, somehow, should be inscribed on a tablet. And
yet it left John Crowell perplexed. This was clearly a man of integrity,
and the leap was so small from his professions of faith to a support for
the end of segregation in the South. But Palmer Gaillard resisted that
connection. Kindness was one thing, equality quite another, and he
continued writing letters for the rest of his life, arguing that integration
was a threat to both races—especially his own. He and John Crowell
continued to debate it, with no trace of progress, until the day in 1959
when Crowell got word that the old man was dying.

It was a day he had dreaded for more than a decade—the end of a
life so spirited and grand—and he drove out quickly to the house in
Spring Hill. Palmer was now 103, and he looked so fragile as he lay in
the bed, his breathing shallow and his skin ghost-white. He couldn't
have weighed more than a hundred pounds, and his voice when he
spoke was barely a whisper. The preacher took a seat on the side of
the bed and the old man slowly reached out his hand.

"Pastor..." he whispered, letting the word hang there as he gathered his breath. "I must tell you now, I see now that you were right."

There were just the two of them in the half-darkened room, where
the shadows fell softly on the old man's bed. He didn't say anything
after that, just shut his eyes as the preacher held his hand. The next
morning he was gone.

As the 1950s drew to a close, John Crowell thought often about
that confession, and it somehow gave him a reason to hope. Palmer
Gaillard was such a symbol of the South. He had lived through more
than half of its history, if you began counting time with the founding of
the country, and he had seen everything since the great Civil War—
the temporary upheavals of Reconstruction, and the eventual restoration of his family and his race. He was proud of the legacy he had
sought to pass on—that code of honor and generosity and kindness,
but in the clarity of those final moments of his life, he may have understood that it wasn't enough.

John Crowell thought so. And the question now for the American
South—confronted with the darker implications of its past—was whether
those still living could understand it as well.

Segregation on Sunday

The dream of racial integration in the South still beckons out there somewhere in the distance. The strange thing is, the church is often the last place to find it. Percy Reeves, the Charlotte minister whose church is profiled here, says he's wondered aloud many times: "What does that say about who we are?"

Creative Loafing
1996

For the first few months, he thought it would work. His life, after all, had prepared him for it—this "great experiment" in racial integration. On July 1, 1994, Percy Reeves was installed as the senior pastor at Plaza United Methodist Church. Reeves is black; the church at the time was mostly white—a Christian outpost in a changing neighborhood that didn't really care what the church had to offer. There were a few blacks who came through the doors, but for the most part the membership was declining.

Reeves was determined to turn things around—to reach out to blacks in the neighborhood around him and still serve the needs of the members who were white. Common sense told him it would not be easy, but his faith kept whispering a different kind of message. "In Christ Jesus," he declared in one of his sermons, "all barriers, all partitions come down. The closer you get to God, the closer you get to your brothers and sisters."

Now it's exactly two years later, and the phone is ringing in Percy Reeves' office. On the end of the line is a troubled young man from a black neighborhood who is waging his private war with cocaine. So far, he is losing. But Percy Reeves won't let him give up.

"Man," he says, "I love you to death."

His voice when he speaks is gentle and sure, the way you'd expect a preacher's to be when he's trying to reach out to somebody in trouble. It is clear from that conversation and others that Reeves is beginning to succeed at his mission—or at least half of what he set out to do. He is bringing in blacks from the neighborhood around him, where some of the families are sturdy and strong, while others still struggle with the sins of the street.

In the summer of 1996, Plaza's membership is going up, as a few more people drift in every week. But the bittersweet fact of the matter is this: Even as blacks embrace Percy Reeves, most of Plaza's white members have gone. There are one or two who are still hanging on—who may even hope somewhere in their hearts that segregation on Sunday will not be the norm; not at their church, where they really did try to build something better.

But most people now have given up the fight. Even in 1996, they will tell you, the chasm, somehow, is simply too wide.

Percy Reeves doesn't care for that thought. Now 36, he has lived his life as a child of integration. From the fourth grade on, in the town of Irmo, South Carolina, he went to public school with whites, and many of them became his friends. They played together, and he went to their parties and shared the same kind of small-town values. In high school, he was one of 12 blacks in a class of 600, and the ratio wasn't much better in college.

But Percy didn't mind. He played football at the University of South Carolina—in a backfield that included the Heisman Trophy winner, George Rogers—and in his day-to-day life at the university, he didn't really pay much attention to color.

When he graduated in 1982, choosing seminary over a career in football, a white alumnus helped cover his expenses. That was the way it had always been. He liked white people, they liked him back, and he thought he was ready for an interracial church. The Bible talked a lot about reconciliation, and Percy, in his heart, believed what it said. He had tried all his life to live as a Christian. His father, Roland Reeves, was a country preacher, and Percy's basic understanding of the world was shaped in part by Sundays spent at a white frame church on the main street of Irmo.

In college, his emphasis was evangelical. He was a member of the Fellowship of Christian Athletes, proclaiming his faith along with the others, though he never thought much about being a preacher. Law school seemed to be his ticket, until the day in 1982 when his summer job took him to a housing project.

He was working for the power company in Columbia, dealing with people who couldn't pay their bills, one of whom was an elderly woman in a tiny apartment that was dark and hot with the power cut off. The smell was terrible, and the woman was hungry, and Percy had never seen anything like it. In the country, everybody was more self-suffi-cient. Even poor people had a garden out back, but here in the city, there was a simmering desperation in the projects, fueled by the lack of money and hope, and Percy couldn't get the woman off his mind.

"I came home," he says, "and talked to my father. I said, 'How come the radio preachers never talk about that?' He said, 'why don't you do something about it?'"

So Percy decided to go to seminary. He got his masters from Colgate-Rochester, then his Doctor of Divinity from United Seminary in Dayton, and he worked for a while at some churches up north. But in his heart, he longed for the South. He had never felt quite at home since he left, and in 1994 he asked his football coach, Jim Carlen, to put in a word with the bishop in Charlotte. Reeves was looking for a special kind of church, one where the mission would touch people's lives—addressing itself to the range of human need...physical, spiri-tual; he knew it all tied together in the end.

Carlen passed the word to Bevel Jones, a veteran bishop and long-time friend who had deep feelings about the need for integration. As Jones said later, it was one of the ironies of American Christianity that "the church, of all institutions, should have so much difficulty with the issue—we who are supposed to be the conscience."

But there was a congregation in Charlotte with a special set of needs—a membership that was stagnant at best in a neighborhood becoming more black. Maybe a black preacher was just what they needed, particularly a bright young man from the South who had spent his life in the company of whites. Jones did some checking on Percy Reeves, and discovered that almost everybody liked him.

"In our minds, he was something of a superstar," Donald Haynes, the Methodists' supervisor in Charlotte, told a reporter from the *New York Times*.

The question was whether the church would accept him.

It was touch and go almost from the start. Most members felt great affection for the church—a modest, red brick structure on the Plaza, a major thoroughfare in northeast Charlotte. It was true that the neigh-borhood around them was changing, and as Christians some of them wanted to respond—to let their neighbors know they were welcome. But they didn't want to do anything too radical, and allowing a black man to lead them in worship—to preside at their weddings and listen to their problems—for many of the people was simply too much.

A few of them left before Reeves arrived, and those who remained were divided into factions. Some were eager to make him feel welcome, while others still bitterly resented his appointment.

The latter group was led by Charlie Lamm, a man in his 50s who had been at the church for 27 years. He was chairman of the board at Plaza United, a social service worker by trade, who wanted change on a more modest scale—perhaps a white minister and a black associate.

On the Sunday that Percy first came to the church, Lamm turned away without shaking his hand. The gesture, however, was not in character. By many accounts, Lamm was a man with a volatile temper. But he was also honest and loyal to the church, and much of the anger that he felt at the start was directed not at Percy but at the people who chose him.

In the Methodist church, such appointments are made by denominational officials, not the individual congregation, and Bishop Jones and superintendent Don Haynes will admit today that they did not handle the situation smoothly. They first chose a white man for the vacancy at Plaza, then changed their minds when they learned about Percy. It was flattering, of course, but it also made his situation harder, adding a touch of righteous indignation to the resistance of Charlie Lamm and the others.

Slowly, however, Percy and Charlie began to talk—sometimes about the church, other times about other things. There was a tragedy taking shape in Charlie's life. His wife, Becky Lamm, was in the last stage of cancer, and one day in the autumn of 1994, an ambulance came and took her to the hospital. Percy got the call about mid-afternoon, and rushed immediately to Carolinas Medical. He was there by the time the ambulance arrived, and spent the next 12 hours with the Lamm's. He was fond of Becky—"the sweetest person," he says today—and he could almost feel the pain himself, as the agony of her illness came at her in waves.

"Becky," he said, in one of those times, "would you like me to put a cool towel on your face?"

"Would you please?" she replied with effort.

So he sat for awhile at the side of her bed, adding cool cloths when he thought they were needed, and then when she seemed to be more comfortable, he and Charlie went out for a walk. They talked about the loss that lay just ahead, and the strength that Charlie would have to find in his faith, and that night when Percy got home after three, he decided to write for awhile in his journal. He wrote about his conversation with Charlie, and the cool wash cloth he brought to Becky Lamm. Despite the terrible sadness that he felt, he thought they had crossed the chasm that night—the barrier of color that kept them apart—and now, at last, he felt like a pastor.

That feeling was confirmed a few days later when Becky Lamm died, and Charlie asked Percy to preside at her funeral. And yet there were major differences between them—a basic disagreement about the future of the church. Charlie wanted to keep things pretty much the same. It was fine to bring in some new black members, maybe even alter the service a little, but if change had to come, he was not in a hurry. People, he said, needed time to adjust.

Percy, meanwhile, was starting to get restless. He restrained himself for the first few months. A gifted preacher, he tailored his style toward a white congregation, but as time went by, there were at least two problems with that approach. The first one was that not enough blacks were coming to the church, and as white people drifted away here and there, it meant that membership was declining.

The second problem was much more personal. Percy simply wasn't being himself. Sometimes he and Nettie, his wife, would visit black churches, much like the one in which he was raised. They went most often for the evening service, and sometimes Percy was asked to preach, and whenever that happened Nettie was always struck by the difference. He seemed so free when he preached in the evenings, feeding off the congregation's response, the cries of amen that filled the sancutary.

He longed for something like that at Plaza—more emotion, more passion, the rollicking sounds of a good gospel choir. He could picture a whole new service in his mind. Some of it would be what they had all along, the familiar sounds of old Methodist hymns, the readings from the Bible, but somewhere along the way every Sunday, they would blend in the black traditions as well. In Percy's mind, that only seemed fair. Much too often in pursuit of integration, blacks had been the ones to make the compromises—seeing their schools shut down, for example, so that even in an integrated setting, white children could stay in their own neighborhoods.

Percy thought the church should try to do better, searching for a definition of integration that would somehow aim for the best of both worlds.

But what did that mean? How far should they go to attract black members, and in order to keep the white members happy, how much would Percy have to rein in his style? He and Charlie continued to debate it until a night in November when they decided to go have dinner with the bishop. It was an emotional meeting at the Red Lobster restaurant on Albemarle Road, and even when it ended a few hours later, many of the issues remained unresolved. Percy, however, felt

206

good about it. He had grown to love and admire Charlie Lamm, and he was starting to believe if they kept on talking, they would eventually arrive at a deeper understanding—an accommodation based on mutual respect. But then the next morning, he was greeted with a shock, a piece of news he could barely comprehend. Charlie had died that night in his sleep, the victim of a heart attack at his home.

Percy grieved this time on a lot of different levels. Part of it was simply the loss of a friend, but he knew he had lost an ally as well. He and Charlie didn't always agree, but they were fellow travelers on a journey of faith, and when it came to the issues of Christianity and race, the journey itself was the thing that mattered. As Percy understood it, they might never come to a final destination, but there was a lot to be learned along the way.

The question now was whether the rest of the church had the heart. The signs, for a while, seemed to be pretty good. In December, there was a meeting between the congregation and the bishop—about 90 people in the vaulted sanctuary with its hardwood pews and a little cross down front—and there was a cluster of media people outside. When the meeting ended after nearly three hours, Percy reported "more smiles and handshakes than we had going in."

But a few weeks later, everything went sour. In February, church leaders got together for a planning session, and one of the speakers was the Rev. Harold Bales, a Methodist minister who had spent six years at an inner city church. He had succeeded in attracting a mixed congregation, and he came to share some of what he had learned. Bales, ordinarily, is folksy, low-key, easy to like, and he came to Plaza with an innocent assumption. He thought they wanted to attract more blacks. One of the ways they could do it, he said, while keeping their regular worship at 11, was simply to add another service every week—a gospel choir, more fire from the pulpit, something more attuned to the black worship style.

Many white leaders at Plaza were appalled. "They saw it as dividing blacks and whites," remembers Jim Burr, a white accountant who serves as finance chairman at the church. But Percy thought there was another level to it. It became clear at the February meeting, he says, that he was simply out of step, for he could picture a time somewhere down the road when new black members who were drawn to the church might, in fact, outnumber the whites. The demographics alone seemed to make that clear. In business terms, Percy tried to say, blacks were the emerging market for the church.

Whites recoiled from that kind of talk—from the possibility of being outnumbered—and in the spring and summer of 1995 white flight grew from a trickle to a torrent. Attendance on Sundays hit an all-time low. From 140 active members when he came, Percy found himself preaching to 30 or 40 people at the most. There was another meeting with the bishop that summer—an ultimatum in which a group of 40 members demanded emphatically that Reeves be replaced. They thought he preached too long on Sunday, or didn't listen well, or didn't communicate about church business. And when the bishop refused to bow to their demands, the members announced they were not coming back.

In the despair that followed, Percy went back over everything that had happened—the terrible reversals of the past few months. He knew that in fact he had made some mistakes—little things mostly, like his decision to make some changes in the music.

"I was in the choir," remembers Jim Burr, "and we were not talked to at all. Percy just kind of went his own way."

Some people say it's all for the best. By the winter of 1996, perhaps even earlier, Percy had given up on the goal of integration, and attendance once again was starting to rise. Almost all the newcomers were black, and Percy did his best to make them at home. On Sunday mornings, the gospel choir rocked and swayed with the beat, and the sermons often ran until well after noon, punctuated by the cries of amen. Percy spent a lot of time with the kids, trying to steer them from trouble on the streets, and people were starting to come forward with their problems, treating him once again as a pastor. All of those things were good for the church, but there were still those times, perhaps late at night or in the quiet of his office, when he felt some regret.

They had had an opportunity to do something different, something fine, for at a time when the community was paying close attention, the chance was there to tear down the walls. But the moment was lost in questions of style, and the element of power that was in there as well —a triumph of human nature over faith.

His sermons still echoed back in his mind: "In Christ Jesus, all partitions come down...." Maybe some day, he thought to himself, but not quite yet—not in the church they had called him to lead.